Business Ethics in Islam

Abbas J. Ali

Distinguished University Professor and Professor of
Management, Indiana University of Pennsylvania, USA

Edward Elgar
Cheltenham, UK • Northampton, MA, USA

Published by
Edward Elgar Publishing Limited
The Lypiatts
15 Lansdown Road
Cheltenham
Glos GL50 2JA
UK

Edward Elgar Publishing, Inc.
William Pratt House
9 Dewey Court
Northampton
Massachusetts 01060
USA

A catalogue record for this book
is available from the British Library

Library of Congress Control Number: 2014937813

This book is available electronically in the ElgarOnline.com
Business Subject Collection, E-ISBN 978 1 78100 673 3

MIX
Paper from
responsible sources
FSC® C018575

ISBN 978 1 78100 672 6

Typeset by Servis Filmsetting Ltd, Stockport, Cheshire
Printed and bound in Great Britain by T.J. International Ltd, Padstow

Contents

Figures

Tables

Preface

This book is part of several research projects that seek to bring forth the best of Islamic thinking during the Golden Era of Islam and demonstrate its relevance and implications in today's business world. In particular, this book focuses on the ethical foundations of business and organization. The elements of these foundations are articulated in the Quran and the Prophet's sayings and are also found in treatises and sermons of early Muslim scholars. Though the task of diving into history and examining volumes of resources may appear impossible, the discovery and recognition of business ethics in these works is ultimately rewarding.

The book creatively links these ethics and sanctioned principles to today's world through a genuine reflection on what is original and essential for morally driven business conduct. In its entirety, the book is about business ethics, its theory and practice, and its necessity for safeguarding societal interests and preventing fraudulent practices and immoral conduct. The book accentuates needed elements for an ethical framework that set the stage for ethical conduct and motivates market actors to do their best to observe their individual and collective responsibilities in the marketplace where temptations are abundant and daunting moral dilemmas are mounting.

Without doubt, business ethics has a social and economic significance. Indeed, market actors, more than ever, need to acquire an awareness of prevailing ethical norms and values and develop sensitivity to their significance in business conduct for responsible citizens and moral organizations. This significance transcends place and time, organizations and societies, employees and managers. This makes familiarity with business ethics an ever-present necessity in a world where corporate scandals and corruption have dramatically increased.

Practically, this book is the most original and comprehensive treatment of business ethics in Islam. It explores the thinking of early Islamic scholars on ethics without ignoring modern developments in the field. In their coverage of ethics, these scholars had rich and valuable perspectives. These were scattered in treatises and commentaries and in books that dealt with spiritual and religious issues. Their original treatments of the subject offer an answer to three concerns in today's world: how early Muslims dealt with and confronted business problems, how such perspectives can give the necessary insight for dealing with rising complexities in today's business world, and how relevant these perspectives are for establishing sound ethical systems in modern organizations.

Business Ethics in Islam moves beyond the question of defining Islamic ethical terms and identification of mere normative judgments. Rather, the book is a mixture of practical and theoretical perspectives on ethical and moral conduct. It is an innovative and authoritative source that captures the essence of business ethics and the mechanisms needed for avoiding ambiguous, doubtful, and questionable issues in the marketplace. For this particular reason, the book is relevant to a wide range of groups in the Muslim world and other regions of the world. In writing this book, four groups have been kept in mind: students, researchers, business people, and policy makers. The first two groups disseminate and promote ethics, while the last two use ethical perspectives in conducting their business affairs and in setting boundaries for ethical behavior.

Though the book is aimed at fostering discourse on business ethics, it seeks to accomplish four objectives. First, it offers a framework for exploring a wide range of ethical issues and dilemmas that arise in the marketplace. Second, it raises ethical awareness and sensitivity of various market and non-market players. The book hopes to impart an understanding of the ethical principles in Islam and their significance in a globalized world. Third, the book enables researchers to use Islamic ethical principles to advance research by offering practical solutions to rising ethical problems in the market. It not only provides theoretical perspectives but also certain assumptions and premises that constitute a foundation for hypotheses development. The identification and translation of various classical sources offer researchers access, probably for the first time, to rich but scattered resources. Translation of these passages was at times difficult as we sought to capture the original meaning. Fourth, it enables business people and policy makers to gain a familiarity with business ethics in Islam. This will allow them to acquire the requisite outlook and understanding for applying business ethics and draw useful implications.

The book is organized into ten chapters. These chapters were written in an integrated way to give readers an accurate understanding of the nature of business ethics, its roots, outlook, and implications. The first two chapters focus on the meaning and scope of business ethics, offer a basic framework for understanding and analyzing ethical dilemmas, and specify the sources of ethical problems. The next seven chapters address ethical issues in the context of the market economy and tackle in detail the issues of competition, profit maximization, leadership, work ethics, marketing and consumerism, and human resource challenges. The last chapter traces the roots of social responsibility and provides theoretical perspectives on corporate social responsibility (CSR) and its components in accordance with Islamic prescriptions.

I should mention that while there are various translations of the Quran, I have relied on King Fahd's version published by King Fahd Holy Quran Printing Complex. In addition, I have referred to classical sources throughout the text which normally employ the pronoun 'he'. However, I have utilized the pronoun 'he' as a generic term. In fact, my book is designed for both male and female students, researchers, business people, and policy makers.

In preparing this book, I had to consult with and seek assistance from several individuals. All have been very cooperative and supportive. My sincere appreciation goes to Robert C. Camp, my Dean at the Eberly College of Business, Indiana University of Pennsylvania. Bob has provided considerable support for engaging in intellectual and scholarly activities. Alan Sturmer, Executive Editor at Edward Elgar Publishing Inc., is a talented and professional editor. His natural cooperative tendency and professional instinct make him a valuable asset. In addition, I am thankful to Tori Nicols at Edward Elgar Publishing for her cooperation and understanding.

Furthermore, I would like to thank Dr. Helen Bailie for her careful editing and useful comments on the manuscript. My graduate assistant, Casey Marie Hefferin, did a fantastic job in helping me finish the book, and I am grateful to both Helen and Casey for their exceptional enthusiasm in working with me. In particular, my daughter, Yasmin, despite her young age, understands difficulties in life and has been a source of motivation.

1. The meaning and scope of business ethics in Islam

What are the common business ethics theories? Can these theories provide practical insights into ethical misconduct? Are there ethical guidelines that could prevent fraudulent behavior? Does Islam share a similar outlook on ethics with other monotheistic religions, especially Christianity and Judaism? Does the Islamic faith address ethical business issues? Does it provide guidelines that are sufficient and practical for preventing ethical misconduct? What are the implications of Islamic prescriptions for business people in a globalized world? These and other issues are addressed in this chapter. The objective is to identify, define, and present Islamic business ethics for business people and researchers alike. The chapter includes the most relevant early Islamic perspectives on market interactions and dealings. Furthermore, it sets the stage for identifying how to engage in purposeful conduct in the face of rising market entrapments and material allurements in the marketplace.

The intensity and frequent occurrence of fraud and corruption in the marketplace in recent decades has accentuated the necessity and importance of delineating, clarifying, and identifying business ethics. Policymakers and business people across the globe have questioned increasing incidents of corruption and the persistency of deception despite stiff regulations and the rising vigilance of public agencies, especially in the Western world. The severity of the consequences of corruption, for both organizations and society, has encouraged market regulatory and civic actors to search for a suitable response to the rising challenges of corporate scandals and fraud.

Due to the failure of these actors to limit the increase or spread of corporate scandals and fraud, researchers throughout the world have pondered the possibility that spiritual and religious instructions and traditions may be vital sources in helping minimize or discourage corruption at the individual and organizational level and could generate insight on how to deal with chronic business ethics violations. While the tenets of Christianity (e.g., Abela, 2001; Emerson and Mckinney, 2010; Karns, 2008; Lee, McCann, and Ching, 2003) and Judaism (e.g., Lewison, 1999; Pava, 1998; Tamari, 1991) have been intensively and systematically debated in business ethics and organization literature, studies focusing on Islamic perspectives and Islamic prescriptions in the marketplace are at best scattered and scarce.

Like Christianity and Judaism, Islam tackles market issues and market behavior both directly and indirectly. Some of these issues are business specific and have direct implications. For example, the saying of the Prophet that "Deception and fraud may sell the goods but lose the blessing" (quoted in Al-Ghazali, 2004, p. 30) focuses directly on business interactions and, therefore, its implication for broader business conduct is easy to grasp. On the other hand, some instructions are general in nature, but nevertheless have implications for business affairs. A good example is the Prophet's saying, "He who cannot keep his trust has no faith and he who cannot fulfill his promise has no religion" (quoted in Al-Ghazali, 2004, p. 35). Whether instructions are business specific or are general, they have been analyzed and addressed by early Muslim scholars since the inception of Islam. Both jurists and researchers have highlighted the spiritual and social aspects of these prescriptions, enabling believers to understand that behaving in ethically condoned manners in the market is expected of them.

WHAT ARE BUSINESS ETHICS?

Any understanding of business ethics cannot be realized independent of the general meaning of ethics. Indeed, articulating and exploring the essence of ethics is essential for comprehending the applicability of business ethics in any society. Though ethics is a relative term, scholars and practitioners alike agree that ethics denotes a society's perception of what is right or wrong. Viewed in this general term, tradition, society's evolution and interaction with the outside world, economic conditions and the state of the economic system, government policies, and religion all shape the meaning of ethics. However, while there are certain core issues in ethical systems that are shared across groups and societies, there are others that are cherished by a particular culture and which are deeply and or widely held regardless of time or location.

Shaw (2008, p. 5) argues that ethics "deals with individual character and the moral rules that govern and limit our conduct." Hartley (1993, p. 3) defines ethics as "standards of right conduct." While Islamic tradition and thinking underscores right conduct, it simultaneously highlights the benefits to society as the measure for judging whether a conduct is right or wrong. Naqvi (1981, p. 18) suggests that ethics epitomizes the "common values of a society and determine[s] the preference structures of the members of that society." The linkage between an individual and his/

her community is manifested in ethical responsibility where self-interest is sought to be in harmony with that of the society. This has always been the concern of Islamic jurists, informed ordinary citizens, and enlightened rulers. Whether a sound balance between individual and community interests can be achieved depends primarily on effective utilization of reason and familiarity with and internalization of religious instructions.

In Islam, ethics is the foundation of deep faith, societal prosperity, and individuals' living standards (see Al-Mawardi, 2002 for detail). Without ethical conduct, prosperity and the well-being of individuals are impossible to achieve. That is, good ethics are a prerequisite for achieving a sustainable economy and social goals. The Prophet asserts that good ethics and generosity lead to "complete faith." In terms of economic development, the Prophet articulates the link between ethics, business, and prosperity stating, "Good ethics and being good to one's neighbors contributes to the prosperity of cities and increases development" (quoted in Al-Mawardi, 2002, p. 383). Al-Mawardi (2002) reported that "He who displays bad ethics, his earnings will be severely curtailed." Though these judgments and instructions underscore the centrality of ethics in economic activities and societal welfare, early Islamic thinkers recognized that ethics cannot exist independent of sound judgment, responsible thinking, and reason.

Guided by Quranic instructions, Muslims thinkers understand that people differ in their conduct and that sound reason rather than lack of it allows people to distinguish what is right from what is wrong. The Prophet Mohamed observes, "Reason is a light in the heart; it differentiates between right and wrong" (quoted in Al-Mawardi, 2002, p. 15). The Quran (17:84) states, "Everyone acts according to his own disposition, but your Lord knows best who has the right guidance." Therefore, Islamic instructions recognize that differences in ethical behavior, commitment, and conduct are a natural propensity and that only through reason are individuals able to grasp what is beneficial and what is harmful for self and society. Al-Mawardi (2002, p. 11), a jurist who died in 1058, made a sound argument when he stated that "for each virtue there is a base and for each ethic there is a stream, and the foundation for both is reason." This dialectic relationship between ethics and reason emphasizes that ethics from an Islamic perspective is defined as "specified rules that govern individuals and organizational conduct and seek to ensure generosity, transparency, and accountability in behavior and actions, while safeguarding societal interests" (Ali, 2011, p. 20). These aspects are necessary for understanding the concept and principles of business ethics in Islam.

Abu Talib al-Maki (1995, died 996), a jurist and Islamic thinker, recorded certain business incidents and treatises that demonstrate how business ethics in Islam were much broader in his time than the narrow meaning attached to business ethics in today's world. Al-Maki (1995, p. 554) argued that any trade or manufacturing activity that is inconsistent with the teachings and instructions of sanctioned ethics is not permissible. He advised business people that if they were in doubt as to the ethics of their conduct then they should avoid any action, irrespective of the gain that might be obtained. He stated, furthermore, that if all people strictly observed what is permissible then there would be no differences in behaviors and desires and, therefore, there would be no need for government or religious guidelines to enforce order and articulate the desired behavior (p. 548).

Like the general term ethics, business ethics is variously and often vaguely defined. Hooker (2011, p. 2) regards business ethics as a "conceptual framework for making defensible business decisions that consider all stakeholders." DesJardins (2010, p. 9) views business ethics as "those values, standards, and principles that operate within business." Similarly, Parboteeah and Cullen (2013, p. 5) define business ethics as "the principles and standards that guide business." The standards and principles, however, may differ from one culture to another. For example, the emphasis on maximizing profit in North America may not have the same priority in East and South Asia.

Islamic business ethics are far reaching, as it sets the standard for going beyond what is generally accepted in the marketplace. To adequately present how business ethics in Islam are broader than the currently prevailing perspectives promoted in Western teachings and practices, a reference to some commentaries and incidents which took place during the first seven centuries of the Islamic civilization is essential. These commentaries capture the spiritual bent and morality of the time, but have relevance to business practices in today's world. Below are selected incidents that Al-Maki reported, which demonstrate the wide domain of business ethics.

The Ethics of Selling

Al-Maki (1995) showed the contrast between a good seller and the best seller. He reported that years before sellers had two books for those who bought on credit (p. 518). One of these books had no title and was specifically designed for those buyers who were poor and needy. This was because those who were in distressed circumstances would eye certain goods or produce they liked to eat but could not afford to buy. If a needy customer said to the good seller, "I need to have five or ten kilos of this, but I do not have money," the seller would reply, "Take them and when you earn enough then pay me." The seller would write the name of that person in his book, anticipating that someday the buyer would be able to pay him for the goods. However, the best seller would neither write down the name of the poor person in his book nor treat the total amount as debt. Rather, the seller would say, "Take what you need and pay me only when you are capable. Otherwise, you are free of any obligation."

The Ethics of Contracting

Al-Maki (1995) reported that when a tailor came to Ibn Mubarak (Islamic scholar, born around 726) and informed him that he could make suits for the agents of the ruler and asked, "Does that make me one who enables oppressors?" Ibn Mubarak replied, "It makes you an oppressor, not an enabler. The enablers are those who sell you the needles and threads" (p. 503).

The Ethics of Social Responsibility

Al-Maki reported that when Sari Al Sagdi (Islamic scholar) was sitting one night he was informed that a fire had been set in the market and had burned his store (pp. 91–2). On his way to the market, he met a group of people who told him that other stores had been destroyed in the fire but not his. His initial response was, "Thanks be to God." But he then pondered what he had said and thought, "I thanked God for the safety of my property but did not care about others whose properties were destroyed." So, he distributed everything that was in his store as a charitable act to erase his sin.

The Ethics of Making Profit

Abu Talib Al-Maki (pp. 508–9) recorded that Sari Al Sagdi bought a bin of almonds for 60 dinars and wrote in his account that the profit would be three dinars. The market price, however, increased to 90 dinars for a bin of almonds. A market agent stopped by and expressed interest in buying the bin of almonds and asked its price. Al Sagdi informed him that it would be 63 dinars. The agent told him that he would buy it for 70 dinars. But Al Sagdi refused and insisted on selling it for 63 dinars (to avoid charging more than what he originally thought was fair). However, the buyer refused to pay less than 70 (to avoid making a large profit margin). So, no transaction took place.

The above incidents demonstrate that business ethics in Islam has a much broader reach than the common concept of ethics in today's capitalism. In the market economy, meeting the requirements of the law and acting accordingly is often considered sufficient. However, there are many issues that are not addressed in the law and the legal system cannot take into account all market concerns and behaviors in a dynamic and ever changing business environment. In addition, on some occasions, a business transaction may not actually be harmful to any individual, but from the perspective of an individual or as a spiritual concern, the act may be considered unreasonable, as in the case of selling the almond bin at market price in the incident above. Even when business ethics includes the interests of all stakeholders, it is impossible to account for all the concerns and priorities of those involved in the marketplace. This is why business ethics in Islam has a broad reach; it goes beyond material gain, intention, and utilitarian perspectives. As we discuss in the chapters that follow, business ethics, in the context of Islamic teaching, is molded by spiritual concerns, depth of faith, and one's position and role in this world. The interplay of all these factors produces an outlook that encompasses more than mere material and legal considerations.

THEORIES OF BUSINESS ETHICS

Scholars in the field of business ethics have debated the necessity of having an appropriate measure for judging whether market behaviors and actions are right or wrong. While most of the debate has taken place in the last few decades, scholars have explored various frameworks and perspectives going back to the Greek civilization or the Age of Enlightenment in Europe. In their quest for theory development, classical philosophers and scholars have sought answers from the past to critical questions related to ethical obligations. This does not mean that contemporary scholars have failed to produce appropriate answers and have had to look at history to address a modern dilemma. Rather, it represents an acknowledgment of the thoughtful contributions of civilization and the relevancy of classical philosophical thinking to contemporary matters. Indeed, philosophical perspectives, across centuries, have often been found to be useful in answering concerns and subject matters essential for any functioning society. The philosophical perspectives, however, often differ in tackling matters related to how people should conduct their lives and their responsibility toward society.

Over the years, scholars have recognized three major business ethics theories. These theories vary in their reasoning and conclusions, but all seek to enlighten decision makers and ordinary citizens alike on what is considered suitable for dealing with human behaviors and dilemmas. In the context of the marketplace, these theories attempt to answer what a business actor ought to do in various business circumstances. The three perspectives that guide business actors are: teleological (consequences-oriented), deontological (duty-based), and virtue ethics. Below is a brief description of each.

Teleological (Consequences-Oriented)

This particular approach underscores the significance of the output in deciding if an act is preferable or not. The word teleological is derived from the Greek word *telos* meaning goal or purpose. Whether a business decision is judged to be ethical depends primarily on the outcome. This approach encompasses two major sub theories: egoism and utilitarianism. Egoism treats any action that serves one's interest as ethical. A person, according to this view, is driven by whatever is deemed important to advance his/her interest for the foreseeable future.

Utilitarianism theory states that any act that leads to the greatest good for the greatest number is acceptable and therefore ethical. Implicitly, utilitarianism justifies the means, as long as the results are considered good. While this theory has many shortcomings, the most alarming one is that powerful actors, be they in the market or other domains, may use their supremacy to legitimize their actions, though the means to achieve them are horrible. Even if we assume that mechanisms exist to prevent the powerful from exercising undue influence, there are certain acts, as we see later, that should not be undertaken irrespective of the outcome. Furthermore, a core issue in utilitarianism is that acts which do not benefit the greatest possible number are judged to be bad. Advocates of utilitarianism have not provided adequate mechanisms for documenting the greatest number of gains in their equitable share of the resulting benefits. Likewise, no act is ever right or wrong in all circumstances; that depends on consequences (DesJardins, 2011). The problem that one might face is how to judge whether an action is bad or good. This requires having agreed upon standards for determining if an outcome is bad or good. Standards, however, are different among individuals and in a larger community, or in a globalized world, this becomes highly problematic.

DesJardins (2011) suggested that the most efficient way to measure benefits to the greatest number is found in the principles of free market capitalism. He argued that competition among rational and self-interested individuals is certain to lead to the greatest overall good. This, however, is mere speculation as events in the global economy have repeatedly demonstrated that the common scenario is that a few powerful actors take advantage of the market and consequently reap the economic benefits for themselves. In addition, these actors, according to many critics, use their economic positions to influence government decisions and politicians. That is, in the real world a purely free market economy is far from a certainty. Under such conditions, generating greatest benefits for the greatest number, as envisioned by utilitarianism, is difficult to realize. To counter such problems, Micewski and Troy (2007) proposed that self-interest in business should be tempered by moral duty and the rights of business executives and their self-interest must end where the rights of other stake-holders begin. In that respect, in 2005 (see Ali, 2005), we underscored the importance of character and credibility of market actors in sustaining market stability and emphasized that the prosperity of business people is highly interwoven with the interests of the community.

Deontological Ethics (Non-Consequential)

In contrast to the teleological premise, deontological ethics (deriving from the Greek word *deon* or duty) places emphasis not on outcome but on certain duties and responsibilities. Intentions are central to the deonto-logical approach, as they determine whether or not business decisions are ethical or unethical. Only when business people act from duty do their actions have moral worth (Shaw, 2008). Shaw argues that when people act only out of feeling, inclination, or self-interest, the action has no true moral worth even if that act may be identical with ones that spring from a sense of duty. A sense of duty, which is based on reason, requires that businesspeople are driven by honesty and fairness. Moral reasoning, therefore, is fundamental for revealing principles that motivate people to engage in acts which are desirable and beneficial. Immanuel Kant, the German philosopher (1724–1804), was instrumental in articulating the non-consequential approach. He set three conditions for this approach (see Shaw, 2008 for details): rules do not depend on circumstances or results and do not permit individual exceptions; humans must not be treated as means to ends; and action has a moral worth only if there is a desire to do the right thing for its own sake.

Virtue Ethics

Unlike deontological and teleological approaches, which focus on rules and guidelines that we ought to follow or on decisions to be made, virtue ethics is concerned with the type of person we should be in the context of our relations with others and our positions in society. It divulges the traits that are essential for engaging positively in the world around us. Virtue ethics is related to dispositions that a person displays in relationships and attitudes and is embedded in the values and beliefs that one subscribes to. It seeks to highlight the virtues that lead to a meaningful and rewarding life. How these are acquired, developed, and evolved is part of the domain of virtue ethics. Since virtue ethics do not exist independently of the society and the environment where a person lives, virtue ethics tend to be numerous and may differ, in priorities, among societies.

There are three key elements that represent the principles that drive those who promote virtue ethics (Murphy, Laczniak, Bowie, and Klein, 2005, pp. 31–2). These are: virtues are essentially good habits and in order to thrive they must be practiced and taught to those who are unfamiliar with the concept; admirable characteristics are most easily identified by witnessing and imitating widely acclaimed behavior; and a key to understanding virtue ethics and the discipline it requires is based on the *ethic of the mean* or the optimal balance of a quality that one should seek. Virtue ethics, therefore, differs from previous theories as it primarily revolves around individual character, attitudes, and other dispositions and preferences, including values and guiding norms. These qualities can be taught and acquired, which can induce business people and citizens in general to behave in an ethical way. Identifying these virtues becomes essential to ensure that those involved in market decision making are not only familiar with these virtues but also internalize them.

In the context of Islamic thinking, the question that might arise is, "Are these theories relevant and if so which theory or combination of theories is appropriate?" The point that should be made is that the above business ethics theories have attracted different followers and advocates. Their applications in the business world validate or refute some of their premises. The popularity of each under certain circumstances may not reflect wide acceptance or unqualified validity. This might be the reason that different cultures may take issue with certain elements of each theory or combination of theories. In Islamic thinking, ethics is not a subject that is taken lightly, but it is looked on as a foundation for a just society and for the enrichment of the faith. Ethics is characteristically linked to faith. Thus, it has been addressed extensively both in the Quran and the sayings of the Prophet or *Hadith*. Both sources provide a general outlook for understanding ethics and what is required for individuals as citizens and members of organizations in order to maintain responsible and morally driven conduct.

Both sources, the Quran and *Hadith*, basically constitute religious illustrations and instructions for the faithful and foundations for relationships and conduct, whether in the marketplace or general life. They are not intended to directly offer theoretical reasonings and outlooks. Nevertheless, they provide a genuine reference for theoretical formulation. In reviewing both sources, there is an emphasis on outcome, intention, and character as a basis for judging whether an act is ethical or not. To have an understanding of this; sample documenting instructions offered in the Quran and the *Hadith* are presented below.

The Quran (16:34) warns believers of the outcome of unethical behavior admonishing, "But the evil results of their deeds [overtake] them" and (30:41) "Mischief has appeared on land and sea by [reason] what the hands of men have earned." While these sayings focus on outcome, there are also instructions that underscore the significance of intention (74:18), "For he thought and he determined" and virtues (17:84) "Everyone acts according to his disposition." The Prophet offers clear instructions that are relevant to secular theories in which he articulates intention as a basis for determining whether an act is ethical or not, stating, "The value of work derives from its intention," and "God does not look upon either your appearance or wealth, rather God examines your intentions and actions." And though the Prophet instructs that "Work is judged by its outcome," he elaborates further when he asserts that sincere intention is a prerequisite: "Work is contingent upon intention and to each according to his intention." Furthermore, having a disposition to serve and help others goes hand in hand with intention and in judging whether the act is ethical or not: "The best people are those who benefit others" and "God loves those who benefit others." Of course, benefits take place only when there is an action and when a person is driven by no other interests except a desire for creating value that benefits self and others. This is the reason that the Prophet insists that "God examines your intentions and actions," adding that "God does not accept any claim without action and no claim or action without intention" (quoted in Al-Maki, 1995, p. 308). That is, there is a dialectic relationship between disposition of an individual and intention and action. The first two are essential for an ethical outcome.

Like other early Islamic jurists and scholars (e.g., Al-Mawardi, Al-Ṣâbi, Al-Shatibi, etc.), Abu Talib Al-Maki elaborated on virtues, good outcome, and intention. However, he gave the latter a special place when he stated that intention is "an act of the heart, a prerequisite for action, and constitutes the beginning of it" (p. 313). And since intention is in the heart and no other person knows about it, reward is always multiplied. Furthermore, intention is treated as a condition for good work, thus, no work can be considered ethical without good intention. An ethical act by nature is purposeful conduct and, therefore, there exists a harmonious relation between intention and outcome. Al-Maki explained that intention encompasses two elements: the exact aim of the heart toward work and sincerity. True sincerity, for him, manifests an absence of predisposition to follow desire and hypocrisy. As he stated, "sincerity without work is better than deceitful work" (p. 310). That is, the goodness or badness of any action is the result of honest or bad intention.

In terms of virtue ethics, the Quran specifies three general virtues (3:104): "Let there arise out of you a band of people inviting to all what is good, enjoining what is right, and forbidding what is wrong: they are the ones to attain felicity." Islamic tradition, however, elaborates on ten virtues needed for ethical action. These are: capacity to reason, sound faith, knowledge,

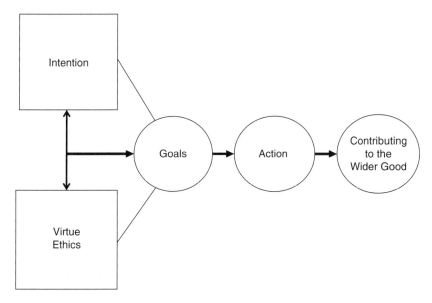

Figure 1.1   The interplay of factors that lead to wider good

forbearance, generosity, adherence to accepted custom, righteousness, patience, thankfulness, and flexibility (quoted in Al-Mawardi, 2002, p. 28). Those with these qualities are gifted with good intention and their actions veer toward serving society. While there is a wide range of virtues, Muslim scholars agree that those who are driven by interests beyond the self are more likely to engage in pursuing goals that deepen commitment to the betterment of society and to a wider sharing of benefits (see Figure 1.1). Nevertheless, the processes that translate goals into actions must be ethical and deemed so by being consistent with serving public interests. There are four means that Muslim scholars have identified (see Al Mahami, 1987, p. 549):

1. means that lead to disrepute are prohibited and must not be used,
2. means for obtaining a permissible act that leads to disreputable action are prohibited,
3. means for a permissible act that is not intended to be disreputable but often leads to it, with the resultant harm being more than the benefit is prohibited, and
4. means for obtaining a permissible act that might lead to disrepute but a resultant benefit is more likely than harm is lawful.

Al-Mawardi (2002, pp. 5–6) illustrated the linkage between intention, outcome, and benefits to society when he stated:

> The importance of a goal is characteristically linked to the significance of the outcome; the magnitude of its consequences is measured by the created benefit, and the priority given to it is contingent upon this benefit, and the care given to it determines how its fruits should be collected. The most important and the most beneficial and useful affairs are those which serve religion and life and by which in this world and the hereafter order is ensured. This is because the righteousness of religion leads straight to worship and the enhancement of life makes happiness widespread.

As indicated in Figure 1.1, in Islamic thinking, goals differ based on personality (virtue ethics) and intention or motivation (duty). Furthermore, while ethics generally explains what should be done, Islamic ethical instructions seek to change behavior in the marketplace and life. Changing conduct takes priority. In fact, the Quran gives examples of certain wrongdoings and sanctioned behavior with the hope that the faithful will observe and pursue righteousness. In terms of personalities, the Quran articulates dispositions of both those who do the right thing and those who are driven by pleasure. Before specifying these personalities, it should be mentioned that the underlying assumption of human needs in Islam is that human beings are complex and dynamic creatures. That is, they are born to strive, to weigh the consequences of vice and virtue, and seek and reach perfection. They have various choices and options in life. These choices have consequences beyond immediate self-interest. Therefore, people of the faith are reminded that they should view their actions in a broad context. The Prophet Mohamed once said, "One has an obligation toward God, self, and family; give due attention to each" (quoted in Glaachi, 2000, p. 59). In Islam, physiological, economic, and spiritual needs are not hierarchically arranged. Rather, they are considered simultaneously. The consideration, however, is influenced by intellectual insight, aspiration, and emotion. Being able to attain a balance in satisfying these needs is a virtue. The Quran (28:77) instructs Muslims to "seek through your wealth the gains of the hereafter without ignoring your share of this life." The Quran, therefore, describes a balanced personality where considerations for this life are not artificially separated from working toward pleasing, fearing, and serving God by acting responsibly and benefiting others.

LEVELS OF EXISTENCE

There are four levels of existence. These levels are in a state of flux and dynamism. People are endowed with mental faculties and a free will to decide what is good for them and their surroundings. That is, people have several options and priorities in life. Choices and priorities are shaped by upbringing, social and economic constraints, knowledge, and perceived and actual opportunities. The Quran specifies and details the levels of existence (e.g., 12:53; 75:2; 89:27–30). The Quran, too, clarifies not only the circumstances that shape the evolution and existence of each level, but also the conditions that induce changes and progress. That is, the psychology of a healthy person changes according to their level of existence. At each particular level, a person exhibits beliefs, values, attitudes, and behaviors corresponding to that stage. As conditions change, the person may progress or regress to a new stage. Subsequently, his/her dispositions, aspirations, values, and behaviors are expected to change. Below is a brief discussion of each in terms of intention and ethics.

Sawala (A Passion for Temptations)

At this level, a person's soul prompts him/her to follow only their desires and to shy away from enlightenment. For example, in the story of Moses, the propensity to evil made Samiri lead Moses's people astray in his absence. When Moses asked Samiri what he had done: "Samiri told Moses, 'I had the skill [of carving], which they did not have. I followed some of the messenger's [Moses's] traditions, but I then ignored them. Thus, my soul prompted me (to carve a golden calf with an artificial hollow sound)" (20:96). Samiri acted in a way that eventually inhibited him from serving the interests of the people and optimized his interests. The fourth Caliph, Imam Ali (AD598–661), described the nature of a person at this stage (1990, pp. 715–16):

> When in doubt, he follows his passions instead of reason and even though he is certain that happiness lies in doing what is good, he disregards this. . . . When there is opportunity to satisfy his passion, he enthusiastically follows it, but he delays seeking forgiveness. If he experiences difficulties, he loses his patience. . . . He is full of talk but avoids action. He competes for things that are insignificant and ignores things that are beneficial. He considers work that is of significance a burden and that which satisfies his passion is of great importance. . . . He is quick in criticizing others but lavishly compliments himself. Time that he spends with the rich for pleasure is more important to him than spending time with the poor remembering God. . . . He fears those people whose actions are not sanctioned by God but does not fear God in his dealings with people.

The primary preoccupation at this stage is with pursuing self-interest. That is, people may possess the mental capacities for differentiating between good and bad, but they lack the capacity to integrate their needs with the rest of their surroundings. Their obsession with self-interest inhibits them from engaging responsibly in actions that serve others, leading to output that is intentionally unethical. That is, temptations overwhelm and blind them from addressing that which is good.

Ammara (The Prone-to-Evil Psyche)

This is a stage where a person is aware that their soul induces them to do bad things and yet offers no resistance to it. At this level, the human soul is a burden with desires and temptations. The Quran (12:53) depicts this personality stating, "Yet, I do not absolve myself (of blame): the human soul certainly incites evil, unless my Lord bestows His mercy." In this context, a person is inclined intentionally and perhaps contrary to self-interest, to engage in wrongdoing. Nevertheless, a person at this stage is willing to confess mistakes under pressure or when he/she understands that conditions are no longer conducive to serving his/her interest. Perhaps this manifests a lack of internalization of the spiritual beliefs. Therefore, intentionally, ethical considerations are not pursued primarily for the sake of a higher goal. At this stage, a person is aware that for actions there are consequences, be they rewards or punishments. However, because the desire for passion overwhelms wisdom, the person is inclined to follow desires.

Lawama (Self-Reproachment)

At this stage, Man is conscious of evil. There is a struggle between good and evil and Man seeks to repent in order to achieve salvation. In sections 75:2 and 75:14–15, the Quran explains the conflicts at this stage of human development: "And I swear by the self-reproaching soul" and "Nay, man will be evidence against himself, even though he were to put up his excuses." Thus, the *Lawama* soul either drives a person toward good and perfection or toward evil action and aggression. In the latter, the person is not inclined to pursue good actions.

People make choices in life and have to live with the consequences, whether these consequences are good or bad. Accordingly, a person at this stage is subject to a continuing internal struggle, hesitation, and frustration. Unlike the preceding stages, the inclination to follow one's desires at this level is not unbridled, as one's will seeks to constrain self. If the will to engage in positive activities overwhelms desires, a person may reach a sense of spiritual fulfillment and contribute to the betterment of society. Intentions are closely pondered and actions taken that are thought to ease life for others, while helping self. This is ensured when a person has clarity of mind. Individuals at this level are generally sensitive to moral and ethical standards, are aware of their weak tendencies, try to resist selfish pursuits, are troubled when things go wrong, and consider what happens to them a consequence of their own choices.

Mutamainna (The Righteous)

This is the ultimate point in human development. At this level, the mind is perfectly in tune with good deeds and a person realizes complete satisfaction and self-actualization. The Quran (89:27–8) says, "To the righteous soul will be said, 'oh soul come back thou to thy Lord, well pleased (thyself), and well-pleasing unto Him.'" Muslim scholars describe this person as one who is content and satisfied with what he/she has, regardless of "abundance or scarcity, prosperity or shortages, prohibitions or permissiveness. It is content without any doubt and does not change heart or deviate from the straight path, and is not fearful during terrifying events" (Al-Jasmani, 1996, p. 16). The fourth Caliph, Imam Ali (1990, p. 475), elaborated that a person at this stage is tempered with magnanimity and practices what he preaches, stating:

> Good deeds are anticipated of them and bad ones are impossible. . . . He forgives those who inflict injustice upon him, gives to those who deprive him, and reaches out to those who desert him. . . . He is calm in the face of calamities, patient when challenged by adversity, and thankful during times of prosperity. He does not violate the rights of those whom he dislikes and does not blindly favor those whom he prefers. He admits the rights of others before there is a judgment against or for him. He is not negligent with what he has been entrusted. . . . He does not ignore a fact when reminded of it. He does not speak ill of people . . . and does not rejoice when others experience misfortune.

According to Shariati (1979), people who reach the *Mutamainna* stage tend "the earth . . . with the power of their industry . . . create a life overflowing with abundance, enjoyment and prosperity" without suspending feeling and all sense of value. They are those in whom the peculiarly human capacity "to perceive the spirit of the world, the profundity of life, the creation of beauty, and the belief in something higher than nature and history" has not been weakened or paralyzed. At the *Mutamainna* stage, a person is responsible and committed to ethical conduct. His/her intentions and actions are one and the same.

The above four levels of psyche are descriptive of personal values and life-styles. The domination by a particular psyche determines the intensity and priority of human needs and behavior. At each level, a person is conscious of his/her actions. This is significantly different from Sigmund Freud's model. Freud, one of the pioneers in studying human psychology, suggested that people, due to their differences in personality, deal with their fundamental drives differently. He postulated that there is a battle between two parts of the soul, the "It" or id (unconscious part) and the "I" proper or the "ego" (an individual's picture of physical and social reality) and the "superego" (storehouse of an individual's values). Freud views the "It" as the hidden or essence of the soul and the "I" as the open and apparent part of the soul. The "It" and "I" are destined to be continuously at war and only "compromise, but never harmony, [can] be achieved between them" (Wilber, 1999, p. 583). This is not similar to Islamic thinking. In Islam, a person is free to choose his/her direction in life, depending on the psyche at a particular stage. The constant struggle or war within oneself, as Freud suggests, is found in the second (*Ammara*) and third (*Lawama*) levels. Even at these levels, the inclination to progress toward "goodness" and "perfection" is always an aim. This is contrary to Freud's assumption that the urge to do things right is not considerably weaker, relative to the urge to do evil. At the last level (*Mutamainna*), people appear to display no uncertainty about their choices in life. The Quran (49:15) explicitly refers to this level by stating that believers are the sincere ones who have "never doubted."

Table 1.1 presents a model of personality and disposition to engage in ethical behavior. It can be seen that the two extremes *Sawala* and *Mutamainna* represent two contradictory tendencies in expected outcomes. The first does not seek an ethical result, though it might take place unintentionally. On the other hand, a person who reaches the *Mutamainna* stage is driven by the desire to serve others and he/she engages in ethical activities that are destined to lead to the greatest benefit. At the stage of *Ammara*, the prospect for engaging in ethical conduct is there, however, the likelihood is not high. In contrast, at the *Lawama* level, the *possibility* of attaining ethical results is relatively much higher. This is because individuals at this stage are aware of their duties and what should be done to rectify wrongdoing.

Table 1.1   Level of existence and ethical behavior

Level of Existence	Preoccupation	Ethical Inclination
Sawala	Passionate pursuit of desires, irrespective of the concerns of others.	Is not a concern.
Ammara	Aware that his/her actions might harm others, nevertheless, inclination is high to follow desires.	Ethical output is not pursued for its sake.
Lawama	Concern with satisfying one's needs and contributing something useful to others.	Ethical conduct is sought.
Mutamainna	Serving society and spreading benefits.	Ethical conduct is a given.

The point is that ethical conduct is shaped by the surrounding environment, expectations, and the personality of actors involved. Not all actions lead to ethical behavior. Though it is desirable that the greatest number of people gain benefits, this is only possible when the *Mutamainna* stage of development is common. In the other stages of personality, there is a constant struggle to create the right conditions where people become more conscious of their role and have the capacity to internalize ethical norms.

ETHICAL FOUNDATIONS AND ASSUMPTIONS

Al-Shatibi (2011), a Muslim jurist (died 1388), identified five types of rules regarding actions and legality: *mubah* (permissible), *wajib* (obligatory), *mandub* (recommended), *mukruh* (discouraged), and *haram* (forbidden). The last two categories (discouraged and forbidden) are within boundaries where the rules are clear and thus any activity within these two categories must be avoided, as the possibility of violating ethical standards is high; for example, gambling, engaging in selling and buying alcohol, charging interest, hoarding commodities, indecent advertisements, and trading in counterfeit goods.

In the case of what is permissible, there is no demand for exclusion or commission and it is left up to the person to choose. Furthermore, Al-Shatibi argued that the permissible category is equal in strength to that of the obligatory and recommended categories, in so far as none of these entail a demand for omission. When the Prophet Mohamed was asked how to cultivate reasoning, his answer was, "Avoid the forbidden, perform obligatory duties, you acquire reason. Seek to go beyond what is required and obligatory in doing good things, your capacity to reason improves and you get closer to god" (quoted in Al-Mawardi, 2002, p. 28).

According to Carney (1983), the fivefold model of duty in Islam is a blend of duties deriving their force from commandments, principles, laws (required and forbidden categories), and acts of virtues deriving their persuasiveness from an attractive ideal of human nature and translated into unique kinds of duties (recommended and discouraged categories). When Carney contrasted the threefold Christian model (recommended, discouraged, and permissible) with that of the fivefold Islamic, he concluded that the fivefold model of obligation appears to "more adequately respond to our moral experience than does the threefold model" (p. 167).

Ethical actions in Islam, however, cannot be understood without a familiarity with three philosophical logics: *Maslaha Aamah*, moderation, and *ehsan*. All three constitute the foundations for ethical conduct and responsible action. They represent the theoretical framework that guides the faithful in conducting their affairs. This framework not only sets Islamic ethical perspectives apart from the other two monotheistic religions, Christianity and Judaism, but also makes it easy to delineate the purpose and scope of business ethics. The first, *Maslaha Aamah*, situates the interests of the people at the heart of business ethics. This is because everything on earth is created to serve people. The Quran (45:12–13) states, "It is God who has subjected the sea to you that ships may sail through it by His command that ye may seek of His bounty and that ye may be grateful. And He has subjected to you as from Him all that is in the heavens and on earth: behold in this are signs indeed for those who reflect." While Christian ethics, especially Protestantism, asserts that love is the way to absolve sins and puts "people at the center of concern" (see Fletcher, 1966, p. 50), it differs from Islamic ethics not only in promoting that ends justify the means, which is outlawed in Islam, but also because Islamic instructions and the logic of *Maslaha Aamah* underscore that everything in this world is created to serve people.

Indeed, the centrality of human beings and the belief that God's approval is contingent on benefiting others makes the relationship between self and societal interests a subject that goes beyond intellectual exercise and is a practical aim for those who seek to observe the principles of the faith. This is the very reason that Islamic instructions underscore the necessity of acquiring knowledge to behave ethically, especially in the marketplace. The Quran (29:43) states, "And such are the parables we set forth for mankind, but only those who understand them have knowledge," while the Prophet observes, "Goodness is a habit. . . . Whomsoever God intends to do good, He boosts his knowledge in religion" and "The most excellent in my community are those who attain knowledge" (quoted in Al-Mawardi, p. 53). Imam Al-Ghazali (2006, died 1111, p. 504) stated, "Be a knowledgeable person who works and you will reach your highest aim."

Knowledge, however, is worthless if it is not utilized in the service of the people. Al-Mawardi (2002) argued, "There is no benefit from knowledge if it is not translated into action. As some learned people indicated, the fruit of knowledge is put to the service of the people. . . . The best knowledge is the one that generates benefit. . . . A perfection of knowledge is applying it" (p. 122). The essence of knowledge should be put in the service of people and the best of knowledge is that which eases people's lives and facilitates their progress. This is because serving people is the primary end of any ethical conduct. As the Prophet observes, "The closest people to God are those who serve people" and "whatever the believers consider a good act, then it is good in the eyes of God. And whatever they deem bad, God treats as bad" (quoted in Al-Maki, 1995, p. 551). The Prophet, too, instructs people to appreciate others and be kind to them stating, "He who does not thank people, does not thank God." The second Caliph, Omer, elaborated on this explaining that "If God likes a person He guides him to be kind to others. Your position in the eyes of God is contingent upon your stance toward people. Whatever God's feelings towards you, is exactly what you tender to people" (quoted in Ibn Abed Raba Al-Andelesy, 1996, died 985, vol. 2, p. 155).

Thus, the logic of *Maslaha Aamah* implies that serving and benefiting people are preconditions for God's approval of any action. *Maslaha Aamah* encompasses two elements: acquisition of benefits and repulsion of harm. Both elements are needed to judge whether an act is ethical or not. Most Islamic scholars argue that applying these two elements leads to the enhancement or advancement of societal welfare. This is because all actions are judged right or wrong upon the serving of public interests (see Al Mahami, 1987, p. 556).

The second logic that represents an outlook and orientation that guides action is moderation. This logic implies seeking a Middle Way. According to Hofstede (1999, p. 43), the rationale for the Middle Way "is that any virtue becomes a sin when extended too far." This is precisely what the Quran (25:67), expressed in terms of spending, states: "Those who, when they spend, are not extravagant and not niggardly, but hold a just balance between those extremes. . . ." Furthermore, in its instructions to believers the Quran (2:143) reminds them to behave justly and act according to what was intended for them: "Thus we have made you a middle-way nation."

The significance of moderation is that it not only enables a person to be steadfast and avoid extreme positions, but it also minimizes troubles and enhances reflection and rethinking of those matters that are important for personal growth and societal cohesiveness. Imam Ali (1990, p. 624), in his letter to his governor in Egypt, elaborated on this when he instructed him "let your preference in all matters be the most righteous (modest) and one that encourages justice and has the approval of the majority of the constituency." In addition, he stated (1990, p. 122), "All extremes lead to nowhere. Only the middle way is the right way. . . . It leads to safety and desired results." Al-Andelesy (1996, vol. 2, p. 199) argued that "The best way is the Middle Way." Likewise, Al-Deinori (1999, p. 381) reported that "Most ethical work is associated with great moderation." This conveys that moderation is an essential foundation for ethical conduct and morally driven actions.

In business conduct, Islamic ethics often highlight the significance of moderation in spending, consuming, leadership, and human resource management. While spending is specified above, and in Chapters 6 and 8, in terms of consumerism, the Quran (7:31) instructs, "Waste not by excess, for God loveth not the wasters." Similarly, the Prophet stated that "He who is prudent in spending will not be dependent on others."

In the context of leadership, the Prophet stated, "Be gentle (to the people) and be not hard (on them), and make (them) rejoice and do not incite (them) to aversion" (quoted in Muhammad Ali, p. 404). Likewise, the fourth Caliph, Imam Ali (1990, p. 402), asserted, "The best people are those who keep to the middle ground. Those are the ones you should follow." And Al-Andelesy (1996, vol. 3, p. 61) stated, "Do not be too lenient so as to be taken advantage of and do not be so rigid that people stay away from you. Being in the Middle Way is the safest action." In terms of human resource management, the Prophet instructed, "Whoever has his brother under his control should feed him from what he eats and should give him clothes to wear from what he wears. Do not impose on them a task which should overpower them, and if you impose on them a task, then help them (in doing it)" (quoted in Muhammad Ali, 1977, pp. 383–4). Thus, in business conduct, Islamic ethics underscores the importance of moderation in building a sound organization and in creating a solid foundation for morally driven conduct. These will be addressed in detail in the chapters that follow.

The third element of the theoretical framework for ethical action is *ehsan*. The philosophy of *ehsan* stems from a recognition that humanity, in order to survive and thrive, has to be inclusive and tolerant, responsive and appreciative to changes and emerging needs. The concept of *ehsan* is the embodiment of goodness and generosity in interaction and conduct, be it on a personal or organizational level. As a projection of goodness and generosity, *ehsan* practically and spiritually encompasses mercy, justice, forgiveness, tolerance, and attentiveness. This means the term conveys a much broader meaning than any of its components, and in the marketplace it represents a philosophical logic that guides participants of the business exchange function to observe the rights of each, while attempting to ease difficulties for others. In a sense, the logic of *ehsan* in its meaning goes beyond what existing stakeholder orientation advocates. For example, Al-Mawardi (2002, p. 169) quoted Sefan ibn Ayneeha (an early Muslim scholar) saying, "Justice means that what is declared and what is kept secret are identical. . . . *Ehsan* conveys that what has been kept secret is much better than the declared deed." Al-Maki (1995, p. 561) viewed it from a different angle stating that "Justice is to take what is right for you and give what is right to others. *Ehsan* is to absolve part of your right and give more than what you owe to others to be among those who do the right things." Though the end results of both views are the betterment of society, the implication of *ehsan* in the marketplace is far reaching and certainly leads to a functional and ethical exchange in the market. And since *ehsan* focuses on relationships among actors of the exchange function, judging whether any action or conduct is right or wrong must stem primarily from the assurance that no market participants are hurt or their rights or those of the society as a whole are ignored. In other words, the philosophy of *ehsan* does not compartmentalize the rights of market actors as rivals and as allies but as significant members of a worthy and religiously sanctioned cause. This implies that interactions in the marketplace are treated primarily as relationships among equals who seek to offer benefits beyond self and immediate interests. The Quran (49:13) states, "The noblest of you in the sight of God are the best of you in conduct."

Accordingly, business ethics is defined as principles and rules that govern individuals' and organizations' conduct in the marketplace. It goes beyond legal and social requirements to include furthering public interest and espousing the philosophy of *ehsan*. Figure 1.2 presents a framework for producing ethical conduct. The elements of the framework include the foundations (commitment to meeting public interests, moderation, and the philosophy of *ehsan*) and the prerequisites for ethical actions (good intentions and virtue ethics). Without a concern for societal welfare and a disposition toward *ehsan*, neither good intentions nor virtues will be cultivated. Thus, engaging in processes or methods that are morally driven and lead to desirable or ethical behavior becomes ordinary behavior. That is, in Islamic thinking, the intent, means, and end results must be consistent and

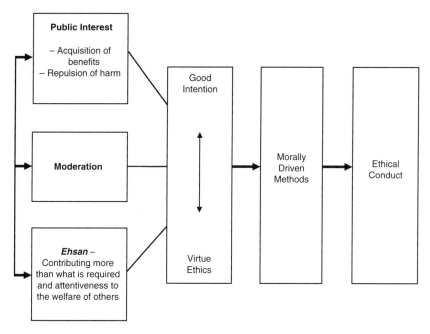

Figure 1.2   Theoretical framework for ethical conduct

moral. It is important to note that the logic of *ehsan* in connection with the element of public interest (generating the greatest benefits, rejection of harm, and promoting the logic of moderation) offers, in theory, a standard of conduct that exceeds what is expected by law or the existing market capitalism ethos.

CONCLUSION

This chapter provides an overview of business ethics in Islam. Ethics, in general, and business ethics were defined. The chapter then offered a brief introduction of existing theories on ethics and presented an Islamic perspective on ethics. It was argued that Islamic instructions offer an integrated framework within which to address business ethics. In this regard, a model for providing greater good to society was introduced.

The chapter, too, discussed the fivefold model of duties. These duties are specified as permissible, obligatory, recommended, discouraged, and forbidden. While business activities are encouraged, certain other engagements are either forbidden or discouraged. In addition, there are some activities which are permissible but under certain conditions they may be situated as doubtful and, thus, should be avoided.

Finally, the chapter presented a model for ethical conduct. The theoretical elements, public interests, moderation, and the logic of *ehsan*, were identified along with the prerequisite components, intention, and virtue ethics. All lead to selection of means that are in harmony with serving societal interests and producing desirable behavior.

2. Sources of ethical problems in business

Though religions are assumed to govern, to a large degree, the moral and ethical behavior of their followers, the violation of ethical standards in the field of business is certainly a common occurrence irrespective of religious teachings. In countries with Muslim majorities (CMMs), this is no exception. From Algeria to Indonesia and from Sudan to Albania, unethical and questionable business behaviors are on the rise. The media has extensively covered, for example, the corruption scandal of the major Algerian oil company Sonatrach, Indonesia's beef corruption scandal, and the Mehran Bank scandal in Pakistan, to name but a few. Among the ten most corrupt countries listed in the 2012 Corruption Perceptions Index (CPI), six are Muslim countries and none are listed among the least corrupt top 20 countries (see Transparency International, 2012).

The World Bank (2013) defines corruption as "Lack of integrity or honesty—especially susceptibility to bribery." The Bank goes on to underscore the devastating impact of corruption stating that corruption:

- Discourages businesses from operating in the corrupt setting, reducing the overall wealth of a country.
- Reduces the amount of money a government has available to pay workers and buy supplies, such as books, medicine, and computers.
- Distorts the way governments use their money, lowering the quality of the services they provide for schools, health clinics, roads, sewer systems, police, etc.
- Allows those with money or connections to bend the laws or government rules in their favor.
- Undermines everyone's trust in governments.

However, the Bank's definition of ethical problems, such as corruption, is surprisingly narrow. As we will see later, in Islam corruption has a broader meaning than simply "lack of integrity." According to the World Bank, lack of integrity is the major component of corruption and, thus, of ethical problems. Lack of integrity is a powerful factor that shapes human behavior and influences a person's inclination to engage in questionable behavior. Across centuries and religions, lack of integrity has been articulated and recognized as an undesirable quality that stands in contrast to virtue and to what is good and cherished. Islam, like other religions, condemns lack of integrity and considers it the reason for most failures in human interactions and relationships. The absence of unethical conduct, from an Islamic perspective, amounts to an ideal society.

Though the Quran and the Prophet have vehemently censured corruption in all forms, corruption is an inescapable fact of everyday life, be it in business or economic affairs. In fact, some types of corruption such as bribes have become endemic. A survey found that in Egypt 64 per cent of the population believed corruption had worsened in recent years; in Tunisia, the proportion was 80 per cent; while in Libya 46 per cent of the population said the country had become more corrupt (Torchia, 2013). While each year the Transparency Report manifests widespread corruption, efforts to limit corruption have also increased. For example, Kuwait, in June 2013, issued an anti-corruption law which severely punishes crimes, including the manipulation of public tenders and auctions, bribery, counterfeiting, forgery, and graft. It also covers financial disclosure and money laundering (Trenwith, 2013). Likewise, Saudi Arabia, in 2011, established the National Authority for Combating Corruption as a national strategy to protect integrity and fight corruption in the Kingdom (Sambidge, 2011).

The Quran (35:10) states, "It is He who exalts each deed of righteousness. Those that plot evil, for them chastisement is terrible; and the plotting of such will be void (of result)" and (17:9) "To the believers who work deeds of righteousness, they shall have a magnificent reward." Likewise, the Prophet declares, "God curses the one who gives and the one who receives bribes" and "He who deceives and plots will go to hell" (quoted in Al-Mawardi, 2002, p. 124). In almost all ethical instructions included in these two sources, the issue of integrity is underscored. Those with integrity are assumed to exhibit moderation and *ehsan* and strive not to harm others. Those with integrity are more likely to either minimize or prevent unethical engagements. But those who lack integrity are easily swayed to follow their desires and commit vice. This was articulated by Al-Mawardi (2002, p. 123) when he wrote: "Excusing the soul deceives it and lures it into engaging in bad deeds. He who says what he does not do is a cheater. He who gives orders to carry out what is unsuitable is a deceiver. And he whose inward belief is inconsistent with his outward behavior is a hypocrite." The longer we persist in acting with lack of integrity, the deeper this behavior is rooted and difficult to overcome.

In this chapter, we will address the factors that stimulate corruption, look at theories of moral development, and examine factors that shape ethically driven business decisions and the forces that facilitate the prevention of unethical behavior. At the heart of the discussion is the issue of self-interest. Though there are many factors which shape an individual's orientations and practices, self-interest remains the starting point for deciphering why people are lured into unethical behavior.

HUMAN NATURE

The disposition to engage in ethical or unethical behavior is linked to human nature. Whether in business or personal affairs, human nature plays a central role in how they are conducted. The concept of human nature manifests differences in people's outlook and conduct. Differences in human nature imply the existence of various needs and approaches that must be satisfied and which necessitate that people cooperate among themselves to fulfill them (Al-Mawardi, 2002). Accordingly, ethical orientations and behaviors vary. This variation is not confined to people from different cultures but is also found within a culture.

Understanding human nature, therefore, is important for deciphering the reasons why individuals engage in dissimilar behavior and how their inclinations are exhibited in various forms. Not surprisingly, researchers have long been fascinated with what makes people react or act in certain ways, what stimulates them to select specific jobs and careers, and how their expectations originate and evolve. Scientists and social scientists have developed their own conceptualization of and approach to human nature. Hence, our knowledge of how human beings engage has expanded substantially over the years. This is evident in the business world where organizations and managers have embarked on various motivational and human resource programs to improve productivity and sustain growth. Since the Hawthorne studies in the late 1920s, the subject of human nature and work environment has been the focus of organizational studies and analysis. Several motivational approaches in the workplace have been developed and applied worldwide, especially in the Western world. Indeed, in the Western world the philosophies of human nature have developed around three traditions of thought: the tradition of reason and nature, the tradition of will and artifice, and the tradition of the rational will (Wrightsman, 1992). Under the tradition of reason and nature, people are part of the natural order of things. They have the faculty of reason through which they can discover the natural laws that govern the universe. Human behavior is subject to these natural laws. The tradition of will and artifice assumes that human beings are ruled by passions and appetites rather than by reason. The third school of thought advances that history belongs to persons of action rather than to persons of contemplation.

Consequently, ideas and passions are realized and articulated only in practice and "only through action do the mind and will make themselves public and visible" (Wrightsman, 1992). These general schools of thought have had a tremendous influence on Western assumptions about human nature in academia and business.

There are also various sets of assumptions concerning the nature of human beings. These assumptions vary significantly in their implications and organizational strategies. They range from the modified trait approach, economic man, to human complexity. Most of these assumptions originated in the West and are shaped either by Christianity and Judaism or secular outlooks. Their popularity in the literature manifests an interest in understanding human motives and psyche in the business world. While Wrightsman (1992) seems to think that his assumptions about and categories of human nature can provide a realistic understanding of human tendencies, Schein (1980) suggests that human nature and motivation are highly complex and are not yet fully understood.

However, the issue of self-interest is also commonly debated in studies concerning human nature. As noted, the reoccurrence of corporate scandals and corruption, along with media intensive coverage of fraudulent behavior, have, in recent years, underscored the necessity for recognizing the motives for engaging in unethical behavior, especially the quest to accumulate wealth in any way possible and irrespective of the harm to others or the society at large. This has brought to the fore the issue of greed and self-interest. While both greed and self-interest are not necessarily harmful at all times, on many occasions they lead to untold harm to society and individuals. The boundaries, however, of harmful and acceptable greed are not easily demarcated. *The Economist* (2002) has suggested that greed can be good if managed properly. Likewise, Wang and Murnighan (2011) argue that greed is not necessarily bad. Their reasoning is that greed is a central driver behind capitalism and competition and that focus on self-interest maximization enables people to figure out the economic benefits of greed.

Unlike in other religions, the indeterminate area between harmful and acceptable greed, according to Islam, is to be avoided. This is in line with Islamic instructions which call for avoidance of any action or transaction where there is a probability of being in the wrong (see Al-Maki, 1995, for detail). However, in the context of greed, the Arab philosopher Abu Othman Ibn Omer Al Jahiz (1998), who died in 868, suggested in his book, *Misers*, that greed is not a totally bad characteristic. It can benefit the self and occasionally benefit others. He provided detailed stories and commentaries on greed delineating, in humorous language, its good and bad aspects by reflecting on daily practices and behaviors of individuals from various social groups (p. 173). He argued that misers are not those who live in a distressed state but are those who are greedy, though they are wealthy; they live on fertile land, but behave as if they are poor. In his book, Al Jahiz presented a letter from a generous, wealthy person to a miser in which he stated, "Those who accumulate wealth but do not spend it should be avoided." The wealthy man added, "People identify a miser as one who is not stingy with himself. He who is greedy, who follows his passions and makes certain to satisfy his desires should be scorned. Moreover, a person acquires the title of a miser if he avoids engaging in acts that accentuate goodness and are appreciated by others" (p. 227). The miser responded ironically in a detailed letter which in part states (p. 250):

> He who wants something is motivated and intensifies his discovery efforts to reach his goal. The bad aspect of affluence is that it deepens thoughtlessness, while the virtue of poverty is the stimulation of thinking. If you seek affluence at the expense of your wellbeing, you become intoxicated with affluence; intoxication is the trait of those who take from others and who are seen as deceivers. If you do not want to have the fate of the lazy and an animal existence and want to combine the soul of the wealthy with the pride and happiness of being rich, if you want the alertness of a sensitive man, a good sense of humor, to have the quality of being able to differentiate between a person who does not like to work for a living and the one who does, then you should become thrifty and ready yourself for any uncertainties and safeguard yourself from any deception.

In quoting the generous wealthy person, Al Jahiz gives a broad definition of greed; a definition that goes beyond the desire to accumulate material things and/or the tendency to be niggardly. This broad meaning includes, in addition to economic behavior, a spiritual and social dimension and a disposition to fear God, to be thankful, to be content, and to be appreciative of others. Furthermore, the generous, rich person appears to differentiate between self-interest and greed, arguing that those who are greedy do not ultimately serve their own interests, as they are looked upon with contempt by others and God does not appreciate their behavior. In his book, Al Jahiz asserts that though greed and self-interest are difficult to differentiate between, there are occasions where a greedy person is not fully aware that by being greedy he is harming his/her self. In this context, Al Jahiz reflects the Quranic (92:8–10) instructions which state: "But he who is a greedy miser and thinks himself self-sufficient, and gives the lie to the best, we will indeed make smooth for him the path to misery" and (3:180) ". . . let not those who covetously withhold of the gifts which God hath given them of His grace think that it is good for them; nay, it will be worse for them. Soon it will be tied to their necks like a twisted collar on the day of judgment."

In describing misers, Al Jahiz presents a portrait of people who are complex in their psyche, but their greed clouds their judgment and thus they undertake activities that ultimately lead to the destruction of their reputation in their community. He writes:

> Why do they call greed enhancement and covetousness thrifty; why do they defend withholding spending as assertiveness; why do they equate spending on the needy to waste; why do they treat generosity as squandering and easing distress as ignorance; why do they persist in their greed and follow practices whereby other people will call them misers, though they do not like this characterization; why do they engage in earning activities though they despise spending? How can they object, though they acquire knowledge, to the contempt of the public; how can they pride themselves, with their depth of knowledge, in what they agree to denounce? . . . What is this contradictory framework of thinking and psychological inconsistency? What is the reason for hiding what is noble and clear and recognizing what is favorable but unclear? (pp. 12–13)

In recent years, scholars have underscored the notions advanced by Al Jahiz in the ninth century. Wang and Murnighan (2011, p. 283) argue that it is almost impossible to identify "when self-interest ends and when greed starts; its exact demarcation remains elusive." In order to understand the miser's conflict with himself, one must understand that in Islamic thinking there is always a struggle between reason and one's soul. When a person has faith and confidence, reason restrains the soul. However, in the absence of confidence and faith, temptation might overcome reason. While Al Jahiz underscored this complexity, he further indicated that the situation, i.e. temptation, appears when a person desires to restrain his/her soul. Thus, those who let their desires determine how to manage their wealth have no one to blame but themselves. He stated, "Wealth is temptation and the soul has desires. Since capital is difficult to obtain, the soul longs for what is unobtainable. And it is a known fact that the soul seeks to accumulate more" (p. 231). However, Al Jahiz qualified this tendency stating, "It is he who lacks thought and vision who is destined to glorify those with wealth." In his arguments and stories, Al Jahiz made a point that greed is a form of corruption. He quoted the second Caliph, Omer, who declared, "Making a poor person wealthy is easier for me than reforming a corrupt person" (p. 264). Though greed is a kind of corruption, it is almost impossible to reform a greedy person. This conveys that in real life eradicating greedy tendencies is a difficult task. This could be the reason that Islamic injunctions, in general, denounce greed. The Quran (104:1–6) instructs, "Woe to every [kind of] slanderer and backbiter who hoards wealth and thinks that his property will make him live forever! Impossible! They will be thrown headlong into *hutamah*. Would that you knew what *hutamah* is!

It is a fierce fire created by God to penetrate into the heart. It will engulf them in its long columns of flames."

LEVELS OF EXISTENCE AND ETHICAL INCLINATIONS

Various scholars who have tackled the issue of human development have underscored the fact that maturity and motivation play a role in interacting with others. Early researchers, such as Erikson (1964) and Graves (1970), explored human existence and the complexity of human nature. In fact, the latter, in a large empirical study that was originally undertaken to support Maslow's theory of motivation and human needs, came up with contradictory results and subsequently questioned the validity and conclusion of the core theory. Erikson (1964), describing the fundamental human developmental stages, suggested that people mature and grow as a result of their handling of various problems and crises. He identified seven stages: infancy, early childhood, childhood and adolescence, adolescence, early adulthood, adulthood and middle age, and middle and old age. At each stage, a person faces different problems and difficulties. For example, at the early childhood stage, an individual struggles with autonomy versus shame and initiative versus guilt. As people mature they face the problem of maintaining effort and interest. In the later stage (middle and old age), individuals attempt to maintain a sense of self-worth and integrity. Erikson assumed that a healthy personality progresses in sequential stages. This, however, may be questioned in other cultures. Moreover, not all individuals go through predetermined specific stages before other stages are completed. The assumption made by Erikson is that ethical inclination and the capacity to differentiate between right and wrong corresponds to each stage.

Graves (1970) speculated that people progress through consecutive levels of "psychological existence" and at each level there are certain values that they prefer. The progression, Graves assumed, is determined by the ability of individuals to acquire and assimilate knowledge and to develop and exercise talents. Depending on the person's cultural conditioning and perception of the opportunities and constraints in the environment, his/her level of psychological existence can become arrested at a given level or can move upward or downward. The level of existence of the mature human being is an unfolding process marked by the progressive subordination of the older lower level of existence to newer, higher-level value systems. Graves identifies six levels for a mature person or groups of mature human beings. These are: tribalistic (a submissiveness to authority and/or tradition), egocentric (aggressive, selfish, restless, impulsive, and, in general, not inclined to live within the limits and constraints of society's norms), conformist (follows existing societal norms and exhibits a low tolerance for ambiguity), manipulative (materialistic, expressive, and self-calculating; they search for avenues to meet their goals but not in an abhorrent way), sociocentric (a high need for affiliation and little concern for wealth; going along with others and serving people takes a priority), and existential (a high tolerance for those who have different values; usually expresses self but not at the expense of others). Unlike Erikson, Graves places great emphasis on values as the major determinant of human attitudes, behavior, and action. Feelings, motivations, preferences, thoughts, and acts reflect the value system at that particular level of existence. Graves sees a distinct hierarchy of needs on each level of the existence model. That is, Graves proposes that there is no idealized state, as mankind continuously evolves.

One of the most widely discussed theories of human development and moral involvement was developed by Kohlberg (1981). Kohlberg suggested a three-level model of moral reasoning and development: two pre-conventional stages (a person is obedient and/or driven by personal gain), two conventional stages (a person is a conformist and/or highly socialized and is driven by obligations toward society), and two post-conventional stages (a person seeks to uphold societal norms and expectations and/or is driven by a worldly outlook where justice and concerns are universal). The first two stages and the last two resemble, to a degree, the Islamic views which were presented in Chapter 1. Kohlberg's first-level pre-conventional stage (unchecked impulsive self-centered behavior) corresponds to *Sawala*, while his last level, the post-conventional level (universal principles of justice, equity, etc.) shares much in common with the *Mutamainna* stage. Kohlberg's secular model, however, differs from Islamic perspectives in its emphasis on hierarchal arrangements. From an Islamic perspective, it is knowledge along with spirituality that regulates rules governing behavior, tempers desires, and guides people away from impulsive urges and toward socially and ethically responsible involvement.

Sources of ethical problems for each level of existence, according to Islamic instructions, are briefly illustrated here (see Table 2.1).

Sawala (A Passion for Temptations)

At this stage, people have no interest in integrating their own interests with those of society's. Their primary emphasis on satisfying immediate desires leads them to engage in temptations. Though these people may try to avoid punishment, their obsession with self-interest blinds them to the consequences of their unbridled desires on themselves and others. Thus, involve-

Table 2.1   Levels of development and ethical inclination

Level of Existence	Character	Ethical Tendency
Sawala	Unconcerned with integrating self-interest with that of others, blinded by following desires at any expense.	Destined to engage in unethical activities.
Ammara	Aware that the soul is inclined to follow desires, but willing to confess to mistakes and misdeeds.	Tendency to be involved in unethical behavior, but attempts to limit harm to others.
Lawama	Has a clear understanding of moral and ethical standards and recognizes their own weaknesses.	Engagement in unethical actions is highly minimized.
Mutamainna	In tune with good deeds; there is no moral ambiguity.	Driven to do good deeds and serve others.

ment in unethical activities is a certainty at this stage. People at this level do not display moderation and disregard *ehsan* and public good. The Quran (23:71) warns that those who follow their desires are destined to create trouble and engage in misdeeds: "Had the truth followed their desires, truly the heavens and the earth and all beings therein would have been destroyed."

Ammara (The Prone-to-Evil Psyche)

Unlike the above stage, individuals at this level are aware that their souls are inclined to follow their desires. Though ethical considerations are overlooked in pursuing desires, a person, nevertheless, is willing to admit to their mistakes and misdeeds. That is, a person is aware that their actions have consequences, be they rewards or punishments. The mere acknowledgment of misdeeds may minimize the impact of their unethical actions on others or at least limit the harm. Though a person may not exhibit moderation in behavior, the person is still aware of *ehsan* and public good, but will not engage in them.

Lawama (Self-Reproachment)

People at this level are always struggling to avoid wrongdoings and misdeeds. They are aware of temptations, but seek to resist them. Individuals at this level have a clear understanding of moral and ethical standards and know their weaknesses. Thus, they tend to take responsibility for their actions and shun temptation. Engagement in unethical actions is, therefore, consciously minimized and moderation in behavior and action are sought. The Quran explains that people at this stage fear engagement in wrongdoing and, thus, attempt to control their desires. It states, " . . . paradise will be the dwelling of those who have feared their Lord and restrained their soul from acting according to its desires" (79:40).

Mutamainna (The Righteous)

At this stage, a person acts righteously as there is no moral ambiguity. Indeed, a perfect consistency between intention and deed takes place and a person is completely aware of his/her role in society and what should be done to serve both self and others. Unethical acts are inconceivable and virtue is the driving force. That is, at this stage a person exhibits moderation, engages in *ehsan*, and seeks the betterment of the society.

Al-Mawardi (2002, p. 173) must have been influenced by the above Quranic classification of personalities in the context of disinterest in avoiding wrongdoing or not when he identified four types:

1. Those who initiate doing what is right. This type represents a munificent person who seeks to maximize benefits to others and uphold societal norms and expectations.
2. Those who emulate. This exemplifies a prudent person who seeks to avoid wrongdoing.
3. Those who prefer not to engage in doing the right things. This represents a person who knows what is good, but is indifferent to the consequences.
4. Those who purposefully seek involvement in unethical acts. This exemplifies a rude and egotistic person.

Morality and ethical discipline are characteristically linked to the evolution of personality. The major assumption in the personality development field is that people have certain values, beliefs, and norms, which in turn determine their attitudes, tendencies, and priorities. However, development theories differ in terms of their perspectives on the nature of each stage. Some theories assume that development of personalities appear to progress in certain directions. That is, these theories consider that development goes through sequential stages. This, however, may be questioned as not all individuals go through predetermined specific stages before other stages are completed. There are various factors in the environment which may influence the progression and there are certain setbacks which make regression from a higher to a lower stage possible. These factors, therefore, influence human ethical outlooks and behavior.

FACTORS THAT SHAPE ETHICAL DISPOSITION IN MAKING DECISIONS IN BUSINESS

According to Islamic perspectives, humans constantly seek to better their lives. Their quest, however, is shaped by various factors and attainment of goals is not a given outcome, as the capacity to reach goals and the goals themselves vary. Early Islamic scholars asserted that gaining knowledge and experience and reaching a specific level of spiritual commitment influence people's outlook and ethical stance (see Al-Maki, 1995; Al-Mawardi, 2002; Ikhwan-us-Safa, 1999). Among the most important factors that shape ethical disposition and decisions are cultural confusion and discontinuity, self-censorship, indifference, authoritarian leaders, tunnel vision, rationalization, and blindness of the heart.

Cultural Discontinuity

From the Mongol invasion of the capital of the Abbasid state, Baghdad, in 1258, the Islamic world witnessed a rapid fragmentation that reached its peak when Western nations colonized countries with Muslim majorities (CMMs). Subsequent occupiers and invaders left their mark on the history and culture of these countries. This was augmented by lack of communication and cultural exchange among various parts of CMMs. With the exception of a few cultural centers, generations upon generations have lost their familiarity with and understanding of genuine Islamic culture, which was once characterized by openness, tolerance, and dedication to hard work and innovation. This has led to economic and social stagnation and with it the rise of flexible ethics that tolerate misdeeds and winning at any expense. British scholar, Rom Landau (1938, p. 8), noted that the financial downfall of the Middle East, for example, was inevitable because of the domination of the West. He stated that "Western greed, disguised as superiority, spread the rumor that without Western administration and financial advisors the Orient was doomed to failure." Landau wrote that Western Powers appointed corrupt indigenous individuals as political leaders to destroy the indigenous people's morale.

Unfamiliarity with cultural principles and history stands out as one of the most important factors that cloud the thinking of those who engage in business and other affairs. Left without a clear perspective on historical events and genuine Islamic views on matters that are crucial for human interaction and functioning, many people engage in questionable business affairs. For example, Islam prohibits any kind of cheating. The Prophet is clear in his injunction: "He who cheats us, is not one of us." Nevertheless, in some parts of CMMs, certain groups advocate that cheating in non-religious affairs is permissible. Likewise, transparency, once cherished in the early years of the Islamic state, is disregarded in business transactions, which leads to thriving corruption. In the business world, these aspects hinder business growth, market trust, and efforts to minimize corruption. For example, among the top 20 countries in developing nations for 2001–10, cited in *Illicit Capital Flows*, are eight nations in CMMs (Global Financial Integrity, 2012). Ranked at the top of these countries are: Malaysia, Saudi Arabia, UAE, Iraq, Qatar, and Brunei.

Self-Censorship

In Muslim societies, there is a tendency among groups or community members to refrain from criticizing, revealing, or informing about others' wrongdoings for fear that this might lead to inflicting unjust damage on the accused or could exacerbate tensions and conflicts. The Quran (49:10–12) instructs Muslims: "Believers, let not a group of you mock another. . . . Let not one of you find faults in another nor let anyone of you defame another. . . . Stay away from suspicion, for suspicion in some cases is a sin." However, at work, self-censorship indirectly leads to a repeat of wrongdoings and may induce others to follow suit. Though the religious injunctions were intended to prevent unsubstantiated accusations and the resultant discord, they were never meant to minimize or to overlook unethical conduct. In fact, both the Quran and the Prophet instruct believers to avoid wrongdoing and to confront those who engage in unethical conduct. The Prophet states, "When one sees a wrongdoing, he has to change it by force, if he cannot, then by voicing concern, and if he cannot, then by denouncing it in his heart; this, however, is the weakest faith."

   In the absence of clear ethical instructions and in an environment of fear and uncertainty, self-censorship may find fertile ground in which to thrive. In business affairs, this can lead to costly consequences and a dysfunctional organizational culture; a culture that obstructs performance and productive involvement. Though scholars in the field recognize the futility of self-censorship, no attempts have been made in CMMs to confront this rising phenomenon. Organizations, themselves, can provide incentives and motivational programs to encourage employees to promote ethical behavior and avoid any involvement that may lead to sustaining a self-censorship tendency.

Indifference

This is different from self-censorship, as it represents a state where a person either does not care about what is going on or attempts to limit his/her sense of responsibility. The first one constitutes a psychological withdrawal and has far-reaching implications for productivity and innovation in an organization. The ethical aspect of this state of mind is that employees do not feel that they are part of the organization and they have little or no stake in its success and growth. This may justify abusing its resources or engaging in questionable behavior. In the second case, employees consciously decide to distance themselves from unethical actions. In an era where organizations are becoming larger and fraud is increasing, many employees may think that they would be better off being indifferent to what is going on in their organization.

Fear of Authority

In fragmented and traditional societies, as in most countries where Muslims constitute the majority, both uncertainty in political and business affairs and clannish outlooks embolden executives and those who are in positions of power. These executives have a say in dictating how things should be run. In many cases, employees have to heed instructions given by executives, though they may be unethical. Employees may fear that they may lose their jobs if they defy an executive's order, believe that it is impolite not to comply with orders, or think that those with authority know what is good for the organization.

This situation exists, as well, in economically advanced countries. In fact, it is considered to be one of the major reasons for the extent of fraud and corruption on Wall Street. *Fortune* magazine (Morris, 2008, pp. 94–5) has labeled this "the wink-and-nod" and has stated that many in the financial sector are under pressure to overstate the value and underestimate the risk "of their trading positions . . . in order to boost their year-end bonuses . . . Bosses want results but not too many details." Motivated by personal gain and the pressures to perform, employees are tempted to engage in questionable practices and overlook risky consequences. The "wink-and-nod" era in business practice has led to serious deceptions and frauds. A number of frauds have resulted in the collapse of corporations, displacement of workers, and hardship for millions of people.

In some parts of CMMs, executives do not need to be indirect when practicing fraudulent behavior; they usually tell employees what they must do plainly. There are two reasons that might explain this phenomenon and one factor that severely limits its application. The first reason is that in

CMMs it is often impossible to differentiate between what is public and what is private. Executives, like most politicians, consider organizational wealth as something that they have a right to. This is especially true in public organizations where the differentiation between what is public and what is private is possibly clearer. The second reason is that most executives and political leaders claim legitimacy by selectively using an instruction from the Quran that sanctions obedience to those who are in power, though the Quran specifies that this is valid only when the leaders are just and fair. The Prophet, for example, asserts that, "Obedience is due only in that which is good" and that "To hear and obey [the authorities] is binding, so long as one is not commanded to disobey [God]." However, there is a potent factor that may deter one from directly ordering a subordinate to carry out a fraudulent or questionable action. This factor is fear of losing face in a highly personalized society. Even among corrupt people there is a degree of caution. They seek to protect their public image and standing in the community by projecting themselves as decent and concerned citizens.

Tunnel Vision

Two fatal problems can lead to making unethical decisions. The first is when individuals focus on limited goals and, thus, ignore other related issues. Focusing on a certain issue often leads to making decisions that have not been adequately evaluated and/or marginalizing certain issues, though this might later prove detrimental to optimization of the original goal. For example, the obsession with removing the regime from power in Iraq in 2003 and in Libya in 2011 did not take into consideration what would be needed to establish sound institutions and governments. This unleashed a chaos that people in both countries still suffer from, especially in terms of safety and economic security. The second problem that might lead to unethical decision making is the lack of a clear understanding of the problem and its consequences. For example, a Saudi Arabian newspaper, *Okaz*, reported that the government had seized a large quantity of meat that was spoiled from one of the major hotels in Mecca (see Al Hasani, 2013). The hotel administration had been focused on making a profit and had ignored the meat's expiration date.

Tunnel vision can be the result of time pressures, the quest to make a profit, lack of adequate information and preparation, limited experience, or absence of discipline and needed foresight. These issues might lead to consequences that harm society. Al-Maki (1995, p. 501) indicated that the obsession with gaining a profit can blind people from seeing what is ethical and what is not. He argued that if people follow the Quranic instruction (28:77), "Do thou good, as God has been good to thee, and seek not [occasions for] mischief in the land: for God loves not those who do mischief," neglecting essential issues would not take place.

Rationalization

This takes place when those in positions of responsibility engage in certain actions that might be considered unacceptable but are actually viewed as not bad or harmful. This is self-justification, which eventually leads to engaging in ethically questionable activities. The rationalization takes different forms. Chief among them: "the action will not hurt others," "the rest are doing it," "no one will notice," etc.

Blindness of the Heart

There are incidents that take place where the action might have harmful consequences. Nevertheless, the members of an organization look the other way. This is not the same as indifference or self-censorship. It is a situation where an individual pretends not to notice unethical behavior and corruption committed by others when it serves his/her interest. The Quran (22:46) warns, "Truly it is not the eyes that are blind, but the hearts which are in the chest." The objective is not to confront or inform anyone about the unethical behavior. In this situation, self-interest may play a major role. An individual may benefit in one way or another by not reporting the incident, or seek to be on the good side of those who committed the unethical act, especially if the individual is a new hire or in a lower organizational position. More importantly, blindness of the heart arises because of two other reasons: lack of moral clarity and unfamiliarity with the organizational ethics and expectations. While the first one is related to character, the second is the result of poor communication of organizational ethics and/or a weak organizational culture.

The above forces, individually and collectively, exercise a tremendous influence on managers and employees within organizations to engage in actions that they might later regret. It should be made clear that sometimes the actions are taken in a hurry and without careful reflection. Furthermore, there may be no ill intent. In any case, these forces are potent and often overwhelm the individual's capacity to reason. However, unethical conduct should neither be ignored nor justified. Not only should the individual be blamed but also the organization, as the latter plays a significant role in shaping the attitudes of those who work within it. Having a strong culture and/or a clearly articulated code of ethics and expectations usually minimizes the tendency to engage in wrongdoing. This, however, does not guarantee that unethical decisions will completely disappear.

What is almost certain is that corrupt individuals will have no incentive to remain in an organization that exhibits a strong culture and an enforceable code of ethics.

COMMON EXAMPLES OF UNETHICAL BEHAVIOR

Unethical behaviors differ in their form and magnitude. Their appearance and frequency also vary among countries. In recent years, the tactics used to engage in unethical behavior have become highly sophisticated. Moreover, in some countries corruption, for example, has become tolerated by higher authorities. In fact, higher authorities' encouragement of fraudulent behavior at lower levels is seen as an effective mechanism for diverting attention from their wrongdoings and in the process adds a sort of legitimacy to otherwise questionable activities. In a report by Reuters (see Al-Salhy, 2013), top government officers in Iraq acknowledged that corruption is widespread among military and intelligence officers stating, "Having paid to secure their positions, senior officers extort from those beneath them to cover the expense, while lower rank officers in turn take bribes to compensate themselves and pay their superiors to go on leave." However, these types of corruption, in comparison to big dealings with multinational corporations (MNCs), are almost negligible. The commissions received from winning huge contracts from governments amount to millions of dollars and those involved are usually well-connected individuals. What follows is a list of common unethical activities in CMMs:

1. **Receiving commissions from MNCs for contracting government agencies.** This is common in almost all CMMs and usually involves huge sums of money. In recent years, the British media have reported on commissions granted by MNCs to influential people in the Gulf region as compensation for their efforts in winning contracts with certain government agencies. For example, the *Financial Times* (see Jenkins and Binham, 2013) indicated that both authorities in England and the US were investigating Barclays for making improper payments to top government offices in one of the Gulf countries.
2. **Stealing from companies.** The decision to engage in such an action is either intentional or because the individual thinks that his/her action is not illegal and does not harm others. This is usually done by lower level employees in the organizational hierarchies. However, when the amount is relatively large this represents determination and planning and is a threat to the future of the company and its position in the market. According to the deputy chairman of a major conglomerate

in the Gulf (see Kanoo, 2006), "In the past, those who wanted to steal had to do so in the dark and away from prying eyes. Unfortunately, today, stealing has become an art . . . . It happens nearly every day."

3. **Violating instructions related to environment protection.** This is a common phenomenon and is found in almost all CMMs. For instance, hazardous materials that carry no warnings or are not in protective containers are often dumped on streets. Though there are several reasons for violating these instructions, the primary two factors are: poor or unenforceable government regulations and lack of awareness among many companies of the risks involved. Both reasons make it almost impossible to educate the public on this subject and to encourage employees to take precautions in protecting the environment. In Bangladesh, for example, medical waste and hazardous materials are found everywhere, even in the capital. Rahman (2012) reported, "Reckless dumping and sale of medical wastes continue to pose a serious threat to public health. Hundreds of children are engaged in recycling these wastes in factories in the old part of Dhaka city. The plastic used in the factories is mostly received from heaps of medical wastes collected by the street urchins from different government and private hospitals and clinics."

4. **Tacit agreements with competitors to manipulate market price.** While this situation usually takes place in certain cities, it is common almost everywhere during religious festivities when the demand is high (e.g., the month of Ramadan). In the United Arab Emirates, for example, the Federal National Council asked the Ministry of Economy to monitor the situation and take corrective action (see Salem, 2013). Likewise, in Indonesia, prices of beef and chicken more than doubled during Ramadan in 2013. The Indonesian Merchants Association "confirmed that in general the price of beef had increased by almost 40 per cent to Rp 120 000 per kilogram, while chicken meat surged to Rp 42 000 from Rp 27 000 per kilogram" (Saudale, Lumanauw, and Putra, 2013). Due to weak legal institutions in many CMMs, competitors often decide to raise their prices at the same time for a variety of reasons.

5. **Leaking information about institutions to outside actors.** This happens frequently through several social networks. Unaware of the consequences and the damage that might be inflicted on the organizations, employees volunteer to disclose to outsiders information related to their companies. On the other hand, disclosing information can be a deliberate act. In its Code of Ethics, the Turkey-based conglomerate Sabanci Holding states, "Private and confidential information includes information that might lead to a competitive disadvantage

of H. Ö. Sabanci Holding Inc. and Sabanci Group Companies, trade secrets, financial and other information that has not been publicly disclosed, employee's personal information, and information within the framework of 'confidentiality agreements' enacted with third parties."

6. **Using company property for personal purpose.** In a society where it is difficult to know where the personal ends and public matters begin, it is difficult to identify with certainty what constitutes violation of abuse of public property. This confusion has been brought to the surface in recent years by the presence of modern organizations. Many governments in CMMs have begun to issue regulations that govern how to use public property. The same is also true of major business organizations. Take, for example, in Indonesia where the government reminded civil servants not to use government vehicles for personal use during the Eid of Ramadan in 2013 (see Sihite and Tambun, 2013). In its decree, the government specified the dates for enforcing the decree, which implied that the use of public property for some types of personal use is widespread.

7. **Deceiving distributors and customers.** Despite clear religious instructions not to mislead or deceive either in personal or business affairs, some individuals harbor and act on their desires to deceive others. Sabanci has articulated in its Code of Ethics its commitment to customers, employees, and suppliers. In terms of its customers, it declares, "we approach our customers with respect, honour, fairness, equality, and courtesy."

8. **Receiving and giving bribes.** Like deception, giving and receiving bribes are prohibited both in the Quran and *Hadith* and vehemently denounced by scholars. Nevertheless, bribery, to a large degree, has become an epidemic in countries like Indonesia, Iraq, and Pakistan, and is flourishing in many other nations. For example, the Saudi Control & Investigation Board, in 2008, charged eight health officials with taking bribes from 13 Saudi and foreign businessmen. These officials took bribes for granting licenses to open new pharmacies, relocating them to other places, and/or transfering their ownership to others (see Ghafour, 2008). On the bright side, there are many individuals who refuse to take bribes, though the amount offered may be huge. A case in point is a report in the Saudi newspaper *Arab News* (2005) where a real estate developer offered a low salary civil servant a large amount in order to obtain ownership of land for his project, but the official turned it down. Companies in CMMs increasingly state in their code of ethics that bribes are prohibited and those who engage in bribery will be severely punished. The Petroleum Development Oman

states that the company "will not, directly nor indirectly, offer, solicit, accept or pay bribes in any shape or form, and requires its Employees to act likewise."

9. **Arriving late to work and/or avoiding performance of duties.** The emergence of this phenomenon in some CMMs stems from two mistaken assumptions. The first is that a job is a privilege rather than a responsibility. The second is that "everyone is doing it, so why shouldn't I?" In countries with large numbers of expatriate employees and workers, national employees tend to leave work to be carried out by expatriates. In recent years, religious leaders have been solicited to issue decrees denouncing this trend. In Saudi Arabia, the Grand Mufti issued a statement declaring, "Workers who are lazy or who sleep during office hours breach the trust they are assigned with, . . . Coming late and being negligent and lax, failing to pull your weight and not fulfilling the public needs are breaches of trust" (see *Arab News*, 2006).

10. **Receiving commissions from mediators.** As a result of increasing business activities with the outside world and increasing use of agents or mediators by foreign companies, individuals within companies often ask mediators to grant them certain amounts of money as gratitude for facilitating contracts with their company, even though the work is part of their normal duties as representatives of their companies. This can be found in working with buyers. In this case, buyers are forced to give a percentage higher than the percentage rate specified in the contract. In the United Arab Emirates, with real estate development experiencing a high growth rate, real estate executives have been charged with taking illegal commissions from the sale and resale of land (see Hartley, 2009).

11. **Selling company properties or government owned companies to relatives and friends well below market price.** Countries, in addition to CMMs, that have embarked on privatization have witnessed an increasing rise in this practice. In CMMs, however, resorting to such mechanisms is often looked on as perfectly fine and legal.

12. **Contracting with bogus companies for large amounts of money.** Executives in both state-owned businesses and the private sector use whatever opportunities are available to generate wealth illegally. These executives often utilize two methods to gain wealth, violating public trust and abandoning professional and moral responsibilities. The first mechanism is to contract a bogus company which subcontracts the operation to a credible company. The bogus company then channels a certain amount of the contract to these executives' (those who granted them the contract) foreign bank accounts. The second is to land a contract with a fake company and share whatever money is

transferred with the executives who then leave the country to avoid legal action. For example, *Iraqi Business News* (2011) in an article entitled, "Canadian Firm Wins $1.7bn Iraqi Power Contract," reported that the Iraqi Inspector General, after inquiries, ordered the cancellation of a contract with a company that was found not to exist (see Kami, 2011).

AVOIDING UNETHICAL DECISIONS

Both philosophers and practitioners have not only tackled the issue of making unethical decisions but also provided normative and applied guidelines for avoiding the temptation or the tendency to make questionable decisions. Aristotle argued, "no blessed man can become miserable; for he will never do the acts that are hateful and mean. For the man who is truly good and wise . . . bears all the chances of life becomingly and always makes the best of circumstances" (1998, p. 21). Early Islamic thinking focused on three aspects that constitute the framework necessary to safeguard against wrongdoing or at least constrain the tendency to participate in unethical acts. These are: character, knowledge, and spirituality. The existence of these factors is essential for establishing a decision making environment where executives and other people in charge are able to recognize possible mistakes and damages that might be committed and, thus, threaten the welfare of others. However, before addressing these aspects, it is important to underscore that any act under Islamic injunction must not harm or lead to harm. The Prophet stated that there should be "No harm or harm-doer." Further he stated, "Not one of you is a believer until he loves for his brother what he loves for himself." The corollary of both sayings is that any decision must benefit society and must not undermine the interests of other members in the exchange equation or larger societal setting. In most business cases, this amounts to idealism. Nevertheless, in Islam, the ideals and reality are often intertwined and it is difficult to draw boundaries between the two. What further complicates the matter is the Islamic consideration of a situation where the decision maker is faced with an uncertain issue. In a case where an act benefits self and seemingly does not harm others, but there is a trace of doubt that this might result in harming others, the faithful decision maker has no choice but to avoid it.

Character

Among the three significant aspects that usually safeguard against the temptation/inclination to engage in a wrongdoing, character clearly stands out. The Prophet stated that among those who are close to God is "One who has the best moral character" and "A person can reach a high status in the Hereafter by his good conduct, though he may be weak in matters of worship" (quoted in Al-Ghazali, 2004, pp. 7–8). In this saying, the Prophet gives priority to moral conduct over ritual religious duties. People may engage in religious rituals, but this does not prevent them from committing wrongdoing. Only a strong moral character can evade making bad decisions. Moral character, as earlier indicated, is either innate or acquired, but in both cases it needs to be cultivated and refined to cope with emerging and evolving issues in the world.

Knowledge

The second element is knowledge. As people acquire knowledge, they are more likely to distinguish between what is important and less important and what actions are appropriate under different circumstances. While knowledge, however, is essential it is never enough to avoid making bad decisions. Though the Quran and *Hadith* underscore the necessity of knowledge, they both warn that knowledge in the wrong hands can be used to spread destruction and maintain oppression. The Prophet stated, "Should I inform you about the wicked people? . . . They are the corrupt learned individuals" (quoted in Ibn Abed Raba Al-Andelesy, 1996, vol. 2, p. 86). Ideally, knowledge, however, is seen as a light that erases darkness and prevents ambiguity. The Quran (29:43) instructs that problems can be understood by those "Who have knowledge." Moreover, according to Mu'adh ibn Jabal, a companion of the Prophet, knowledge allows a person to identify "what is right (permissible) and what is wrong (prohibited)" (quoted in Ibn Abed Raba Al-Andelesy, 1996, p. 77).

Spirituality

This element strengthens character and enables learned individuals to utilize knowledge in the service of that which is good. That is, spirituality eases the application of knowledge to serve society, thus benefiting the largest possible segment of the population. In his sayings, the Prophet articulated this when he stated, "A believer's decency or civility is his religion, his tolerance is his wisdom, and his lineage is the goodness of his character" (quoted in Al-Ghazali, 2004, p. 9).

The existence or absence of the above elements determines to a large degree the propensity of an individual to make ethical/unethical decisions. However, in a world that is constantly changing, fraud and corruption evolve accordingly and those who commit them often think that they will not be caught, that they will find loopholes in existing regulations, or that they are well ahead of the legislator's thinking. Four current changes in the business world make the application of some Islamic prescriptions problematic. These are: globalization, expanding the roots of a business, the rise of professional managers that run businesses, and the increasing role of governments in the economy. The globalization of business not only enlarges the geographic space of competition and multiplicity of businesses, but also enables partners from various cultures and nationalities to cooperate and enter various forms of alliances. This multiplicity of space and partnership allows businesses to meet the demands and requirements of various stakeholders. These demands involve making decisions that certainly violate Islamic ethical instructions. For example, the Hotel George V in Paris, among other hotels that are owned by Muslims, or hotels that operate in some CMMs sell alcohol and/or have gambling casinos. The owners of these hotels are driven by business concerns, even though the activities are inconsistent with Islamic injunctions.

One of the most important changes is the expansion of businesses beyond their local communities. As a result of these expansions, increasingly, most managers and those in position to make decisions are from different cities or regions within a country and even from neighboring countries. These individuals do not have personal contacts with members of the community and do not have intimate knowledge of buyers and suppliers. Thus, they may make decisions that are not sanctioned by the community. Likewise, the rise of professional managers constitutes a departure from the intimacy that owners usually have with members of their immediate communities. These professional managers may not be in a position to make decisions that incorporate *ehsan* and to give preference to those who are needy and poor. More importantly, as many governments in CMMs are actively involved in business affairs, the reservation that many early Islamic scholars had in dealing with rulers or their representatives are just as valid these days (see Al-Maki, 1995), as many government officials are often not to be trusted.

CONCLUSION

In this chapter, we explored issues that are expected to be on the minds of the general public and those in positions of responsibility. Rapid changes in business at the national and international levels and the spread and frequent reoccurrence of fraudulent behavior make it difficult to prevent unethical action. In discussing the role of self-interest and greed, it is noted that greed may paradoxically hinder self-interest.

The issue of human development was covered briefly, with an emphasis on the meaning and scope of the subject in Islamic thinking. Though we underscored some similarities between Western thinking and Islamic typology, we made it clear that there are certain differences and these differences situate Islamic perspectives as useful guidelines that may shed light on how to constrain tendencies to make unethical decisions. Furthermore, factors that shape an ethical disposition in making decisions in business are outlined and their impact is underscored. In doing so, a reference was made to original Islamic sources and we underscored their views on ethical behavior and how to counter unethical behavior. In addition, common unethical decisions were specified and reasons that they were made discussed.

Next, three elements of a framework for ensuring ethical decision making were identified. These elements, though interrelated, have their own justifications and implications. Individually or collectively, these elements if present constitute a powerful force by which fraud and corruption can be prevented. Their weakness or absence leads to fostering questionable conduct. As we see in the chapters that follow, ethical conduct in today's world is difficult to sustain and decision makers will increasingly face the struggle between temptation and their responsibilities toward their organizations and society.

3. Islamic ethics and free market economy

Though ethics in Islam focuses primarily on behavior and relations among people, its coverage of the exchange function and entitlements and responsibilities in the marketplace underscores the intertwining relationships between people's welfare and business activities. Indeed, the three elements of the ethical framework—public interest, moderation, and *ehsan*—set the stage for ethical conduct that is in line with optimal utilization of purposeful economic activities that ensure a balance between self-interest and societal welfare. Furthermore, the moderation elements, while safeguarding against both conspicuous spending and miserliness, highlight the virtue of responsible spending without ignoring the need to save for the future and invest in worthy projects.

Traditionally, most of the writing on free market economy in Islam has attempted to show the link between Islam and capitalism. This is not the case in this chapter. The objective is to show that, based on the issue of moderation, market exchange and function must observe ethical principles that prevent any intentional harm to members of the exchange function and to stakeholders. This might be ideal but, according to early Islamic thinkers, the further members of the exchange function drift away from ethical principles the less stable the market will be. Thus, in this chapter, several issues pertaining to the nature of free market economy will be examined in the context of Islamic instruction.

FREE MARKET ECONOMY

There are four components of Islamic ethics that reinforce free and just exchange in the marketplace. These are: effort, competition, transparency, and morally responsible conduct. Collectively, these components offer a practical framework for safeguarding the interests of stakeholders and in cases where these components are observed they ensure orderly market function. Competition is essential for functional market transactions. But, as it will be seen later, Islamic perspectives on competition are different from those that prevail in a capitalistic system.

In terms of strengthening positive engagement in the economy and motivating market participants to invest and expand, the Quran underscores the importance of private property (4:29) and the sanctity of societal welfare (4:114). While the issues of competition, effort, and private property are found in capitalism, the emphasis on responsible conduct and societal welfare places Islamic perspectives on free market economy apart from capitalism and ruinous competition that is aimed at displacing or driving competitors out of the market. This may explain why, from the early days of the Islamic states, there has been an emphasis on free transactions and exchanges in the marketplace. The conditions for free transactions are discussed later. However, the Quran (4:29) specifies that any transaction must be an outcome of mutual agreement, free of any deception or coercion: "Let there be amongst you trade by mutual good-will." The Quran (2:279) links free transaction to morally responsible conduct. In the case where there is deliberate deception, it warns of severe consequences. However, in the case of repentance, the Quran (2:279) states, "Ye shall have your capital sums: deal not unjustly, and ye shall not be dealt with unjustly." That is, justice in the marketplace is a necessary condition for a thriving economy and market. It is for this reason that it was stated: "He who displays bad ethics, his earnings will be severely curtailed" (Al-Mawardi, 2002, p. 383). Both justice in the marketplace and transactions must be based on mutual goodwill and serve as a foundation for the Islamic instruction that pertains to market exchange; there should be no harm to players in the marketplace. This implies that market entry should be unrestricted for those who are capable and willing to participate in economic activities, competition should be morally driven, and pricing should be the result of market conditions, i.e. supply and demand.

Moreover, free exchange requires not only transparency but also knowledge of the market and its function. While this requirement is essential for avoiding engagement in prohibited or unjust operations, its economic significance stems from the fact that it eases transactions and allows market players to have access to economic opportunities without any impediments. These players are assumed, as we will show later, to freely engage in market activities and the state should facilitate their operations, while offering them the needed security.

ETHICAL ASPECTS AND MARKET FUNCTIONS

In light of the ethical framework, introduced in Chapter 1, ethics in the marketplace is linked to religious and personal obligations. These cannot be separated. The Prophet once said, "No faith is true unless the heart is true; and no heart is true unless the tongue reflects it." This is the reason that Al-Mawardi (2002) grouped ethics into three major categories: the ethics of religion, the ethics of this world, and the ethics of the soul. In the marketplace, these all interact, depending on their harmony, either in enhancing or impeding market function. Though there are various factors that may strengthen or weaken commitment to ethical standards, in the marketplace the ethics of responsibility, appreciation, and gratitude constitute the safety valve for appropriate and moral conduct.

There are certain responsibilities that individuals and institutions should meet in order for the market to function optimally. These responsibilities, however, as we discussed in previous chapters, must be guided by an appreciation of those who are members of the exchange function and for what has been achieved and the promise of what will come. The reasoning is that God's approval of an individual's action is contingent upon the individual's service to society and gratefulness for what has been attained. This makes any endeavor in the marketplace a continuing challenge, as it must include observation of rights and duties without inflicting damage in the marketplace and obstructing the exchange function. As individuals in the exchange function display and practice good ethics, those who concur with them multiply, they have fewer enemies, and their most difficult tasks are easier to carry out (Al-Mawardi, 2002, p. 383).

The ethical aspects in the context of a free market economy are grouped, for clarity, into three categories: personal, government, and economics. These categories intend to highlight ethical issues pertaining to each subject. Nevertheless, in practice these subjects are interrelated and the ethical framework addressed in Chapter 1 underscores the totality of the ethical systems. Personal aspects are influenced by government stance and guidance and both are influenced by religious economic prescriptions. Al-Mawardi (2002, p. 11) observed the dialectic relationship among these categories and stated that "Though people differ in their aspirations, abilities, needs, and objectives, God has made it possible for them to work together. He has enabled people to recognize that what governs their conduct encompasses two dimensions. The first is, what is validated by reason is reinforced by religion law. The second is, what is intuitively justified by reason religious law makes it obligatory." Therefore, conduct in the marketplace is not divorced from the personalities of the individuals, the norms that govern groups, and the religious prescriptions for worldly and spiritual affairs. Below is a brief description of each category.

PERSONAL QUALITIES

Though there are several characteristics under the personal category, the most relevant are lying, cheating, deception, sincerity, forgiveness, and differences in abilities. Each of these items is critical for judging whether a conduct is ethical or not. In the section below, we highlight the perspectives of Islamic teachings on each.

Lying

Among the issues that all Muslim scholars agree lead to severe consequences and must be avoided is lying. The Quran (3:61) declares, ". . . invoke the curse of God on those who lie." The Prophet Mohamed indicated that it is possible for a person who has faith to be a coward or even a miser but never a liar. Lying is the source of all unethical deeds and miserable acts, as it has appalling consequences and ultimately leads to animosity and in a state of animosity there is no security or relaxation (Al-Mawardi, 2002, p. 11). In the marketplace, moreover, lying spreads distrust among market players and institutions and leads to waste of time and resources. It is for this reason that Muslim scholars agree that the motives for lying are always unjustifiable. Al-Ghazali (2004) stated that lying is a great sin and when a person is known to be a liar his word is no longer credible, no one will trust what he says, and people will look at him with contempt.

Cheating and Deceiving

According to Islamic prescriptions, truthfulness is a prerequisite for morally responsible transactions. The Prophet states, "He who cheats is not one of us." This makes it obligatory in the marketplace to avoid deception and fraud. The rationale, according to the Prophet, is that cheating obliterates the blessings of God and obstructs the path to prosperity.

Sincerity

Islamic instructions stress that sincerity in the marketplace has two dimensions: kindness to people and purposeful conduct. According to Al-Maki (1995), the first is met when a person has faith in God and avoids inflicting harm upon others. The second one is performance of duties guided by knowledge so no damaging elements affect performance.

Forgiveness

This incorporates both generosity and overlooking wrongdoings committed by others with the hope that in the future they will avoid repeating such behavior. Al-Mawardi (2002) classified forgiveness into two categories: contracts and rights. He explained that an ethical person in entering a contract with others should ease agreement, avoid arguments, and be free of deception and cunning. He further indicated that one's rights encompass two aspects: personal affairs and finance (debt). In personal affairs, one should not engage in rivalry with others in order to gain a better position and or a better rank. This leads to competition over minor issues and bad reputation and behavior. The financial aspect has three elements: debt forgiveness, debt reduction, and extension of due dates until difficulties are eased. All these initiatives facilitate transactions, increase trust and cooperation among market players, and reinforce smooth market function.

Differences in Abilities

While the Quran instructs that people are equal in creation, it recognizes that they differ in their capabilities and, thus, vary in their roles in the marketplace and in creating wealth. The Quran (6:165) states, "He raised you in rank, some above others, that He may try you in the gifts He hath given you" and (46:19) ". . . to all are [assigned] degrees according to the deeds which they [have done], and in order that [God] may recompense their deeds." Thus, rewards or punishments should correspond to performance and capability so justice in the workplace is assured.

THE GOVERNMENT'S ROLE

In debating the role of the government in the market, it should be mentioned that the centrality of private property and the right to act freely in the market are important components of Islamic economic thinking. This recognition is reinforced by underscoring both the psychological and natural tendencies of mankind toward obtaining wealth and owning property. The Quran (89:19–20) declares, "And ye devour all inheritance with greed, and ye love wealth with an inordinate love!" In addition, the Quran (67:15) stresses the freedom to engage in economic activities stating, "It is He who has made the earth manageable for you, so traverse ye through its tracts and enjoy of the sustenance which He furnishes."

The role of the state in the economy, however, is limited. This is because the state in the context of Islamic instructions has three primary functions: it facilitates trade and economic activities, provides protection to and ensures the safety of market players, and prevents oppression or harm from taking place in the market. A detail of such functions is provided in Chapter 8. Nevertheless, in this section, it is important to note that the role of the state from an Islamic perspective goes beyond what is promoted by capitalism. Guided by moderation and public interest, the state is expected not only to refrain from giving preference to certain market players over others, but also to make certain that no player is placed in a disadvantaged position through market manipulation or cut-throat competition or to make a profit at any expense. For example, the Abbasid Caliph, Al-Mustershid, instructed his chief justice regarding the role of the market supervisor, the *Muhtasib*, stating:

> Give adequate consideration to the function of market supervision, as it represents the greater public interest by offering wider comprehensive benefits to people, protecting their wealth, organizing their affairs in an orderly manner, and swiftly dealing with sources of corruption. Make sure that the *Muhtasib* does not exceed his boundaries and take the necessary steps to ensure that his deputy is familiar with the level of prices, investigates the type of commodities and their availability and scarcity, sits in the hub of the market to make sure that prices reflect the mechanism of demand and supply, does not deviate from moderation, does not give advantage to certain market players whether in a state of plenty or shortage, gives considerable attention to the regulation of weights, and recognizes those who cheat in measure from those who do not. . . . until they observe the right measure. (quoted in Al-Anbari, 1987, p. 344)

While this instruction articulates the duties of the *Muhtasib*, it also indicates the responsibilities and the limits of the government in the economy. There is always fear that abuse of power by the state is not only a possibility but a living reality and thus avoidance of it must take priority. The Prophet underscored this fact by his refusal to set prices when he was approached to determine the price of certain commodities.

The government's role is also exhibited in four areas: property rights, taxation, development, and social welfare. These subjects are commonly debated in capitalistic societies. In the context of Islam, these are treated within the framework of public interest, moderation, and *ehsan*. That is, while there is an emphasis on the role of the state in the marketplace, it should not be viewed independent of the general framework that aims at establishing equilibrium in economic and social affairs. Below is a brief discussion of the ethical dimensions of each subject.

Property Rights

This is an integral element in any economy that is destined for growth and innovation. In his farewell address the Prophet stated, "Regard the life and property of every Muslim as a sacred trust. Return the goods entrusted to you to their rightful owners. Hurt no one so that no one may hurt you." The Islamic reasoning for protection of property rights stems from the following: to encourage people to take initiative and ensure that they gain the fruits of their efforts, to reinforce trust in market transactions and operations, and to motivate people to engage in useful and beneficial activities that contribute to economic growth and prosperity. The Quran (4:29) instructs, "O ye believers! Devour not each other's property among yourselves unlawfully save by trading by mutual consent." The prohibition also applies to copyrights. Abu Talib Al-Maki (1995, p. 540) recorded an incident that was told to him by a faithful individual who stated, "A person dropped a paper which had useful sayings and subjects and I wanted to read and copy it. But [a religious scholar] . . . reprimanded me saying that this was not permissible without obtaining permission from its owner." Al-Suyuti (1996), in his book, *History of Caliphs*, recorded that the Abbasid Caliph, Al-Mansur (AD754–75), wrote to his judge in Basra, Iraq, Swar ben Abdullah, saying: "Look at the land that is a source of conflicting claims between a military commander and a merchant and give it to the military commander." The Judge wrote back that the evidence showed that the land belonged to the merchant and he would not take it from the merchant without clear evidence. Al-Mansur again ordered him to give it to the military commander. Swar ben Abdullah wrote to Al-Mansur that it belonged to the merchant and it would not be given to anyone else without the merchant's consent. After receiving the Judge's letter, Al Mansur stated, "O God, justice prevails in the Kingdom as my judges lead me to the right path."

Taxation

In his treatise on taxation, *Book on Taxation*, Abu Yusuf (N.D., died 798) stated that the purpose of levies is to reform the affairs of people and prevent oppression (see Shelaq, 1990). In general, taxation seeks to ensure that the welfare of the public is taken into consideration and that no injustice is imposed on market players that obstruct them from engaging in economic activities. This implies that a moderate tax is imposed on economic activities so no market actor is denied the opportunity to invest or grow or is forced to move to other more amenable places. This point was underscored by Ali Ibn Esa, a chief minister during the Abbasid era, who wrote to one of his deputies that imposing tax on crops before cultivation, especially when based on a best case scenario of full yield, impedes agricultural development and productive farming (see Al-Sabi, 2003, p. 363).

Ibn Khaldun, a medieval Arab sociologist, argued that when taxes exceed certain levels this can lead to the ruin of a business and the state. He stated (2006, p. 218):

> When tax assessments and imposts on citizens are low, they are motivated to work hard and engage in various economic activities. Economic growth thrives and financial returns increase, as low taxes generate satisfaction. As the economy flourishes, the base of imposts and assessment becomes much broader. Consequently, the amount of total tax revenue increases. . . . When imposed taxes on subjects exceed what is fair and become a burden, people have less incentive to work, as there is no hope of gaining reasonable benefits. This occurs when people compare the amount of taxes paid to the received benefits and fruits of their labor. Thus, many might find engaging in economic enterprises unrewarding. This leads to a shrinking of the tax base and the total amount of collected taxes will be small.

Like earlier Muslim scholars, Ibn Khaldun elaborates on the psychological and business effects of imposing high tax on business people. In addition, he does not overlook the ethical aspects and the harm that is inflicted upon the population by tyrant rulers. These rulers have no interest in the welfare of the public and care only about covering the expenses of their huge apparatus and meeting their demands for luxury items.

Economic Development

In terms of development, the state has four primary functions: facilitator, promoter, distributor, and sponsor. These four functions tend to ease economic development and ensure public benefits and economic growth. In terms of a facilitator, the fourth Caliph, Imam Ali (1990, p. 635), in his letter to his governor in Egypt, stated:

> Let your primary concern be the development of the land rather than the collection of taxes. Improving farmland is essential for obtaining needed revenue. He who seeks taxes without cultivating farmlands will obstruct economic development, deprive people of prosperity, and will never last long in power . . . . Even when you face a shortage of revenues, because you have used them to alleviate hardship in your constituency, regard this as an investment, as it will boost development and enhance the power of your government. The people will praise you and appreciate your efforts and you will feel satisfaction in spreading justice and gain confidence in their support for your projects.

The state should play an instrumental role in promoting opportunities for working or investing. It was reported that the Prophet showed people who did not have jobs or skills what to do in order to avoid poverty and begging. It is the duty of the state to cooperate with the private sector and to identify or prioritize economic opportunities and encourage companies to benefit from them.

The Prophet sought to distribute the wealth of the state among the people with the objective of alleviating poverty and encouraging people to own property so they could contribute to productive activities. In his instructions to two men who he sent to govern Yemen he stated, "Be gentle [to the people] and be not hard [on them], and make [them] rejoice and do not incite [them] to aversion" (quoted in Muhammad Ali, 1977, p. 404). Furthermore, the Prophet stated, "He who cultivates land that does not belong to anybody is more rightful [to own it]" (quoted in Sahih Al-Bukhari, 1996, p. 508). The functions of distributor and sponsor were carried out, on a large scale, during the rule of the second Caliph, Omar (589–644). Caliph Omar made it a duty to distribute public funds to the needy and the rest of the population. Furthermore, he insisted that the conquered land should be "the property of the state and not of the conquering forces, and former occupants of lands . . . not be dispossessed" (Numani, 2010, p. 261). The Caliph attempted to avoid a concentration of wealth in the hands of the few and to reward those who cultivated the land. During his era, too, the state sponsored the building of canals, public roads and bridges, and the establishment of major cities like Kufa, Basra, and Fustat.

Social Welfare

Muslim scholars underscore the ethical responsibility of the state to provide an adequate level of living to the poor and those who are in disadvantaged positions. The reasons are that the economic well-being of the society and the goal of social harmony are unreachable if there is a sizeable segment of the population that experiences economic hardship. Likewise, when prosperity and economic benefits are widely shared, economic revival and growth are a natural outcome. Indeed, Islamic scholars (see Ahmad, 1995; Al-Sadr, 1983; Glaachi, 2000) argue that it is part of the state's responsibility to safeguard the welfare of the needy and the poor. The Quran (59:7) states, "Whatever God grants to His Messenger (out of the property) of the people of the towns, belongs to God, the Messenger, the kinfolk, the orphans, the destitute and to those who may become needy while on a journey, so that it will not only circulate in the hands of the rich ones among them" and (93: 5–10) ". . . soon will thy Guardian-Lord give thee (that wherewith) thou shalt be well-pleased. Did He not find thee an orphan and give thee shelter (and care)? And He found thee wandering, and He gave thee guidance. And He found thee in need, and made thee independent. Therefore, treat not the orphan with harshness; nor repulse the petitioner." The Prophet asserts that a person is entitled to three rights: food to strengthen existence, clothes to cover self, and a house for shelter (Al-Maki, 1995, p. 382). The responsibility of the state relative to the poor is further articulated in a letter that the fourth Caliph, Imam Ali (1990, p. 668), sent to the governor of Mecca. He stated, "Look at the revenues God has placed at your disposal and disburse them among the needy, especially those with many dependents and those who are deprived, in order to eradicate poverty and despair. Whatever is left, you should send to us to distribute among the needy at our end."

As part of social welfare, religious instruction encourages people to give *Sedakah* (charity) to the needy and other organizations that support social and economic justice. The Prophet declares that "*Sedakah* is incumbent on every Muslim." The Quran (2:267) instructs, "O you who believe! Give in charity of the good things you earn and of what we have brought forth for you out of the earth, and do not aim at giving in charity what is bad." This, however, does not necessarily mean that since individuals are obligated to pay *sedakah* the state does not need to engage in social welfare.

ECONOMIC ASPECTS

The ethics of economic activities stem from the understanding that everything on earth is created to serve mankind. The bliss that God bestows on a person, group, or society is contingent upon ethical commitment to avoid wrongdoing and to serve the largest segment of members in the society. He who has gained the approval of God and the appreciation of the people lives in a state of complete happiness and sustenance (Al-Mawardi, 2002, p. 295). The ethics of economic activities is found, therefore, in serving public interests. Below is a list of certain economic and market activities and motives. Each is briefly discussed with an emphasis on its ethical dimension:

Spending

In Islamic economy, spending in moderation is a virtue. Thus, the Quran (59:9) instructs the faithful to be generous: "And those who are saved from the covetousness of their own souls, they are the ones that achieve prosperity." While the Quran instructs the faithful not to be miserly, it encourages people to spend only according to their ability. It states (65:7), "Let him with abundance spend according to his means, and the one whose resources are restricted, let him spend accordingly." Spending, in Islam, as was articulated by the Prophet, is a duty essential for a functioning society, as it facilitates prosperity and the broadening of sustenance. He stated that God tells the faithful: "Spend and I will reward you more, do not be tightfisted or I restrict your sustenance" (quoted in Al-Maki, 1995, p. 60). While spending might be in line with public interests and *ehsan* principles, it must be undertaken in moderation. The Quran (25:67) articulates, ". . . and those who, when they spend, be neither extravagant nor miserly" and (17:27) "Surely squanderers are brothers of Satan." Spending in Islam takes three forms (Mahmud, 2000): consumption (spending on personal needs), investing (part of an income that is utilized to take advantage of business opportunities and expand business capacity), and spending on charitable activities (amounts that are spent on activities and or meeting religious and civic duties, such as alms and contributions to causes that further public interests). These three forms of spending create a dynamic economic environment where the rights of society and individuals are kept in a fine balance. However, earlier Islamic thinkers differentiated between a wastrel and squanderer. For example, Al-Mawardi (2002) argued that a wastrel is one who is ignorant about the amount to be spent, while a squanderer is one who is ignorant of where the money should be spent. Though neither are virtuous, a squanderer is worse than a wastrel. This is because squandering wealth can hurt oneself and others and the squanderer does not know where to spend. Al-Jahiz (1998, died 868, p. 22) argued that "He who does not know where to spend on inexpensive items, will not know how to be watchful in spending on luxurious goods." Al-Jahiz (p. 240) underscored the value of moderation and balanced activities when he stated:

> He who is modest in behavior, his thinking is balanced, he engages only in thrifty activities, and his actions tend not to be extreme. This is because a balanced activity does not produce only a sensible one, just like those which are irregular lead to asymmetrical outcomes. Admonishments do not stop he who is disposed to do bad things and whose aim is focused on squandering.

Saving

In the early days of the Islamic state, when economic activities and needs were relatively simple, the aims of saving took three forms: protection from unforeseeable events, taking care of rising business needs, and finding better opportunities for increasing wealth. The state's role was to make sure that resources were distributed fairly among the population and that the needy were provided with the essentials to ensure their dignity. The state, however, encouraged people to save so they would not be dependent on others. The Prophet stated, "He who is prudent in spending will not be dependent" (quoted in Al-Nawawi, 2001, p. 300). The virtue of saving, moreover, is emphasized by religious instruction. The Prophet stated that "God does not like for you to gossip, intrude, and waste capital" (quoted in Al-Nawawi, 2001, p. 395). Abu Talib Al-Maki (1995) made a powerful justification, from a religious perspective, for saving money. He indicated that saving is a virtue and that the amount of saving should be commensurate with the risk involved and or the nature of planned activity. Al-Jahiz (p. 241) argued that "maintaining wealth is more difficult than obtaining it." He further stated that "One should be vigilant in investing any part of his wealth in a venture unless it offers a better opportunity" (p. 242).

Investing

Investing is considered an instrument for furthering societal prosperity and revitalizing economic growth. The Prophet stated that "For a person who is indifferent to money, beneficial wealth is like a spring water" (quoted in Al-Mawardi, 2002, pp. 336–8) and that "Capital with good return is just like a high quality breeding mare and productive date palms." In Arabia, at that time, the breeding of unique Arabian horses and date palms that produced more yield were good sources of revenue and economic prosperity. Investing in projects with high returns has implications beyond economic success. Al-Jahiz articulated this reality when he stated, "Learn that investing money is a mechanism for generosity, strengthens your faith, and enhances your friendship with others. He who loses his wealth, others will neither fear nor want to be associated with him. And he who is not feared and with whom people do not want to associate is not taken seriously by others. So make an effort in your work in order for others to respect and obey you in matters of religion and worldly affairs" (quoted in Ibn Abed Raba Al-Andelesy, 1996, died 985, vol. 2, p. 326). Investment of capital is critical for economic growth and the creation of wealth: "God will bless your wealth though you engage in trade and commerce even without making a profit" (Abu Talib Al-Maki, 1995). Capital to grow has to be invested and it is these business transactions and investments that lead to prosperity. A ninth-century Muslim scholar, Maruf Al-Karkhi (died 815), argued that "Capital grows through transactions (like pastures)" (quoted in Jasim, 1990, p. 83). That is, the ethics of investment is that any type of investment, as long as it does not harm people and does not violate religious prescription, must be pursued. This is necessary for the continuing improvement of economic affairs and for reducing poverty. For these two reasons, investment is a necessary market activity that leads to lawful gains and capital growth.

Competition

In Islamic economic thought and relative to competition, four principals have been underscored. First, mankind is disposed toward competition and has a desire to win. Al-Mawardi (2002, p. 217) stated, "Competing and the aspiration to win are part of human nature." Second, competition should be guided by *ehsan* and those who engage in *ehsan* are rewarded. The Quran (55:60) states, "Is there any reward for good—other than good?" This implies that no harm should be done in any transaction. Third, no competitor should induce a market actor to buy from him after that actor has entered into an agreement with another seller. The Prophet instructs, "A seller should not urge someone to cancel a bargain the latter has already agreed upon with another seller, so as to sell him his own goods" (quoted in Al-Bukhari, 1996, died 870, pp. 477–8). Fourth, markets are an arena for players to act freely in and benefit from their transactions. The Quran (62:10) instructs, "Disperse through the land and seek of the bounty of God." Muslim scholar, Hassan Al-Basri (died 728) stated, "Markets are just like banquets, those who attend them obtain benefits" (quoted in Al-Maki, 1995, p. 523). In their treatment of competition, early Muslim scholars took note of the Quranic sanction on competition. The Quran encourages competition (*munafasa*) stating literally (83:26), "Let competitors compete." However, competition should be based on advancing public interest and observing *ehsan* and moderation in business conduct.

Contract

An important element of an ethical business transaction is contractual agreement. This was delineated both in the Quran and in the sayings of the Prophet. Contractual agreements seek to reduce uncertainty in transactions and make certain that neither party's rights or duties are overlooked and that promises are fulfilled without serious misunderstandings or disagreements. The Quran (2:282) instructs, "To write (your contract) for a future period, whether it be small or big, it is more just in the sight of God, more suitable as evidence, and more convenient to avoid doubts among yourself. But if it be a transaction which ye carry out on the spot among yourselves, there is no blame on you if you reduce it not to writing. But have witnesses whenever ye make a commercial contract and let neither scribe nor witness suffer harm." Indeed, the Quran (5:1) makes it obligatory to meet promises and agreements stating, "O ye who believe! Fulfill (all) obligations" and (17:34) "fulfill (every) engagement, for (every) engagement will be enquired into (on the day of reckoning)." The Prophet warns believers that they should not say anything that they do not intend to execute and not violate promises in transactions. He states, "Muslims shall be bound by the conditions which they make" (quoted in Muhammad Ali, 1977, p. 310). Al-Mawardi (2002, p. 542) argued that any contract should have at least four qualities: easy to execute, articulated content that minimizes hesitation, free of ill feelings that may result in backbiting, and free of deception and cunning.

Profits and Earnings

Though Islamic instruction sanctions business transactions and earnings, it also regulates them. The regulations are intended to safeguard the interests of market players and society at large. Certain boundaries for permissible actions are specified and the limitations are identified. Al-Maki (1995, p. 502) indicated that any earnings from business transactions should not be a result of cheating, thievery, corruption, confiscation, cunning, or deception. Al-Maki argued that how earnings are achieved should be known by acquiring market knowledge and being familiar with religious guidelines. The earnings or profits should not, therefore, be higher than what the market dictates and should not be to other market actors' disadvantage. According to Islamic scholars, "He, who participates in market operations and prefers his wealth at the expense of others, does not display honesty in his transactions with others" (quoted in Al-Maki, 1995, pp. 501–2). It is for this and other reasons that Islamic instructions, as explained in the next chapter, recommend a modest profit and do not condone profit maximization.

Hoarding

Hoarding, whether of money or commodities, is considered harmful to the welfare of society. This is not only because it leads to a reduction in money circulation and lost opportunities but because it obstructs free exchange in the marketplace. The Quran (9:34) declares, "there are those who hoard gold and silver and spend it not in the way of God: announce unto them a most grievous chastisement." The Prophet says, "He who withholds commodity is a sinner." Early Muslim scholars argue that hoarding gold, silver, or important commodities just for the sake of increasing one's own welfare and accumulation of wealth is a disservice to society and one's fellow men (see Al-Mawardi, 2002, p. 354). This is precisely the reason for outlawing hoarding. The Prophet declares, "He who brings goods to the market is blessed and the hoarder is cursed" and "Shame on the hoarder; when the price is low he is sad and when it is high he rejoices" (quoted in Glaachi, 2000, p. 16). Abu Talib Al-Maki (1995, died 996, p. 508) recorded that a grain merchant sent a shipment to his agent in Basra, Iraq. He told him that the commodity had to be sold on the day it arrived. The agent consulted with local merchants who told him they expected the price to go up the following Friday. The agent hoarded the shipment and sold it on the Friday, thus doubling the profit. When the agent informed his boss of his activities, the latter was angry and told his agent: "you violated our order and committed sin by hoarding . . . give the full amount of the sales to the poor in Basra, as I do not like to be party to hoarding."

Monopoly

Like hoarding, monopoly is outlawed. The general Islamic law pertaining to market exchange is that transactions and trade are encouraged (Ahmad, 1995; Glaachi, 2000; Mahmud 2000); the exceptions are few and are in the domain of what is considered harmful (e.g., selling and buying alcohol, gambling, etc.). Hoarding and monopoly are viewed as mechanisms that restrict free trade, access to opportunities, and lead to harming players in the market. This was articulated from the inception of Islam and the establishment of the state. In a letter to his governor in Egypt the fourth Caliph, Imam Ali (1990, p. 638), ordered him to be aware of "those who monopolize commodities and dominate markets. This harms the general public and distorts the image of the ruler. Prevent monopoly as the Prophet, peace be upon him, did."

Usury or Riba

This type of economic form and for practical matters all types of interest are outlawed in Islamic law. Though this subject is covered in Chapter 6, it is important to point out that the prohibition took place earlier in Islam and that both the Quran and the Hadith of the Prophet Mohamed have specifically addressed it. The imposition of interest is thought to be contradictory to the principles of *ehsan*, moderation, and public interest. Before Islam, the rich and merchants in Arabia utilized interest to gain phenomenal wealth and to severely limit the economic freedoms of those who borrowed money. Thus, it was viewed at that time as a menace to justice and to the economic viability of the community. The Quran (2:276) declares, "God will deprive usury of all blessing, but will give increase for deeds of charity" and (2:278) "O ye who believe! Fear God and give up what remains of your demand for usury, if ye are indeed believers."

CONCLUSION

Islamic economic prescriptions encourage ownership, free exchange, competition, and gainful activities that lead to economic prosperity and a stable society. Nevertheless, like Judaism, Islam places certain limitations on economic activities in order to protect weak actors in the market exchange and to safeguard the rights of the poor. The Quran recognizes that people have a strong desire for wealth accumulation and seeks to steer them toward utilizing their wealth in the service of society without endangering their rights.

Effort and competitive spirit are also praised by the Quran as instruments to advance economic progress and eradicate poverty. The latter is perceived to be a serious obstacle for spiritual and economic viability. However, the Quran acknowledges that people differ in their capabilities and involvement and, thus, they are rewarded accordingly. Furthermore, while Islamic prescriptions encourage commercial and financial activities, these instructions have certain guidelines for articulating what is permissible and what is forbidden in the marketplace.

While the state's role in the marketplace is limited, some guidelines and regulations are deemed important to prevent abuse and fraud. These are set to protect market actors and reduce uncertainty in the market. The state is assumed not to favor any market actor over others and not to influence market function with the goal of benefiting certain actors. Though the state has responsibilities toward the society, these exceed issues of security to include economic, spiritual, and social commitments. This is because in Islam the spiritual environment is not assumed to flourish without economic prosperity and the safety of the people.

Morality in the marketplace, however, remains the most important protection against abuses and corruption in the marketplace. One of the most interesting aspects of Islamic economic and moral teaching is that those individuals who defend others and safeguard the rights of weak actors act as God's guardians on earth. This assigns special roles for those who are morally driven and motivates them to persistently uphold what is right and avoid what is bad in the marketplace. This recognition of intrinsic motives is essential for adequate functioning of the market and for deepening trust among market actors.

4.   Ethics and profit making

In recent years, the debate over the role and ethical responsibility of organizations in society has intensified. There are those who believe that organizations are not equipped to deal with social issues and that they should focus on their primary business by producing goods/services and generating high profits for their stockholders (see Friedman, 1970; Ottaway, 2001). Others, however, assert that business organizations are economic actors that assume social and political roles and accordingly they have a responsibility that goes far beyond the economic domain (see Barton, 2011; Porter and Kramer, 2006). The report by the *Financial Times*, and other major media outlets, that executives in Britain have been prioritizing profits over principles and putting financial goals above ethical considerations has fueled discussion on the goals and profit making of corporations in the business world (see Groom, 2011). This concern is not new and, among other issues, has situated ethics at the center stage of discourse on the role of business in society. As we indicated in the previous chapter, the attitude toward this matter is influenced by many factors, including the stage of economic development, religion, and openness. The interplay of these factors shapes how people in certain civilizations/societies and time periods deal with business issues and emerging or pressing events; religion, however, remains a determining force in ethics formation and application. Indeed, each religion has its own set of values and beliefs, which in turn determine what is considered right and wrong and the standards upon which a behavior/conduct is judged.

In this chapter, several issues related to profit and profit maximization motives are addressed. Specifically, a brief survey of the literature and a discussion of the stance toward profit making in Islamic thinking is provided. The emphasis, however, is on the place of profit making by market actors and the attitudes toward profit maximization in Islamic thought. As we have done in previous chapters, references to original Islamic texts and treatises are included, not only to put things in an appropriate historical perspective, but also to gain a clear understanding of the ethical justifications in Islam toward profit making and business operations. Thus, the focus is on the religiously sanctioned boundaries of business conduct, whether or not Islam sanctions profit drive, and how it views profit. That is, the objective is primarily to answer the question: Is profit an end goal of business activity or a means to a broader end?

INTRODUCTION

Organizations and management studies have examined organizational performance and how religion shapes executive behavior (e.g., Graafland, Kaptein, and Schouten, 2006; Lee, McCann, and Ching, 2003). These studies have, in recent years, been driven by the popularity of spirituality and sustainability concepts and their implications among practitioners and researchers. In their studies on the importance of religious beliefs on ethical attitudes in the marketplace, Emerson and Mckinney (2010) credited the attention focused on the reoccurrence of financial crises and marketplace misconduct to a rising interest in spirituality, morality, and religion. The authors have asserted that the importance of religion in one's life is much more significant than mere religious affiliation in shaping ethical attitudes.

Scholars have argued that in today's marketplace it is impossible to regulate executive behavior and that morality and ethics are instrumental in restraining one's urge to engage in corrupt or questionable acts (see Ali, 2005, 2008a; Emerson and Mckinney, 2010). These scholars, along with Pava (1998), suggest that religion-based and or spiritually driven ethics motivate individuals to incorporate the highest human and spiritual ideals into their business conduct. These ideals can be manifested in the work-place environment, customer relations, pricing and profit margins, recruiting and promotion, and competition in the marketplace.

While many of these issues are discussed in various sections in the book, here the issue of profit earnings in the marketplace is highlighted and differing perspectives are provided. There is a general agreement that business organizations cannot survive without profit. However, there is disagreement among religious and business scholars and practitioners on the level of profit. Should profit be moderate or excessive, minimum or maximum, fair or exploitative? Three camps have emerged in recent years pertaining to profit making and reasoning. These are the moralists, the economic efficiency advocates, and the organizational responsibility proponents.

In contrast to those who propose that profit maximization is a wrong concept (Drucker, 1974; Li, 1964), there are those who argue that executives and their corporations must seek profit maximization (Koplin, 1963; Friedman, 1970). On the other hand, there are those who, driven by secular (e.g., Sibley, 2009; Dierker and Grodal, 1996) or religious (e.g., Karns, 2008) motives, postulate that excessive profit is not only undesirable but also inconsistent with optimally serving society. The third group promotes the notion that profitability is only one concern among many goals that ensure the survivability and viability of business organizations (Freeman, 2000; Grant, 1991).

Primeaux and Stieber (1994) have made a powerful argument that not only is ethics at the heart and center of business but also profit and ethics are intrinsically related. This linkage helps to focus attention on the role of corporations in society, the objective of the firms, the nature of profit, and situates the latter as a moral concern that is relevant to societal welfare and prosperity. For this particular reason, some scholars have attempted to address the subject of profit maximization in terms of religious teaching and or philosophy.

Primeaux (1997) and Primeaux and Stieber (1994) have moved beyond economic efficiency and focused on the behavioral aspects of profit maximization. These studies, while highlighting the importance of profit maximization, assert that it symbolizes the contribution of business to communal and personal well-being. Likewise, these studies have contributed to understanding the role and objective of the firm with an emphasis on moral responsibility and ethical conduct in the marketplace. This particular development has situated the subject of profit maximization at the center of the study of ethics and subsequently has framed decisions regarding profit, not only in terms of efficiency but also in the context of responsibility and contribution to society.

THE ETHICS OF EARNINGS AND BUSINESS CONDUCT

Like other religions, Islam specifies certain prescriptions and business instructions. Some of these instructions, especially in the context of earnings, place Islam apart from other religions. Some Islamic prescriptions are general; others are specific and tackle issues that relate to daily activities in the marketplace and to exchange functions. While the specific prescriptions leave no room for the faithful but to observe the instructions, the general instructions can be adaptable to changing business and economic conditions. An example of a specific order is the Quranic instruction (4:29), "Eat not up your property among yourselves in vanities, but let there be amongst you trade by mutual good-will." A general order could be (Quran 2:275), "God hath permitted trade and forbidden usury" and the saying of the Prophet, "Seeking earnings is a duty for every Muslim." The general, in this case, gives believers more room to consider what type of trade or earning is sanctioned and should be pursued.

That is, in the marketplace, ethics plays a significant role in setting the boundaries for accepted conduct and in preventing fraud, corruption, and questionable behavior. The centrality of ethics in business conduct manifests a deeper regard of the Muslim faith for the role of ethics in the business world; a precondition for economic growth and prosperity. Naqvi (1981) asserts that ethics determines business conduct and behavior and that economic considerations should be subordinate to ethical priorities. That is, the value of any business action stems from its contribution to the general welfare of the society. For this particular reason, ethics not only determines the boundaries of conduct but also dictates whether certain economic activities are legitimate or not. Ethics, therefore, takes on a broader domain of influence in the marketplace, including a wide range of issues from interest to monopoly and from pricing to profit margin. This broad governing of business affairs accentuates the social dimension of organizational activities, making it fruitful for business executives to factor in social consequences to their decision making process. Ethics, however, is neither entirely fixed nor divorced from the prevailing law. Al-Mawardi (2002) explained that there are two types of ethics in relation to law: one is dictated by reason and, thus, it becomes legal as it is approved by the law, and one is justified by reason and the law makes it obligatory.

This dialectic relationship between ethics and the law indicates that no business action is independent of its social milieu. This explains why in the early days of the Islamic state, in the seventh century, knowledge of religion-based ethics was set as an essential prerequisite for market actors. The second Caliph, Omer (590–644), declared: "Only he who is a religiously learned person can sell in our market" (quoted in Asaf, 1987, p. 224) and Al-Shaybani (1986, p. 42), an Islamic jurist (died 804), argued that "If a person wishes to engage in commerce, he should learn what is necessary to safeguard against usury and fraud." Possibly the reason for such emphasis was that an ethically guided businessperson would avoid blunders by aligning his/her act in the marketplace with societal benefits.

The theoretical framework, described in Chapter 1, has three pillars: *ehsan*, moderation, and public interest. These pillars influence perspectives on profit making and on earning levels. *Ehsan* implies goodness and generosity in interaction and conduct, be it on a personal or organizational level. As a projection of goodness and generosity, *ehsan* encompasses mercy, justice, compassion, social responsiveness, forgiveness, tolerance, and attentiveness. These aspects constitute the standards by which to judge whether or not a transaction is ethical. Likewise, these aspects characteristically uphold the pillars of moderation and public benefits. Indeed, any transaction must be aimed at avoiding imposing harm on those involved in market operations. The Prophet Mohamed's saying, "*Al-Din*

Al-maamala" (Religion is found in the way of dealing with other people), serves as a reminder that everything on earth is created to enhance the well-being of the people. That is, judging whether any action or conduct is right or wrong must stem primarily from its benefit to people and society. Moderation conveys avoidance of excessiveness and encourages humbleness. This applies to all transactions, including pricing and earnings. The Prophet states, "May God have mercy on the man who is generous when he buys and when he sells and when he demands" and that God rewards those who "give respite to one in easy circumstances and forgives one who is in straitened circumstances" (quoted in Muhammad Ali, 1997, pp. 294–5).

The interplay among the three pillars (*ehsan*, moderation, and public interest) sheds light on the nature and essence of Islamic ethics. In fact, as we show later, it elucidates why the issue of profit is situated at the heart of Islamic ethics. In Islamic teaching, not only is the universe created for the sake of mankind, but the worth of any human being is determined by his/her relation and service to others. The Quran (49:13) states, "The noblest of you in the sight of God is the best of you in conduct." Likewise, the Prophet declares, "The best of people are those who benefit others" (quoted in Al-Barai and Abdeen, 1987, p. 144). Good intentions in business transactions are considered a virtue and a necessity for morally driven conduct. The Prophet instructs that "He who does not oppress people in transactions, does not lie, and fulfills his promises is a noble person whose justice is confirmed and his friendship is required" (quoted in Al-Maki, 1995, p. 429). Furthermore, the aim of business exchange and involvement is to create value to society and to serve one's interests, while serving the community (Al-Ghazali, 2006, died 1111; Al-Maki, 1995).

In the context of earnings, there are three factors that should be kept in mind: divinity of earning, *sedakah*, and the multiplication of reward for engaging in ethical activities. These factors collectively set the boundaries for ethical conduct relative to earnings and profit making. Below is a brief discussion of each in the context of earnings.

Earnings as a Divine Duty

Earnings take on a great value in Islamic teaching and tradition. The Quran (78:11) states that one should "make the day as a means of subsistence." The Prophet further elaborates on the virtue of earning when he declares, "Among the sins are sins that cannot be recompensed by prayer and fasting . . . [but are wiped out by] a commitment to earning a livelihood" (quoted in Al-Shaybani, 1986, p. 39, died 805) and "A person who makes an effort to support himself and thwart dependency on others and avoids asking people for help is on the path to God" (quoted in Al-Maki, 1995,

p. 499). Furthermore, Al-Shaybani (1986, p. 29) argues that the continuity and survival of humanity is contingent upon making a living. Probably, in making earning a divine duty, the Islamic faith motivates the observant to participate in economic activities and ensures that able members of society contribute positively to societal well-being.

Sedakah

Though this term is often translated as charity, its religious legal term exceeds the common literal meaning of charity in the West. In its broader meaning, *sedakah* encompasses the tangible and intangible, material giving and non-material connection. Indeed, *sedakah* is either linked to earnings and or to almost all aspects of business, be they interaction, material compensations, or intangible rewards. The Quran (2:67) states, "O you who believe! Give in charity of the good things you earn and of what we have brought forth for you out of the earth." The Prophet said, "If you do not ease the lives of people via your wealth, then ease their lives by being pleasant to them and behaving ethically" and "Give knowledge or direction as *sedakah* to your colleague to guide him" (quoted in Al-Mawardi, 2002, p. 322 and p. 127 respectively).

Sedakah signifies any sincere or beneficial deed. The term is a derivative of *sedak* (truth) or righteousness. While both Islam and Judaism place considerable emphasis on *sedakah*, in Islam it has two forms—obligatory and voluntary. The two forms of *sedakah* are specified in the Quran (9:60): "Charity is only for the poor and the needy, the collectors appointed for its collection, those whose hearts incline to truth, the ransoming of a captive, and those in debt, and for the way of God and for the wayfarer." In regards to the obligatory form, like the monetary, only able people are expected to engage in it.

The broader meaning of *sedakah* was articulated by the Prophet Mohamed who when asked about it provided the following clarification (see Muhammad Ali, 1977, pp. 209–11):

1. It is obligatory: "*Sedakah* is incumbent on every Muslim." Furthermore, the Prophet asserted that in business affairs, *Sedakah* must be given to wipe out sins or mistakes (see Al-Maki, 1995, p. 513).
2. It can be monetary or non-monetary, for he who has anything to give "He should work with his hands and benefit himself and give *sedakah*." But if he cannot find work, then "He should help the distressed one who is in need." In the case that he is not able to find such a situation then "He should do good deeds and refrain from doing evil—this is *sedakah* on his part."

3. It is morally binding and broad in its application: "Every good deed is *sedakah*" and "A removal of that which is harmful from the road is *sedakah*." Al-Maki (1995, p. 514) reported a saying attributed to the Prophet, "He who gives a loan for a certain due date, he receives *sedakah* for each day until the payment due date."

The Multiplication Factor

Philosophically, the logic of *ehsan* constitutes the principal factor that shapes and reinforces one's disposition to engage in what is good and beneficial to society. However, there is a reward for engaging in *ehsan*. The Quran (6:160) instructs, "He that doeth good shall have ten times as much to his credit. He that doeth evil shall only be recompensed according to his vice." This reward induces believers to go beyond what is required legally or what constitutes a just act. The reasoning behind this was articulated by the tenth-century jurist Al-Maki who argued that *ehsan* is much broader than justice. The latter implies that one should acquire one's right share and give what is their right share to others. In contrast, *ehsan* implies that a person may forsake some of his/her rights for the sake of societal welfare while acting generously by giving more than what he/she is required to do. The reasoning is based on a narrative attributed to the Prophet Mohamed who stated that God forgives an individual's sins if that person is engaged in giving "respite to the one in easy circumstances and forgives one who is in straitened circumstances."

It is binding for believers to act according to *ehsan*. This implies that they have to act generously and ethically, as this will lead to reward. The Quran (42:23) underscores this stating: "And if anyone earns any good, we shall give him an increase of good in respect thereof." The Prophet reiterates responsible behavior stating that God has "mercy on the man who is generous when he buys and when he sells and when he demands" (quoted in Muhammad Ali, 1977, p. 294).

Therefore, the multiplication factor in reward is characteristically linked to involvement and participation according to the logic of *ehsan*. However, in a business environment and in relation to profit, the multiplication of reward encompasses five significant issues:

1. Investing of capital is critical for economic growth and the creation of wealth. "God will bless your wealth though you engage in trade and commerce even without making a profit" (Abu Talib Al-Maki, 1995, died 996). The second Caliph, Omar (590–644), declared, "Invest the wealth of orphans in areas that generate profit" (quoted in Al-Maki, p. 520).

2. Engaging in business is critical for the continuity and thriving of a community. However, economic endeavor must generate income to market actors and enable and motivate them to serve their community: "When people no longer do business in order to make a living and when they cease all gainful activity, the business of civilization slumps and everything decays" (Ibn Khaldun, 1989, p. 1332–406).
3. The return on capital is important for personal growth and security. Al-Jahiz (1998, died 868, p. 256) argued that "The betterment of wealth is superior to poverty." Furthermore, he stated, "I like wealth because I detest poverty and I hate the latter as I fear that I might lose my dignity" (p. 202).
4. Business activities must be driven by the purpose of easing burden and avoidance of harmful activities. The Prophet stated that a person should "help the distressed one who is in need. . . . [and] should do good deeds and refrain from doing evil" (quoted in Muhammad Ali, 1977, p. 209). The intention of the business and conduct, therefore, takes precedence in Islamic ethics. This was articulated by the Prophet Mohamed who declared, "The value of work is derived from the accompanying intention, rather than its results."
5. Profit is an outcome, but its amount should not be the overriding factor in business affairs (Al-Maki 1995; Raghib, 1995).

The above five issues demonstrate that while economic activities are sanctioned in Islamic ethics, the scope of these activities and their purpose have to further the welfare of the community while enhancing the economic security of the person. Ibn Abed Raba Al-Andelesy (1996, died 985, vol. 2, p. 331) argued,

> He who cares about worldly affairs demands three things which cannot be realized without the addition of another four factors. The three things that he seeks are prosperity, social prestige, and good living until the end of life. These are realized by the following: obtaining wealth through respectable approaches; safeguarding it; investing; and spending wealth in ways that enhance one's living standard, brings satisfaction to family members and relatives, and ensures a blessed hereafter life. If he loses any of these four factors, he never reaches the three things that he has sought to achieve. If he does not work, he does not gain an income for living, and if he has work and wealth but does not take care of them, he ends up with no income. If he does not invest his wealth and just spends it, gradually his wealth will be depleted . . . If he participates in gainful activities, protects and invests his wealth but does not spend his income in the right ventures, he will be in the same position as a poor person with no money, as his wealth will be squandered without any benefit as if he had kept his water down a drain.

Therefore, how one conducts his/her business and the means of acquiring wealth are important considerations when understanding business

ethics. Though legitimacy of an economic activity is essential, it is insuf-
ficient if harm to others is a possibility (Al-Maki, 1995).

The aforementioned issues, in the context of ethics, highlight five
aspects of business conduct. First, involvement in business is a blessed
activity and while profit is the reason for any venture, it is a predictable
outcome for a business and should never be viewed as the overriding
factor. Second, selecting the appropriate ventures for investment is a must
for a business to thrive. Nevertheless, one should give serious attention to
how money should be spent. Third, even though the profit margin might
be low, it is much better than nothing. Over the years, through dedication,
discipline, and creativity, a business thrives and grows. Fourth, the value of
any business venture stems from its contribution to society. Thus, the ultimate measure of the worth of a business is the value it creates for society.
Fifth, in conducting business affairs, one should keep in mind that ethical
and morally responsible conduct are essential for satisfying spiritual needs
and obtaining God's blessings.

PROFIT MAXIMIZATION OR PROFIT MODERATION

In their debates on profit and economic systems, Muslim scholars have
argued that when the purpose of a business does not serve society, the business loses its legitimacy (Al-Sadr, 1983; Chapra, 2001). The latter asserts
that the goal of profit maximization leads to unfair business practices and,
therefore, does not serve the society at large. It is likely that this justification is derived from two Quranic (16:90) prescriptions: "God commands
justice" and (2:143) "we have made you a middle way nation." While the
first underscores fairness, the second instruction calls for moderation and
avoidance of an extreme stance or behavior. Both are assumed to further
societal interests and ease burdens on market actors, especially those
who are in urgent need. Though Islamic instructions sanction market
competition, property rights, and ownership in general, and limit government interference in the marketplace, they, nevertheless, seek to prevent
market abuses, be they deception, manipulation, or monopolistic attempts.
Indeed, during the early years of the Islamic state, scholars, jurists, and
the government gave considerable attention to market functions and
delineated unethical business practices guided by the Quranic instruction
(2:279): "Deal not unjustly, and you shall not be dealt with unjustly."

However, because many countries with Muslim majorities have been
integrated into the global capitalistic system and since many Muslim business scholars have been exposed during their college studies to concepts,
terminologies, and models developed in the West, especially the US, they

tend to uncritically accept the premise of profit maximization (e.g., Rizk, 2008; Samad, 2008). Some business corporations, thus, have blindly incorporated this goal in their conduct. In Saudi Arabia, for example, Kayed and Hassan (2011a, b) have found that the private sector in the Kingdom is driven by profit maximization rather than Islamic prescriptions. The Saudi-based Amiantit Group, in its mission statement, states that achieving a higher profit is a major goal. Likewise, the UAE-based corporation Emirates Group states, "we are focused on maximising profit margins."

The question that should be raised is, "does Islamic teaching sanction the concept and practice of profit maximization?" Most contemporary economists and jurists agree that the concept of profit maximization may not be consistent with the overriding objective of optimally serving society and avoiding exploitation (Chapra, 2001; Hassan, 2002; Metwally, 1980). Their argument postulates that maximization of profit can be either the result of monopoly or hoarding in the marketplace, which leads to manipulation in the market. Glaachi (2000, p. 62) stated, "If we say that the purpose of production is to achieve material benefits and maximize profit, ignoring the goal and cherished values of the society, the economy will be a captive to this concept. Thus, all compassionate meanings will be erased from the spiritual ideal, cultivation of the soul, altruism, friendship, kindness, for the sake of wealth worshiping."

In addition, profit maximization, as a motive and drive, may contradict the logic of *ehsan* and generosity in business dealing. For example, Al-Ghazali (2006) judged that it is commendable when a business person, guided by *ehsan*, lowers prices when they sell to the poor and customers in distress and pay higher prices for purchases from poorer suppliers to enable them to survive market competition. Al-Ghazali, in his reasoning for passing this judgment, relied on the Prophet Mohamed's saying, "God bless a person who is benevolent at selling and buying" (quoted in Al-Qurni, 1987, p. 120).

This promotion of fair and just transaction is substantiated by a narrative recorded by the tenth-century jurist, Al-Maki (1995, p. 509). He reported that there was a textile merchant who had two different grades of cloth: one was sold for 400 dirham and another for half of that amount. The merchant left his nephew in the store when he went to pray. A customer came and asked to see the 400 dirham cloth. The boy showed him, by mistake, the one that was sold for 200 dirham. The customer approved it and paid for it, thinking it was the one which cost 400. On his way back from the mosque, the merchant saw the customer outside of the market looking at what he had bought. He asked the customer, "How much did you pay for this?" The customer replied, "Four hundred." The merchant told him that it was not worth that much, only 200. The customer indicated that in his city, the cloth was sold for 500. The merchant replied, "Telling the truth is much better than material gain" and paid him back 200 dirham. Later the merchant asked his nephew, "Do you fear God; are you not ashamed of yourself gaining such high profit disregarding the public interest?" The boy replied, "He bought it with full consent." The merchant replied, "Even if he agreed and approved, you should do for others what you wish for yourself."

In another narrative, Abu Talib Al-Maki (1995, p. 508) also recorded that a merchant bought a container of almonds for 60 dinars and wrote in his book that he would sell it for 63 dinars. A few days later, the price for a container of almonds increased. An auctioneer approached him and offered him 70 instead of 63 dinars. The merchant declined the offer, telling the auctioneer that this was not acceptable because the profit margin would be too high. But the auctioneer insisted on paying the prevailing market price of 70 dinars. No transaction took place as both thought that their respective offer was fair and both of them thought that accepting his counterpart's offer would be unfair and unjust. This tenth-century narrative conveys that both market actors were driven by moral and ethical principles and neither wanted to be perceived as exploiters, despite the fact that they were transparent. Furthermore, it appears that at that time market actors gave considerable attention to their market reputation and their standing in the community.

The two narratives above highlight the fact that in a traditional society and in a community governed by ethical instructions, a market reputation for being decent and generous is critical for success. Indeed, the narratives demonstrate that both actors view themselves as members of a broader community where their welfare and that of the community are interrelated and harmoniously co-exist. Furthermore, it reveals that action and decision making in an Islamic setting are anchored in ethics. Business people, therefore, are concerned about their market reputation and their standing in the community. Their integrity is a social capital and, thus, they seek to safeguard it when conducting business and in dealing with customers. Their active involvement in the market, business survivability, and gains are a measure of their rightful contribution and perceived as a reward for good deeds. The Quran (18:46) declares, "Wealth and sons are allurements of the life of this world: but the things that endure, good deeds, are best in the sight of thy Lord, as rewards, and best as [the foundation for] hopes." Indeed, the preceding discussion clarifies that in Islamic ethics profit maximization is not the ultimate goal; serving customers and creating value for market actors and the society at large constitute the primary goal.

Among contemporary management scholars, Peter Drucker (1974, p. 60) was a pioneer in advocating that profit is not the purpose of business organizations stating, ". . . profitability is not the purpose of but a limiting factor on business enterprise and business activity. Profit is not the explanation, cause, or rationale of business behavior and business decisions, but the test of their validity." Similarly, Karns (2008) argued that profit is an essential means to the end of serving mankind but not the ultimate goal of business activity, as set forth in the shareholder wealth paradigm.

If profit is the test of the validity of a business and evidence that the business is creating value for society, then how do Muslim teachings and early Islamic scholars treat and view profit? It is important to state that the primary concern of Islamic teachings in the early years of the Islamic state was that just, transparent, and fair dealings in the marketplace were secured and that no exploitation was to occur. The Quran (11:85) instructs believers, "Nor withhold from the people the things that are their due" and (2:279) "Deal not unjustly, and ye shall not be dealt with unjustly." While these are general guidelines, the Prophet Mohamed was more specific, emphasizing that in the marketplace justice is an overriding motive for avoiding exploitation and protecting market actors. The Prophet identified four conditions for market transactions to be just (Ali, 2011). These are: in marketing exchange, there should be "No harm or harm-doer"; "Those who declare things frankly will not lead to each other's destruction"; "It is prohibited for anyone to take over the property of another without consent"; and "Sell commodities at the market price." These conditions, along with Quranic instructions, set certain limitations on profit levels and the need to engage in free exchange and stimulate economic activities.

In reviewing the literature on profit levels from the early years of the Islamic state, the following perspectives and judgments appear to offer a clear understanding that profit maximization is neither sought nor is desirable:

1. Business operations can thrive by focusing on investment and operation even when profit is low. Small profits and commitment to operations will lead to growth. Imam Ali, the fourth Caliph (died 661), stated, "Do not discard the low profit margin, so you will not be deprived of more profit" (quoted in Ibn Al-Josie, 1995, died 1177). Similarly, the third Caliph, Othman (577–656), when asked how he became rich, explained, "I did not turn down any margin of profit" (quoted in Al Jahiz, 1998, p. 269). This was also reiterated by a companion of the Prophet, Abdulrahman ibn Awf. He was a merchant who, when he was asked about his financial success, indicated that he "never turned down a transaction even with very little profit" (quoted in Al-Maki, 1995, p. 520). The medieval sociologist, Ibn Khaldun (2006, p. 311), articulated the role of small profit in business growth

      when he stated, "Many times a little [profit] is much." It is recognized, however, that without profit, "Business . . . merchants do not engage in trade and they lose their capital" (p. 313).

2. Capital to grow has to be invested and it is business transactions and investments that lead to prosperity. A ninth-century Muslim scholar, Maruf Al-Karkhi (died 815), argued that "Capital grows through transactions (like pastures)" (quoted in Jasim, 1990, p. 83). Ibn Abed Raba Al-Andelesy (1996, vol. 2, p. 330) stated, "The best wealth is that which generates return rather than losses." That is, market transactions are blessed activities which yield gains and lead to capital growth.

3. Profit earnings can be better realized during the early start of the market. The Prophet states, "Engage in transactions early and be lenient in your pricing, as leniency produces better profits" (quoted in Al Deinori, 1999, p. 287). Traditionally, market buyers and sellers interacted in the early hours. Merchants who did not sell their commodities during that time risked losing customers. Therefore, instead of holding out for higher profits a merchant was better off financially selling at market price.

4. Profit earning levels are linked to quality and availability of an item. Ibn Khaldun (2006, p. 312) articulated this when he stated, "Trading in commodities that are found in faraway countries and where there is a great risk in transportation is more advantageous and profitable for merchants. This is because the shipped goods are few and rare . . . When goods are in demand and there is a shortage in the market, their price is high." Profit must be the outcome of transactions which are carried out freely in the marketplace and should not result from harming others. The Prophet Mohamed instructs, "Pricing belongs to God's domain. He provides and withholds sustenance. Therefore, I shall not determine pricing for fear that I will be questioned in the hereafter for possible harm done to any actor in the market." Imam Al-Ghazali (2006, p. 411) argued that it is the duty of the market actor to show *ehsan* as his sales volume "is contingent upon his price; if he lowers his price, his customers will increase and vice versa."

5. Profits, however, are influenced by the amount of risk involved. If risk is great, the profit should increase accordingly. That is, profit level should correspond to the degree of risk involved (Glaachi, 2000, p. 112).

6. The government should protect actors in the marketplace and prevent manipulation. The fourth Caliph, Imam Ali, stated that "Buying and selling should be conducted in mutual consent . . . and fair prices for both buyer and seller. If anyone engages in monopoly after you have abolished it deal him severe but not excessive punishment." This is because in Islamic teaching hoarding and monopoly are prohibited

as both lead to higher prices and obstruct access to needed goods. The Prophet states, "He who hoards commodities is a sinner." Governments or rulers, however, should not enter the market to compete with private business, as this can result in a market actor who "consumes his capital and forces him out of business" (Ibn Khaldun, 2006, p. 220).

The prohibition of the desire and practice of profit maximization seeks to ensure just and fair transactions in the marketplace and, consequently, safeguards the interests of the broader community. Furthermore, the prohibition impels market actors to avoid what is considered unethical engagement, especially when resorting to deception and manipulation. The unethical engagement includes what is referred to as doubtful (gray) areas, where market actors are not certain whether a transaction is clearly permissible. Thus, faithful business people are encouraged to forsake profitable opportunities if there is a feeling that they are not in line with the religiously condoned practices.

CONCLUSION

In this chapter, the concept and practice of profit maximization is examined in terms of Islamic teaching and ethics. Since Islamic business ethics and prescriptions place considerable emphasis on the continuity and the welfare of the community, profit maximization is not condoned for fear of exploitation, obstruction of market function, and wrongdoing. Islamic teaching generally approves of lawful earnings and profit levels that do not lead to exploitation. Therefore, excessive pricing and or harm to the community are not looked upon positively. In fact, the evidence provided in the chapter demonstrates that while profit is a positive outcome for fostering economic prosperity and enhancing the welfare of the society, nevertheless, profit maximization is clearly perceived as antithetical to Islamic concerns with societal welfare and ethical conduct.

5. Leadership

According to Islamic thought, the absence or presence of a just society is characteristically linked to the nature of leadership. This belief has shaped the psyche of Muslims for many centuries and guides their aspirations for farsighted and morally disciplined leaders. While the debate on the feasibility of attaining such leadership is not expected to reach a conclusion, the fact remains that ethical leaders are thought to steer organizations/groups to the right path, thus minimizing chances for setbacks and turmoil.

The role of leadership in promoting purposeful and productive relationships in the context of a business organization has seldom been given priority in business ethics studies. This stems, perhaps, from the almost chronic upheavals that have characterized Muslim societies since the end of the Rightly Guided Caliphs' era in 661 and the deepening of fragmentation after the Mongol invasion, which led to the collapse of the capital of the Abbasid caliphate, Baghdad, in 1258. Historically, while traditionally theological and philosophical studies have placed special emphasis on political and religious leadership, only in recent decades have countries with Muslim majorities witnessed the presence of large-scale domestic-based business organizations. In small business organizations where the owner/manager is in direct contact with customers and other market actors, one's reputation in the marketplace, be it social or business, is essential for continuity and for a thriving operation. The owner/manager's reputation is shaped based on ethical conduct and the relationships with others. In large organizations, this is difficult to maintain.

The lack of debate about leadership in the context of business ethics, however, does not mean that leadership issues have been ignored. In fact, the subject of leadership is often a topic in Islamic discourse, with a primary focus on the business conduct of market actors. Underscoring the role of these actors, in the context of market conduct and morality, was thought to safeguard societal welfare. That is, in early religious commentaries and treaties, the emphasis was on stressing *ehsan*, modesty, and benefits to society and highlighting desirable behavior in the market, religious expectations, and the principles of the faith.

Generally, in Islamic thinking, leadership is viewed as a primary factor in generating productive and thoughtful relationships among members of society. It is in this quest that leaders have had to creatively maintain a balance of priorities, clarify possibilities, inspire followers, and maintain a focus on achieving goals. These, however, require trusted relationships which are manifested in active interaction, dialogue, persuasion, action, and reflection. In this chapter, we reflect on leaders' responsibilities, the theory of leadership based on early Islamic perspectives, and the role of leaders in enhancing ethical conduct and morally driven behavior.

THE NATURE OF LEADERSHIP RESPONSIBILITIES

As we indicated in previous chapters, early Islamic thought underscored the importance of leaders and leadership in shaping attitudes toward worldly and spiritual issues, while enhancing commitment to do what is good and beneficial. Faced with mounting challenges of limited resources in Arabia, strong rivals who controlled the trade routes and were intent on defeating the new faith, persistent tribal ethos and traditions, along with simmering rivalries among his followers, the Prophet had to articulate the message of the faith in a coherent way and build sound foundations for a thriving state in the face of a hostile environment.

Leaders' responsibilities cannot be understood without being viewed in terms of ethical foundations: public interest (acquisition of benefits and avoidance of harm), moderation, and *ehsan*. These foundations not only shape the conduct of a faithful leader but also define the responsibilities of the leader within his/her organization and society at large. In the organizational context, the Prophet underscored two functions: task and human relations. He declared, "God instructs me to be considerate and responsive to people, and to focus on carrying out duties" (quoted in Al-Mawardi, 2002, p. 532). Unlike contemporary studies on leadership functions, the Prophet did not dichotomize leaders' responsibilities – either task or relationship oriented. These responsibilities are broad in nature and emphasis on one does not preclude the other. Rather, depending on the event, a leader may have to set priorities. Both, however, have to be addressed within the framework of ethical foundations.

Figure 5.1 depicts the relationship between the three foundations and the two responsibilities. While public interest dictates that in dealing with individuals or followers societal benefits should be ensured and harm must be avoided, moderation and *ehsan* play a significant role in assessing the capabilities of a subordinate or a group to carry out their tasks and duties. That is, an individual should not expect to be burdened with tasks that far exceed his/her ability and conditions. The Quran (2:286) states, "On no soul doth God place a burden greater than it can bear." In addition, *ehsan* necessitates

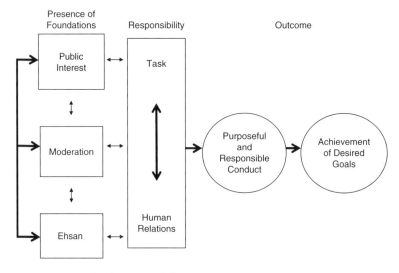

Figure 5.1   Leaders' responsibilities

that leaders must be sensitive to prevailing conditions that followers experience and generosity requires not only that the rights of followers are not ignored or dealt with unjustly but that followers receive more than what is required as their rights. In the interplay between the foundations and responsibilities, the latter is transformed so as to be in the service of the followers and the facilitating factor for optimizing relationships between leaders and followers, thus contributing to achieving the desired goals. It is this optimization which situates leadership responsibility on an idealization level; difficult to reach but always sought by the faithful.

Responsibilities of an ethical leader are exceptionally broad and can be direct or indirect. Nevertheless, a responsible leader who fears God considers them to be moral duties that have to be carried out in a morally driven way. While this is difficult to validate, Muslim scholars across centuries have agreed that one of the most just leaders was Omer Ibn Abdulaziz (died 720) who stated, "As I assumed the leadership of the Muslims, be they black and the red, I thought about the hungry poor, the sick without shelter, exhausted with inadequate clothing, the marginalized and oppressed, captives, senior citizens, those with many dependents but with limited resources, and those like them across the country and in the peripheries and I know that God holds me responsible for them during the day of judgment" (quoted in Al-Suyuti, 1996, p. 198). Though Abdulaziz articulated his responsibilities in broad terms, the essence is that in assuming a leadership position, one should not abandon any responsibility, even if it is a remote one or directly the responsibility of a deputy. That is, leadership has a spiritual dimension and essentially represents a moral contract between the leader and God. Accordingly, in making certain that the performance of their duties is ethically conducted, leaders must reflect on their actions and hold themselves responsible for any wrongdoing. The Quran (16:93) declares, "but ye shall certainly be called to account for all your actions" and (17:14) "sufficient is thy soul this day [of Judgment] to make out an account against thee."

Leaders, in what they do, are accountable to themselves, their followers, and God. A responsible leader holds himself self-accountable. This was articulated in the saying of the Prophet Mohamed: "Before you are asked to account for your actions, show accountability toward yourself" (quoted in Al-Mawardi, 1986, p. 189). Being self-responsible and reflecting on what has been done enables a leader to overcome weaknesses, avoid future mistakes, reinforce correct action, and ensures the respect of followers. Al-Mawardi (2002, p. 560) asserted that when a leader reflects on his behavior, he might find that what he did was desirable or that he had made mistakes or did not fully carry out appropriate actions or did more than what was intended. Imam Ali (1990, died 661, p. 694) stated, "He who assumes the position of an imam has to educate himself first before educating others. He should set an example for others before instructing them."

Accountability to followers manifests a commitment to pleasing God and demonstrates that a leader is one who is fully responsible. Answerability to followers is a virtue and manifests confidence and moral clarity. The Prophet instructs, "What you love for yourself you should love for others" (quoted in Al-Ghazali, 2006, p. 395). That is, a leader must be driven in his actions by what is good for his followers, optimize their welfare, and avoid doing them harm. The Prophet states, "A leader who intends to deceive his followers, God will deny him paradise" (quoted in Al-Suyuti, 1996, p. 711). Caliph Yazid Ibn Al-Waleed (701–44), who was known to be pious, articulated the meaning of responsibility and the accountability of a leader to his/her followers when he stated:

> Oh followers, it is my promise to you that I will not build a palace, reroute rivers, hoard money, or give wealth to a wife or son, nor transfer wealth from one country to another before making sure that the needs of the poor are met and those with special needs are taken care of. If there is extra, I will transfer it to the next country in need. I will not keep troops on the field too long . . . and will not overtax non-Muslims. . . . I will make payments on time. . . . If I fulfill my promise, you should listen and obey and I will seek your support and assistance. But if I do not meet your expectations you have the right to depose me and if you see or know someone who is known as being decent and a reformer . . . and

you want to give him your allegiance, I will be the first to follow his leadership. (Quoted in Al-Mawardi, 1986, pp. 134–5)

Among the faithful, the belief that a person is in the end accountable to God for everything he/she does is a powerful motivational factor to do good and avoid wrongdoing. Indeed, for those who are guided by spiritual goals, God's injunction to help others and confront misdeeds is a motivation for taking care of those who are under their direction and making certain that their actions are morally driven. The Quran (3:30) warns, "On the day when every soul will be confronted with all the good it has done, and all the evil it has done, it will wish there was a great distance between it and its evil. But God cautions you [to fear] him and God is full of kindness to those that serve him" and (75:14) "Nay, man will be evidence against himself." Those who serve God and seek his reward must treat followers with justice and be responsive to their needs and aspirations. The Prophet states that "People are God's creation, and the one that is loved by God is the one who is beneficial to His people" (quoted in Al-Suyuti, 1996, p. 280). The second Caliph, Omer, informed one of his deputies: "God's view of you is contingent upon how the public views you. Whatever you do for the people is what God accounts you for" (quoted in Al-Andelesy, 1996, vol. 2, p. 155). Al-Andelesy, quoting a noble person, stated that people are "the witness[es] of God against the ruler and His monitors of those who deviate from the right path" (p. 155).

The aforementioned responsibilities demonstrate that, from an Islamic perspective, a leader's legitimacy and the scope of his activities are closely intertwined with the approval of his followers. As such, a leader is responsive and his actions beneficial to society. This particular subject is addressed in detail in the section that follows. Muslim scholars agree that justice and avoidance of oppression stands out as the best guarantee for ensuring ethical and moral behavior.

Al-Suyuti (1996, p. 277) quoted Caliph Omer Ibn Abdulaziz saying, "Whenever I confront a great problem, I often trace its sources to oppression committed by my deputies." While competency is an important quality, in the absence of justice it loses its value. The Quran instructs those who are in a position of authority that they should act justly (38:26): "So judge between people with justice and do not follow [thy] desire." The Prophet Mohamed, furthermore, argued that leadership should be bestowed on people who are competent. This was articulated in his saying that leadership is a "trust and on the Day of Judgment can be a cause of humiliation and repentance, except for one who meets their obligations and [properly] discharges the duties attendant thereon."

In terms of political leadership, Al-Mawardi (2002, p. 221) specified seven responsibilities. These are:

1. Safeguarding the faith and encouraging followers to act according to its principles without overlooking it.
2. Safeguarding the boundaries of the state and public properties from enemies or those who seek to take over wealth or gain at the expense of others.
3. Developing the nation and upgrading its infrastructure and its roads.
4. Managing public wealth wisely without changing the just way it is accumulated and dispensed.
5. Addressing grievances evenly and passing judgment among people justly.
6. Ordering a punishment without exceeding the limits or overlooking due process.
7. Selecting deputies from a pool of qualified individuals who are known for being trustworthy.

These responsibilities encompass seven dimensions: spiritual; security/ defense; economic growth and development; finance and wealth distribution; social and societal welfare; legalistic; and human resources. Any leader, according to Al-Mawardi, who is incapable of upholding the ethical aspects of responsibility, especially avoidance of oppression and maintenance of justice, should be removed. Oppression is seen as an effective mechanism for the economic destruction and corruption of people. On the other hand, justice is considered a pillar for safeguarding this world. Without it there can be no betterment of human well-being.

The *Ikhwan-Ul-Safa*, (1999, vol. 3, pp. 174–5) or the Brothers of Purity, who rose in the tenth century, indicates that a political leader has primarily ten responsibilities. However, the *Ikhwan-Ul-Safa* argues that carrying out these responsibilities is possible only if a leader understands and knows his people's rights and is endowed with reason, as both knowledge and reason enable a leader to act in a way that sustains justice and upholds laws. The ten responsibilities are:

1. Follow up on and be concerned with the affairs of the people in order not to overlook their problems, whether these problems are related to the young or old.
2. Treat people according to their deeds.
3. Apply justice evenly and without exception.
4. Avoid brutality.

5. Reward both knowledgeable and ignorant people accordingly in terms of rank and compensation.
6. Select and appoint representatives and subordinates who have the best reputations and are independent to supervise and conduct people's affairs. That is because whatever subordinates do, people will attribute to the leader; if subordinates spread justice or oppression, people will hold the leader responsible.
7. Select advisors from those who share a similar faith and outlook. Advisors who do not share a leader's outlook may not be sincere in their advice.
8. Select a *wazir* or first minister who is the best in terms of faith and worldly affairs. The selection should be from people who have good reputations and are noble.
9. Protect the rights of the weak and the oppressed.
10. Make sure that people who were wronged are given justice.

PERCEPTION OF LEADERSHIP

Before reflecting on the Islamic perspective of leadership, it might be appropriate to briefly look at the state of the literature. In the West, current studies on leadership provide a rich view on the nature and aspects of leadership. While the majority of the research agrees on the centrality of leadership in meeting goals and moving forward, the literature offers a wide range of perspectives, often contradictory, on what constitutes effective leadership. As Hunt and Conger (1999) assert, the range in new leadership conceptions is quite broad. While this state is necessary and healthy, it may unintentionally lead to ambiguity and generalization. Recently, Howell and Shamir (2005) reviewed the literature and concluded that most leadership theories have been simple, unidirectional, and have focused almost exclusively on a leader's personality and behavior. In the process, the role of followers and the cultural environment that gives rise to leadership has often been neglected.

Traditionally, most research on leadership places considerable emphasis on specific attributes (e.g., Blau, 1963; Dow, 1969; Stogdill, 1974). Identifying attributes were thought important when differentiating effective leaders from others. Friedland (1964) and Wolpe (1968), among others, consider social and historical contexts as critical in determining leadership. Hughes, Ginnett, and Curphy (2006) assert that leadership is the result of the interaction between a leader and his followers. Willner (1984) argues that leadership is neither personality-based nor contextually determined but is largely a relational and perceptual phenomenon. Conger and Kanungo (1987) agree with Willner and view leadership as an attribution phenomenon. The authors suggest that leadership is attributed by followers who observe certain behaviors on the part of the leader within organizational contexts. They propose that attribution of charisma to leaders depends on four interrelated components: the degree of discrepancy between the status quo and the future goal or vision championed by the leader, the use of innovation and unconventional means for achieving the desired change, a realistic assessment of environmental resources and constraints for bringing about such change, and the nature of articulation and impression the management employs to inspire followers in the pursuit of the identified vision.

Howell and Shamir (2005) argue that in the context of charismatic leadership there are two types of relationships: personalized and socialized. The first relationship is based primarily on followers' personal identification with a leader. The socialized relationship revolves primarily on followers' social identification with the group or organization. This approach attempts to answer most of the shortcomings in leadership theory – especially the charismatic leadership process. Nevertheless, the approach does not offer any direct link to societal culture. Peterson and Hunt (1997) make a serious attempt to address leadership theory from a global and historical perspective. The coverage, however, is primarily focused on the US and the linkage between leadership and culture is neither clear nor systematic.

Societies differ in their perception of leadership and the effectiveness of a leader. Hofstede (1980, 1999) attributed such differences to cultural values. He argued that values are specific to national cultures, never universal. Values represent what is desirable and generally they are a preference of specific states of affairs over others. These broad tendencies are ranked hierarchically according to their relative importance. Societies differ not only in their values but also in the way they rank these values, i.e., a value system. A value system helps in establishing priorities, solving conflicting demands, and categorizing leaders. Shaw (1990) suggests that each culture appears to categorize leaders differently. He argues that cultural perception of whether or not a person is a leader involves simple categorization. In fact, he proposes that in each culture there are pre-existing leadership prototypes and expectations which are a potential source of variation across cultures. The attributes and practices that differentiate cultures from each other are predictive of a leader's attributes and behavior (House, Javidan, and Dorfman, 2001). Recent empirical studies provide support for such a proposition. Brodbeck (2000) led a group of researchers to study cultural variations of leadership prototypes across 22 European countries. The results indicate that leadership concept is culturally bound. Clusters of

European countries that share similar cultural values are found to share similar leadership concepts that may differ from other European clusters. Nordic countries, for example, rank highly the attributes of outstanding leadership, such as integrity, inspirational, visionary, team integrator, and performance. In contrast, managers in Latin countries rank the attributes of team integrators, performance, inspirational, integrity, and visionary, in order as the most desired.

As was previously mentioned, leadership in Islam is perceived to be the most significant instrument for the realization of an ideal society. The ideal society is based on justice and compassion. Both qualities are an integral part of leadership. Al-Suyuti (1996, p. 195) cited, "If the head is healthy, the body is fine" or "If the leader is morally disciplined, followers will not commit wrongdoing." Similarly, Al-Mawardi (2002, p. 219) indicated that "The ruler, in his own right, is a leader with followers. . . . If he is an oppressor, no one will govern with justice. But if he is a man of justice, no one will dare to oppress others." In Islamic thinking, neither creativity nor order can be sustained without justice and compassion. That is, justice "is the mainstay of a nation" (Imam Ali, 1989, died 661). Leaders are held responsible for promoting and enforcing justice. The Quran (4:58) instructs its believers: "When ye judge between people then ye judge with justice." Indeed, the thriving of justice is closely linked to the subject of leadership and leaders.

It should be noted that Muslims hold the early period of Islam (about 622–61) as the most just, compassionate, and ideal era of Islamic history. Muslim scholars argue that during those early years Islamic society most closely resembled an ideal state. The conditions for such an ideal state did not reoccur until the era of Caliph Omer Ben Abdul Aziz (717–20) and for a short period of time during the Abbasid Empire (750–1258). Muslim scholars claim that justice was then fairly meted out and leaders were morally guided and responsible. Therefore, a sense of idealism evolved in the psyche of most Muslims, resulting in a deeply seated infatuation with what is termed a Prophetic leader, as opposed to the Caliph model of leadership. Both concepts will be discussed later.

Leadership is defined as a process of influence, shared in nature, whereby a leader and followers engage in certain activities to achieve mutual goals. At the outset, it should be mentioned that the traditional view of leadership in Islam is that leadership is a shared influence process. Leaders are not expected to lead or to maintain their roles without the agreement of those who are led and, at the same time, decisions made by these leaders are expected to be influenced by input from their followers. The process is dynamic and open ended and the ultimate aim is to sustain cohesiveness and effectiveness. The Quran clearly calls for a leader to be flexible and receptive to followers and states (88:21–22), "Thou [go on] reminding;

thou art only a reminder. Thou art not, over them, a compeller." The foundation for understanding and leadership has to be fundamentally based on wisdom and spirited debate, otherwise followers become resentful and dissatisfied. The role of a receptive leader is captured in the Quranic instructions which state (16:125), "Argue with them in manners that are best and most gracious" as (3:159) "Wert thou severe or harsh-hearted, they would [break] away." The leader is obliged to exemplify openness, a willingness to listen, and compassion in dealing with subordinates or followers. For example, during the course of a public meeting, an individual criticized the second Caliph, Omer. Some in the audience thought the criticism was harsh. Omer's answer was that it was the duty of the leader and his followers to listen to each other and to voice concerns. He was quoted saying, "When followers do not participate and provide input, they are not contributing something useful. And we are not useful if we do not consent to their contributions." Omer thought that public participation is fundamental and, as the Prophet Mohamed insisted, that it is a policy choice. Omer, however, pursued the matter further when he informed followers: "When you see me engage in a wrongdoing, straighten me out." In this context, the shared influence is not only built on a "two way influence," through dialogue and debate, but also on the right of subordinates to take a proactive role in confronting and correcting their leader. This foresighted model was possibly founded on the Prophet Mohamed's instruction, which made it mandatory that followers not blindly follow leaders: "Obedience is due only to that which is good."

Before reflecting on theoretical perspectives on leaders and leadership in Islamic thought, it should be pointed out that since the era of the Rightly Guided Caliphs (632–61), the subject of leadership has been fiercely debated. However, no consensus has been reached among scholars about what specific qualities leaders have or the traits that predict who will emerge as a leader. Nevertheless, the Quran provides certain qualities that must exist for a person to be a leader. The Quran (28:26) instructs that in selecting leaders the preference should be for those who are "competent and trustworthy." Competency includes the physical and intellectual capacity to carry out responsibilities and optimally serve the community. This is reemphasized in the Quran (12:55): "Set me [in authority] over the treasuries of the land; Verily, I am a (faithful) keeper, knowing well." The underscoring of trustworthiness (faithfulness to followers and the cause, reliable, and ethical), and competency (having the needed skills, foresight, and vision) conveys the message that leadership is not independent of its milieu, but a dynamic and continuous interaction with followers and the forces in the environment that may serve as either enablers or impediments, and often both, for optimal achievement of goals.

Indeed, competent leaders have the capacity to safeguard the interests of followers with pragmatism and imagination. Both are essential for inspiring followers and enhancing trust in their leaders. Pragmatism implies avoidance of extreme stances and an inclination to serve followers in the most realistic and beneficial ways. On the other hand, imagination demonstrates not only foresight but also the will to venture unto new terrains to safeguard the interests of the public and minimize future threats, while building the foundations for coping with future challenges. That is, a leader must be committed to carrying out his/her current duties with utmost adherence to moderation and *ehsan*, but also to prepare followers for what difficulties might lie ahead and to cope with emerging challenges. This process deepens trust between leaders and followers. This is especially pertinent as trustworthiness is an attribute that people bestow upon a person, manifesting not only a confidence in the leader but also a proven leadership. The Prophet Mohamed reflects on this relationship when he states, "The best of your leaders are those who you like and who like you and the worse are those who dislike you and who you loathe" (quoted in Al-Mawardi, 2002, p. 223).

The concept of leaders and leadership has evolved across centuries and has been largely influenced by the nature of power structure and sectarian allegiances. To be sure, however, the evolution of leadership has been shaped by powerful events, dynasties, rulers, and individuals. These forces have had a considerable impact on reshaping the image and religious conceptualization of what leaders should be. In traditional Muslim societies, proper religious justifications and assertions have been utilized for sustaining and validating power and authority.

The perceptions and realities of leadership have evolved dramatically in the Muslim world. These dramatic changes in the concept of what constitutes a leader and leadership have been most likely influenced by the rise and fall of ideology (faith) and openness in society. As the following discussion shows, the Islamic view of leaders and leadership has been in a state of alteration. While degrees of strength of faith and openness have primarily influenced these changes, outside forces and instability have accelerated the trend. The changing nature of leadership in the Islamic context has gone through three stages. Since the focus in this book is on ethical aspects, only two stages, according to almost all Muslim scholars, that reflect true Islamic thinking and practices are addressed. These are: the Prophet Era and the Rightly Guided Caliphs. These stages are considered by Muslim thinkers and authorities to capture the essence of Islam and genuine practice.

THE PROPHET ERA (610–32)

The Prophet Mohamed combined the authority of a religious leader and a statesman. Under his leadership, profound cultural and political changes took place in Arabia. Karen Armstrong (1992) argues that the immediate spread and acceptance of Islam reflected the unique message of Islam and was clearly a reflection of the genius of Mohamed. She suggests, however, that the Arabs were not sufficiently developed for a sophisticated Islamic monotheism. She states (p. 53), "Christianity took root in the Roman Empire where Jewish communities had paved the way and prepared the minds of the pagans. But Mohamed had to start virtually from scratch and work his way towards the radical monotheistic spirituality on his own." The Prophet believed that a leader must have three qualities: *Rehema* (mercy), *ehsan*, and *adel* (justice). Once these foundations were met, race was not an issue in selecting a leader. As he asserted, "Listen to and obey whoever is in charge, even though he is an Ethiopian [black]." Prophet Mohamed developed a pattern of behavior that facilitated a cultural change in Arabia that not only altered ethical priorities but set the stage for establishing law and order in a chaotic society:

1. He developed a vital community of believers and envisioned what this community should be like. While faith was an important instrument in energizing his followers, the Prophet had to engage in other dramatic social changes: he established a new form of social association (*muakhat*—two Muslims were paired together and declared brothers, replacing the traditional blood relationship). He announced that faith would replace blood as the basis for social relationships (Siddiqui, 1987). Furthermore, the Prophet understood that Arabs are highly individualistic, unreceptive to centralized authority, and sensitive to direct orders. Therefore, contrary to prevailing practices of show of power, he declared that he was not a compeller, but a messenger of God; that his job, primarily, was to preach, warn, remind and guide, do good, and avoid vice. In doing so, the Prophet situated himself as an impersonal conveyer of the new faith. The Quran (17:15) declares, "Who receiveth guidance, receiveth it for his own benefit; who goeth astray doth so to his own loss."

2. He created a social order in Arabia where faith was treated as the only acceptable standard by which to construct and identify groups; differentiation was no longer based on tribal identity and or wealth-based social status. He stated that there are no differences among people "except in piety." The Quran (49:13) instructs, "The most honored of you in the sight of God is (he who is) the most righteous of you." By

underscoring the new social order, the Prophet sought to achieve three objectives: put an end to social fragmentation and division in Arabia; create an outlook and relationships to facilitate the propagation of his message; and ensure identification with and loyalty to his leadership.

3. He promoted his message in two stages. Initially, he focused only on disseminating the message of Islam and creating an environment to facilitate cultural change. Once the new community became large and a city-state was established, instructions regarding law and order were specified. Furthermore, cooperation among members of the Muslim community was encouraged and brotherly relationships were extended far beyond the original Muslim community. When various regions in Arabia and the surrounding areas adopted Islam, the Prophet assigned *walis* (governors), local administrators, and market commissioners among others to govern. These were given autonomy in running their affairs (Siddiqui, 1987).

4. He introduced a mechanism of consultation to solve disputes and govern the thriving community. He stated, "Consultation prevents regrets and is a safeguard against blame" and "If you consult a wise person you will benefit, and if you ignore his advice you will be regretful" (quoted in Al-Mawardi, 2002, p. 473 and p. 475, respectively). The Quran (3:159) states, "Consult them in affairs [of the moment]. Then, when thou hast taken a decision, put thy trust in God."

5. He linked every action of an individual to the service of mankind, stating "He who does not thank people, does not thank God," and "The best of people, are those who benefit others." The Prophet's words consistently reminded members of his community that cooperation and doing good were essential for solidarity and prosperity. He declared, "This community is in good standing and is blessed by God as long as its learned people do not go along with the desires of rulers, its decent people are not sacrilegious, and its good people do not empathize with the wrongdoers. If they do, then God will not bless them and will enable oppressors to control and subject them to severe torment" (quoted in Al-Mawardi, 2002, p. 132).

6. He introduced innovative organizational concepts and practices to a society that was driven by a tribal ethos where the rich and powerful had absolute power and were expected to be served. He demonstrated that a leader's primary job is to make sure that community interests are safeguarded, stating, "The leader is the servant of followers" (quoted in Al-Suyuti, died 1505, p. 362) and "A ruler who having obtained control over the affairs of the Muslims does not strive for their betterment and does not serve them sincerely shall not enter Paradise" (*Sahih Muslim*). By asserting that a leader is a servant to his followers,

the Prophet intended to end the exploitation of the weak and the poor by the powerful tribal chiefs and other powerful and wealthy people, to breach the walls that divided the community, to unify the community, and, most importantly, institutionalize the process of benefiting others as a norm.

7. He underscored the link between ethical conduct and the prosperity of the community stating, "When the best of you are the leaders, the wealthy among you are generous, and your affairs are managed in consultation among yourselves, then what resources are currently available [on earth] will be sufficient and there will be no need to search for additional ones [deep inside the earth]" (quoted in Abu Dawod, 1996). The Prophet also declared, "If God wishes a comfortable life for people, their leaders will be forbearing, their judges knowledgeable, and their wealthy generous" (quoted in Jasim, 1987, p. 185).

8. He promoted freedom as a means of energizing the people, enabling them to regain their dignity, motivating them to carry out responsibilities, and enhancing their loyalty, stating, "Wicked people do not accept mistakes, do not accept excuses, and do not forgive" (quoted in Al-Barai and Abdeen, 1987). The Quran (10:99) declares, "If it had been thy Lord's will, they would all have believed—all who are on earth! Wilt thou then compel mankind, against their will, to believe!" and (29:18) "the duty of the messenger is only to preach publicly [and clearly]." Furthermore, the Prophet associated oppression with sinful acts and considered oppressors to be the enemies of God. He warned that "The most tormented person at the Day of Judgment will be he who was an oppressive ruler" (quoted in Al-Mawardi, 2002, p. 226). The Quran (40:18) states, "No intimate friend nor intercessors will the wrongdoers have, who will be listened to."

9. He established various forms of alliances. These alliances were aimed at ensuring safety and stability and certain principles were observed in an environment that had once been characterized mainly by the absence of law and order. More importantly, he sought alliances to strengthen and spread the faith. Alliances with Jewish communities and other tribes in different geographical localities were intended to build the foundation of the faith and convey the message to a wider audience (Jasim, 1987).

The Prophet Mohamed viewed leadership as a process of shared influence. In his general conduct of affairs, whether religious or otherwise, he utilized a public open forum where members of the community had immediate input and contributed on the spot to civic and administrative matters. He instructed his representatives by saying, "God blesses those who benefit others." That is, leadership is valid only when it results in benefiting society, regardless of the setting. He was reported to have said, "Everyone of you is a leader and every one of you shall be questioned about those under your supervision; the Imam is a leader and shall be questioned about his subjects; a man is a leader in his family and he shall be questioned about those under his care; a woman is a leader in the house of her husband and shall be questioned about those under her care; and a servant is in charge of taking care of his master's property and shall be questioned about those under him." In this broad concept of leadership, the Prophet implied that shouldering responsibility is essential for cohesiveness, smooth performance, and improving the welfare of the society. In addition, Prophet Mohamed highlighted two necessary qualities for leadership: persuasion and moderation. In terms of persuasion, the Prophet Mohamed asserted the necessity for debate and argument. Moderation was viewed as an avoidance of extremism and seeking the middle way was considered the optimum state, as supported by the Quran (2:143): "Thus we have made you a middle-way nation."

THE RIGHTLY GUIDED CALIPHS (632–61)

There were four Caliphs during this period. Their sayings and practices are relevant to understanding the nature of leadership and organization. During that time, the community was in the early stage of development, politically and economically. Ideology (faith) was a potent motivational factor. Accordingly, allegiance to the group and identification with the faith was strong. The first Caliph, Abu Baker, in his inauguration speech, defined what a Muslim leader should be. He stated, "I have been given authority over you, but I am not the best of you. If I do well help me, and if I do ill, then put me right. . . . The weak among you shall be strong in my eyes until I secure his right if God wills; and the strong among you shall be weak in my eyes until I wrest the right from him. . . . Obey me as long as I obey God and his apostle, and if I disobey them you owe me no obedience" (quoted in Armstrong, 1992, p. 258). During this period there was a consensus that the quality of a leader was primarily built on three foundations: the approval of followers, justice, and performance. Imam Ali (1990, p. 622) succinctly stated, "Good leaders are known by what their subjects attribute to them. So, the best action, for you, is the one that benefits others." The four Caliphs, in general, reaffirmed that leadership is a shared influence. This was captured by a saying attributed to the second Caliph, Omer: "If you see me doing wrong, then put me right." Most importantly, at this stage, despite an attempt to the contrary during the era of the third

Caliph, Othman, the Muslims and Caliphs viewed the role of Caliph as a secular position. Though Caliphs served as successors to the Prophet, they could not be considered heirs or a replacement for him (Arkoun, 1986; Ashmawy, 1992). In Islam, the government is considered a civic system that is entirely built on the will of the community. The community's approval of how things should be run is the only validation that the leader should be in power. This understanding differentiates the traditional Islamic concept of the leader and government from that of Christianity and leadership. The latter views the leader as having a divine order. This was articulated in (Romans 13:1), "Let everyone submit himself to the ruling authorities, for there exists no authority not ordained by God" and in (Matthew 16:19) "And I will give unto thee the keys of the kingdom of heaven: and whatsoever thou shalt bind on earth shall be bound in heaven: and whatsoever thou shalt loose on earth shall be loosed in heaven."

RELATIONAL LEADERSHIP THEORY

While the elements of public interest, moderation, and *ehsan* constitute the foundation and the guiding principles for leaders in their interpersonal relationships and social interactions in a dynamic setting, desired outcomes are contingent upon the positive involvement of followers and conditions in the environment. This state can either facilitate performance and achievement of goals or can create certain obstacles that ultimately make it impossible to move forward and meet objectives. While most of the literature focuses on leaders' or leader-followers' interactions (see for detail Uhl-Bien, 2006), environmental conditions play an instrumental role in either facilitating social and personal interactions or the emergence of a leader. Indeed, Arabia before the rise of Islam experienced a power vacuum, absence of law and order, and the rapid decline of the two empires to the east (Persian) and to the north (Roman).

Uhl-Bien (2006), reviewing the literature on leadership, argued that as a process, leadership is relational in nature. She argued that leadership as a relational process is a social influence when it contributes to the emergence of a social order and to the rise of new attitudes, values, and goals, i.e. change. These two conditions may shed light on the nature of leadership in Islam and help to better understand leadership phenomena in general. Nevertheless, Islamic perspectives, as viewed within the framework of public interests, moderation, and *ehsan*, present a broader view of the nature of the leadership process. While leadership in Islam is deemed relational, it is inherently a moral phenomenon and trust. That is, neither the leader nor followers are ignored; the worthiness of a leader stems primarily from ethically pursuing the interests of followers and meeting their aspirations.

Often misunderstood in the debate on leadership in Islam is the role of followers in creating and reinforcing leadership relationships. Though theoretical perspectives and early practices in the Islamic state articulated how relationships, whether interpersonal or social interactions, should be, the practice of leadership for centuries has primarily focused on the leader, with little, if any, credit given to followers. This situation, while obstructing theory articulation, has severely paralyzed business and state-owned organizations and prevented them from optimally utilizing available resources for the advantage of the people. Relational theory of leadership, with its emphasis on interpersonal and social interaction, attribution of certain qualities to leaders, and the role of the latter in bringing about genuine transformation of followers' attitudes and organizational effectiveness, can eradicate many organizational ills. The elements of relational leadership were often exhibited in Islamic traditions through various Quranic messages and sayings of the Prophet and his immediate successors. These are outlined below:

1. The bond between leader and followers is contingent upon attentiveness to and the treatment of and responsiveness to followers' needs. The Quran (3:159) instructs, "Wert thou severe or harsh-hearted, they would [break] away." As was reported previously, the Prophet made attentiveness to each a condition for strengthening the bond, stating, "The best of your leaders are those that you like and who like you and the worse are those who dislike you and who you loath."

2. Highlighting that leadership can occur in any direction in a relational leadership; relational processes are essential for relational leadership (see Rost, 1991; Uhl-Bien, 2006). The Prophet underscored this when he stated, "Every one of you is a leader and every one of you shall be questioned about those under his supervision; the Imam is a leader and shall be questioned about his subjects; the man is a leader in his family and he shall be questioned about those under his care; the woman is a leader in the house of her husband, and shall be questioned about those under her care; and the servant is a leader when taking care of the property of his master, and shall be questioned about those under his care." The second Caliph, Omer, farther emphasized this aspect when he stated, "If you see me doing wrong, then put me right."

3. Accentuate certain duties and responsibilities that both leader and followers must undertake in order for the relationship processes to be further reinforced. The fourth Caliph, Ali, elaborated on the reciprocity between a leader and followers when he commented (Imam Ali,

1989, p. 245), "God has made it an obligation for his creatures to observe their obligations toward each other. He made them equitable and interdependent. The greatest of those obligations are the mutual rights of the ruler and the ruled. God has made them reciprocal so that they constitute a basis for their cohesion."

4. Underscoring that responsibility lies with the collective and not just the leader (see Fletcher, 2004; Uhl-Bien, 2006). The first Caliph, Abu Baker, asked people to give him a salary and to decide the amount (see Al-Maki, 1995, p. 37). Furthermore, he stated, "I have been given authority over you, but I am not the best of you. If I do well help me, and if I do ill, then put me right . . . Obey me as long as I obey God and his apostle, and if I disobey them you owe me no obedience" (quoted in Armstrong, 1992, p. 258).

5. Leaders are different from their followers only in terms of the amount of responsibility they have and their accountability to the general public. The first Caliph, Abu Baker, underscored this when he stated that he was not better than others except in terms of responsibility. The second Caliph, Omer, articulated this when he compared the role of a leader to a person who is selected by fellow passengers to be responsible for managing their travel expenses saying, "We are similar to passengers who give their travel funds to one of them to manage. Does this person have more rights than the rest? . . . No" (quoted in Al-Deinori, 1999, p. 94).

6. Followers attribute certain qualities to leaders and if these qualities in a leader are absent, followers should not select that person to lead. The fourth Caliph, Imam Ali (1990, p. 542–3), succinctly stated, "Good leaders are known by what their subjects say about them. So, the best deed is the deed that benefits others." Furthermore, Imam Ali stated (p. 256), "If the elected person rejects or contests his [followers'] decision, they will bring to his attention the issues that need to be addressed. If he persists in his deviation, they will fight him for not following the consensus of the Muslims."

7. There is a dialectic relationship between the qualities of followers and their leaders. Leaders mirror the prevailing characteristics of their followers. Al-Maki (1995, p. 557) indicated that if the followers exhibit good qualities, their leaders are decent and follow God's instructions. However, "If followers are corrupt, their leaders will resemble them."

Thus, leadership in Islam is viewed as a social process where followers and their leaders engage in reciprocal relationships. These relationships generate a dynamic setting where mutual influence takes place resulting in optimized benefits to the members of the community. The mutual influence assures that both leaders and followers have certain obligations toward each other and these obligations should uphold ethical norms and commitment to that which is desirable.

ISLAMIC MODEL OF LEADERSHIP

In line with the aforementioned theoretical perspective, leadership in Islam is assumed to be shaped by societal norms and culture, followers' expectations, and a leader's commitment to ethical foundations (public interest, moderation, *ehsan*). The societal norms and the culture constitute the primary forces that influence the social process and thus they either sustain or undermine ethical conduct. However, though cultural norms are assumed to be shaped by the Islamic ethical foundations, cultures in many countries with Muslim majorities vary in their adoption of these foundations. Though followers' expectations are influenced by prevailing cultural values, they either impose certain limits on a leader's action or tolerate the leader's inclination to act freely and without any account-ability toward their followers. This is particularly true when followers are indifferent, unfamiliar with their faith and early traditions, or are depend-ent and cannot think of better alternatives. On the other hand, a leader's commitment to ethical foundations measures the degree to which a leader is willing to accept these foundations as a guiding principle in his/her rela-tionship with followers. The foundations, as was argued before, constitute for the faithful a powerful force that guides their actions and relations with others. However, like many guidelines, they are often ignored or violated in practice. This enlarges the gap between the ideal and reality, especially as many people publicly utter statements that represent these foundations.

The daily uttering of Islamic principles and Quranic instructions have been instrumental in maintaining rich traditions across generations and across vast and dispersed geographical areas. This, however, has created an inclination among most Muslims, especially the religiously informed ones, to be infatuated with the ideal forms, even when they know that these ideal forms are contradicted by reality. Those who are infatuated with ideals may develop a tendency to overlook contradictory practices and persistent violations of Islamic teachings. Their preoccupation with daily affairs and difficulties most likely accounts for their lack of attention to their leaders' conduct. Ignoring what leaders do has become commonplace when, apart from learned individuals, the general public maintains a longing for ideals while disregarding the reality that their leaders are neither committed to nor observant of the core foundations of Islamic teachings. The gap, there-fore, between the ideal and reality has widened.

In the context of leadership, Muslim infatuation with ideals has hindered the development of sound and practical leadership theories. This is because when ideals are treated as identical to practice, rather than merely constituting the criteria by which practice is to be judged, disappointments and frustrations take place. Furthermore, infatuation with the ideal in an authoritarian environment may solidify autocratic tendencies among individuals in authority. That is, the notion of indispensability finds a fertile ground in this environment. The infatuation of Muslims with the ideal and their longing for a just leader and society plays a significant part in their daily lives. Idealism in Islamic culture is considered a necessary social element. As such, in the face of their current relative economic and political failures, people in countries with Muslim majorities still bemoan the loss of a glorious past and hope for a bright future. This infatuation with idealism is a powerful force that often prevents Muslims from dealing practically with contemporary world events. It could be, however, a potent factor in energizing their activities and revitalizing their economies. Under conditions of normalcy, the longing for the ideal and the powerful presence of hope can reinforce high expectations.

The three elements, culture, followers' expectations, and a leader's commitment to ethical foundations (public interest, moderation, *ehsan*) are essential for understanding relational processes and the practice of leadership in business and other worldly affairs. Though ethical foundations are assumed to influence leadership, it is the interplay among these factors that shapes the processes. Indeed, the interplay produces three major scenarios. These are:

1. There is a harmony among culture, followers' expectations, and a leader's commitment to ethical foundations. Under this possibility, the leadership model that emerges is that of a great man; the prophetic model. In the business world, this resembles a transformational leadership and leads to optimal realization of organizational goals and those of its major stakeholders, primarily the employees and customers. The Quran specifies that the role of a leader is to guide rather than to oppress, to teach rather than to ask for blind compliance, and to remind instead of punish. The Quran (16:125) instructs, "invite [all] to the way of thy lord with wisdom and eloquent preaching and argue with them in ways that are best" and (51:55) "But remind: for reminding benefits the believers." However, knowledge and intellectual capacity are needed for transformation to take place. The Quran (29:43) states, "And such are the parables we set forth for mankind, but only those who understand them who have knowledge."

2. Ethical foundations are weak, though existing cultural norms value empathy and social support. Followers may voice certain needs but

these are neither coherently nor assertively presented. A leader generally attempts to comply with his followers' expectations. Under this state, the leader is a benevolent authoritarian, as he/she may show some sensitivity to followers' concerns and needs.

3. There is an inclination on the part of the leader to overlook ethical foundations. This is especially true if it is a weak culture where values and beliefs are neither widely shared nor deeply held and followers are generally submissive and apathetic to what is going on. The emerged leader is generally an absolute authoritarian; a tyrant. Muslim scholars often argue that the presence of tyranny is predictable when Islamic teaching is ignored. To validate their point, they refer to a saying attributed to the Prophet Mohamed: "The caliphate after me will last thirty years, then it will revert to being a tyrannical authority" (see Al-Maki, 1995, died 996, p. 241; Al-Ghazali, 2006, died 1111, p. 454; Ibn Khaldun, 2006, died 1406, p. 281). The first Caliph equated tyranny with a monarchy, stating, "The most tormented people in this world and the hereafter are Kings. . . . A king is never content with what he has and covetous in what is in the hands of others. . . . Does not learn from experience and does not display trust in any person . . . after me will come an oppressor king" (quoted in Al-Deinori, 1999, pp. 624–5). The Quran warns against this tendency stating (88:21–22), "So thou [go on] reminding; thou art only a reminder. Thou art not, over them a compeller." Furthermore, the Quran (27:34) instructs, "Kings, when they enter a country, despoil it, and make the noblest of its people its meanest; thus do they behave." A king is portrayed as one who is a tyrant and does not observe ethical foundations and followers' demands.

The presence of each model has its own ethical consequences. Under the transformational model (great person), a ruler is expected to act in a way that generates the greatest possible benefits to the people and makes it possible to transform the thinking and practices of followers. Under these conditions, it is assumed that the number of people who are knowledgeable and driven by the desire to do what is good will increase. As Al-Maki (1995, p. 556) stated, "If the number of people who are good and decent believers increase, goodness will be more widely spread . . . The foundation for the presence of ethical conduct is a just leader." On the other hand, the presence of benevolent authoritarian and or absolute authoritarian (tyrant) leaders encourages the rise of unethical conduct, corruption, and mischief. This antithesis to Islamic leadership persists, though conditions might change as events evolve.

CONCLUSION

In this chapter, the ethical foundations for leadership are identified and presented in terms of the business and historical evolution of Islamic thought. While the concept of leadership in Islam is deeply rooted in the teachings of the faith, highlighting its nature and ethical dimensions in today's world takes on a significant value. This chapter, therefore, presented the foundations and pillars of leadership. In addition, responsibilities of leaders are classified and their ethical dimensions are elaborated on.

More importantly, the chapter discusses relational leadership theory and provides historical incidents and examples to evidence that in Islamic thought a relational approach is valued and applied as preferred practice that ensures the presence of a just society. Guided by this perspective, the chapter presents a model of leadership. Three scenarios are identified and, accordingly, three possible models are suggested: transformational, benevolent authoritarian, and absolute authoritarian. It is argued that the transformational leadership model is more in line with Islamic teachings and the early practices during the first half century of Islam.

The presented model of leadership neither focuses on specific situations nor on leaders as individuals. Rather, it views leadership as a shared influence process. There are dynamic interactions among a leader's commitment to ethical foundations, cultural values and norms, and followers' expectations. The interplay of these forces leads to the type of leadership that emerges. Since the underlying purpose in Islam is to benefit people, any leadership that results in endangering the welfare of the people or creating hardship for them is considered to be unethical.

6. The ethics of banking and financial services

The historic growth of Islamic banking in various parts of the world has brought to the surface certain financial concerns. These concerns range from the validity of Islamic financial instruments to the nature and challenge Islamic banking faces in a free market economy. The allure of Islamic financial instruments is real and in response conventional commercial banks, like Citigroup, have begun to offer Islamic financial services. Simply put, this is because rising segments of customers demand them. These particular segments are either driven by spiritual, economic, safety, or psychological reasons or, most likely, Muslims in the West who seek a kind of spiritual peace of mind or who view religiously guided financial transactions as a means to minimize doubt about the legitimacy of their financial affairs. In countries with Muslim majorities, the Islamic financial sector has experienced a dramatic increase in the number of institutions and numbers of products they offer, as many people find that sector more attractive than conventional banking. In Malaysia, for example, the rate of growth in Islamic banking is between 20 and 25 per cent (Yousef, 2011a). In Pakistan, Islamic banking shares about 10–11 per cent of the market and is expected to reach 22 per cent by 2020 (Rizvi, 2013). However, three of the most important factors that have accelerated the growth in Islamic banking in recent years are the rapid rise of indigenous corporations in global business (e.g., Qatar, Saudi Arabia, Malaysia, Turkey, and UAE), the rise of a Muslim middle class with sizeable wealth, which should be invested, and the 2008 financial crisis.

According to the *Financial Times*, Islamic finance is relatively new and has witnessed rapid growth. Even Britain is determined to be a world hub for Islamic finance in the coming years (see Moore, 2013). In *Bloomberg*, Leonid Bershidsky (2013) reported that Islamic finance is growing "50 per cent faster than traditional banking" and that religious-compliant "assets worldwide stand at $1.8 trillion, up from $1.3 trillion in 2011." In this chapter, ethical aspects of financial and banking services are highlighted. In particular, the chapter confronts several issues related to the possibility of embedding ethics in a sector where temptations are extremely high relative to other economic sectors.

The chapter, therefore, does not address Islamic economy, its elements, and objectives. Rather, it reflects on ethical limitations and instructions necessary to guide banking and financial actors to behave in a responsible way without ignoring their professional obligations and duties toward their organizations and selves. The present chronic economic and financial crisis has situated ethics as a primary factor for understanding the nature of these crises. Thus, addressing ethical aspects has become a pressing issue in the quest to attain a deeper sense of stability and trust in market functions. Indeed, financial transactions have become instrumental in obstructing or accelerating economic growth within a nation and across the globe. Ignoring them may open the gate for tragic economic events and ultimately deepen the sufferings of society.

The Quran portrays wealth as a necessity in life that can be used to further what is good, such as helping those who are in need and undertaking activities that ensure the prosperity and well-being of the people. Nevertheless, it warns that a desire to accumulate wealth can lead to negative consequences that can hurt one's self and others. The Quran (18:46) states, "Wealth and children are [but] adornment of the worldly life. But enduring good deeds are better to your Lord for reward and better for [one's] hope," (104:1–3) "Woe to every scorner and mocker who collects wealth and [continuously] counts it. He thinks that his wealth will make him immortal. No! He will surely be thrown into the Crusher" and (2:280) "And if the debtor is in difficulty, grant him time till it is easy for him to repay his debt. But if ye remit it by way of charity, that is best for you if ye only knew." Thus, Islamic tradition and prescriptions view wealth as either temptation and an unworthy desire or as an instrument that can be used to enhance society. While this duality of boundaries is applicable to Christianity and Judaism, in Islamic teaching the boundaries of what is positive are much broader. This emphasis on doing good can be difficult, as greed and desires are powerful motivational forces for gaining wealth. However, those market actors who have needed market knowledge and are gifted with self-control are able to avoid these temptations.

ETHICAL FOUNDATIONS

Islamic ethical foundations are at the core of ensuring that financial behavior is conducted within the sanctioned boundaries. The foundational elements (public interests, moderation, and *ehsan*) have three functions: to engage in activities that will not harm the general public, avoid extreme positions in financial dealing, and to be generous with other actors in financial dealings. These functions are briefly discussed.

Avoiding Harm to the General Public

This implies engaging in activities that secure interest and avoid harm to others. According to Al-Shatibi (2011, died 1388), it is imperative that market actors refrain from what is prohibited, as prohibited acts are inherently injurious. Likewise, permitted acts are beneficial, as everything in this world was created to serve mankind. That is, they are associated with ethical conduct, especially when individuals seek to utilize wealth to promote what is good and alleviate the distress of others. The latter is considered to be one of the noblest acts that lead to paradise. The Prophet stated, "The angels met a soul of a man from among those before you (and) they said, 'Hast thou done any good?' He said, 'I used to give respite to those in easy circumstances and forgave those who were in straitened circumstances.' So they forgave him" (quoted in Muhammad Ali, 1977, p. 295).

Avoiding Extreme Positions

This takes the form of borrowing, spending, lending, and investments. Indeed, moderation in financial behavior is the reason for the prohibition of *riba* (interest) and bribery. People are advised to avoid borrowing such that debt becomes a burden. The Quran (7:31) instructs, "Eat and drink, but waste not by excess, for God loveth not the wasters" and (4:5) "To those weak of understanding, give not your property which God has assigned to you to manage, but feed and clothe them therewith and speak to them words of kindness and justice."

Be Generous with Others

It is recommended that actors in financial dealings go beyond what is legally binding or contract conditions for the sake of relieving hardship. This is an act of charity and part of the general moral norms meant to govern all interactions in the marketplace. It is also part of social responsibility and is aimed at enhancing the vitality of the market and market trust. The Prophet stated, "Take what is your right in full or less than that; God will forgive your sins" and "He who lends someone money for a specific time, receives charity [reward from God] for each day until the due date. If, however, he grants the debtor additional days after the due day, for each day he receives charity equal to the amount of the loan" (quoted in Al-Maki, 1995, p. 514).

ROOTS OF BANKING IN THE EARLY YEARS

In the early days of Islam, money, be it gold or silver, was used as a mechanism for exchange and for measuring the amount of alms or *zakat*. Al-Maqrizi (1999, died 1442) reported that the Prophet imposed alms on the wealthy; five dirham on five pure silver pieces of money and on each 20 dinars, half a dinar. While successive governments issued money, no comprehensive attempts to mint a uniform currency were reported until Caliph Abdil Malik (died 705) assumed power. Al-Maqrizi indicated that it was during the era of Caliph Abdil Malik that the state minted money (e.g., dirham and dinars) across the land. The active involvement of the state in issuing money enabled markets to function smoothly and eased, at the time, commercial transactions.

Banking services were limited, in the early days of the Islamic state, to money exchange and lending. These were performed by individuals or small partnerships. The Prophet Mohamed recognized the significance of these two functions, lending and money exchange, and sought to prevent exploitation and abuses. In terms of the first, he indicated that to be valid the exchange must take place at the time of the transaction, stating that if the exchange is "from hand to hand, there is no harm in it; otherwise it is not permissible" (quoted in Sahih Al-Bukhari, 1996, p. 466). Al-Ghazali (2004, p. 412) specified that an ethical banker "seeks the correct way, gives trust to its rightful owner, avoids *riba*, approves delaying payment, does not sell bad currency, commits to right measures, avoids cheating and exploitation, and often checks his measures to make sure they are in the right order."

Three issues related to banking were often discussed in the early years of the Islamic state: debt, *riba* (interest), and investment to facilitate commercial activities. The ethical aspects of each of the items are explored below.

Debt

The prevailing general view in the early years of Islam was that debt was not only a financial burden but those who could not repay their debts on time would suffer socially and psychologically. Furthermore, debt might lead to misunderstanding and conflict. Thus, the Quran (2:282) instructs, "O you who have believed, when you contract a debt for a specified term, write it down." This is required so neither party to the debt contract forgets the loan or the conditions that govern it. The Prophet stated that the timely payment of one's debts by an able debtor is a virtue. He warned, "Delay of payment of a debt by a well-to-do person is injustice" (quoted in Muhammad Ali, 1977, p. 320).

While debt, under normal conditions, may be a necessary instrument for furthering commercial activities, a person should be careful not to borrow money beyond what he/she has the capacity or the means to repay on time. For this very reason, the Prophet stated that "debt hurts the reputation of decent people," while the second Caliph, Omer, argued, "Beware of debt. as its start represents agony while its end constitutes sadness" (quoted in Al-Andelesy, 1996, p.196). Therefore, debt from an Islamic perspective does not lead to goodness and may result in undesired consequences. This is different from capitalism, as even healthy and cash rich corporations are encouraged to engage in borrowing. Foroohar (2013, p. 22) states that in recent times the philosophy which views greed as good has begun to take root and that corporations are being pushed by big investors to borrow. She goes on to explain the reasoning: "Debt . . . wasn't always considered a bad thing—if companies weren't using cash and assets productively, why not lever up and give money back to investors? The tax code, which increasingly came to favor debt over equity, thanks to the efforts of the financial lobby, only made such tactics more tantalizing."

Interest

The prohibition of interest or *riba* has social and economic dimensions. Socially, it creates a class of lenders who take advantage of a broad segment of the population, especially the poor and those in need. These groups are dependent on the mercy of lenders and may be heavily burdened for a large part of their lives. Furthermore, the rise of the lender class hinders social harmony and integration, while weakening social bonds. Al-Maki (1995, p. 525) reported that those who take *riba* are socially disdained by the rest of the population and it is much better for a person to spend the whole amount of gained *riba* on those who are in need, so he might be forgiven. He reported that upon the death of his father, who was a rich man, a son went to a far-away city to collect his inheritance from his father's agent. When he was told that the agent had accumulated 16 000 dinars using his father's 4000 dinars through *riba*, he took the principal, 4000, and left the rest.

Economically, engaging in activities that involve imposing *riba* is considered to be unproductive. This leads to misallocation of resources, prevents the generation of jobs, and accordingly increases unemployment. It can also lead to higher prices, as there will be less investment in activities that entail risk and or take a longer time to collect.

Investment

Banking services have been instrumental in promoting commerce and trade since the rise of the Islamic faith. While *sukuk* (Islamic bond) and *hawalah* (primarily, transfer of debt from one party to another) were common in facilitating economic activities, informal notes written by bankers to known parties in distant places to finance certain trade activities were often used. In either case, the Quran instructs that a contractual agreement is necessary. The Prophet stated, "Whoever contracts a debt intending to repay it, Allah will pay it on his behalf [granting him the means to pay it], and whoever contracts a debt intending to waste it, Allah will bring him to ruin" (quoted in Muhammad Ali, 1977, pp. 38–9). This implies that investing or using borrowed money in trade generates profits, serves market needs, and enables the debtor to repay the debt. That is, the objective of borrowing or engaging in any sanctioned economic activity should focus on the better use of wealth in its broader social context. The better use of wealth not only serves those who are partners in financial transactions but also society at large, as it creates jobs and stimulates related economic activities.

In addition to its economic benefits, early Muslim scholars argued that betterment of investment, represented in increasing wealth, has three personal and social functions. First, it allows a person to spend on good deeds, engage in activities that lead to piety, and help those who are in need (Al-Mawardi, 2002). Second, betterment of wealth ultimately results in preserving the two most desired revered pursuits: religion and reputation (Al-Mawardi, 2002, p. 532). And third, the betterment of wealth is a manifestation of nobility. Al-Maki (1995, p. 521) quoted an early Islamic scholar, Waheb Ben Al-Aswad, saying that nobility is "taking care of parents and betterment of wealth."

CLASSICAL INSTRUMENTS OF ISLAMIC FINANCE

In the search to develop financial instruments and mechanisms to avoid prohibited practices, reduce risks and uncertainty, and generate the greatest benefits to society, Muslim scholars, over the centuries, have explored various possibilities and alternatives to conventional banking and financial activities. Due to market expansion, the rise of firms' roles in daily activities and the search for a larger segment of the population for alternative investment opportunities in accordance with Islamic principles, financial scholars have devised various forms of instruments to meet or attract Muslim customers.

Several scholars have identified alternatives for transactions that entail *riba* (see Asaf, 1987; Glaachi, 2000; Iqbal, 1997). These instruments are promoted as effective mechanisms to minimize harm to society and ensure economic vitality and stability and have been invented to cope with

emerging economic realities, such as world economic integration, technological innovations, and financial deregulations. The emphasis here is on
selected classical instruments. The illustration of these instruments sheds
light on the scope and intention of ethics in financial services. They are
briefly identified below.

Murabahah (Mark-Up on Sales)

This constitutes profit sharing. In this case, the lender (mostly a bank)
will buy a specific commodity from a third party for a person according to specifications identified by the latter. Both the lender and the
client agree in advance on the amount of profit that will be added to the
capital. The client pays the capital provider the agreed on installments or
lump sum payments. Therefore, profit making is based on the following
conditions:

1. a promise from a prospective buyer (client) to buy a specific
   commodity,
2. a promise to obtain and sell the commodity by the lender (intermedi-
   ary) for the client, and
3. a contract for selling, for a profit, the commodity.

   The title for the commodity will be transferred to the client once the
latter has paid all the debt, the capital, and profit to the lender. During the
transaction, the lender assumes the risk. Though this might be similar to
a loan with fixed interest to buy a property, it is argued that the intention
is not to impose interest but to assume the risk of buying a commodity by
having an agreed upon profit.

Mudarabah

This is a type of investment partnership. It is completely different from a
transaction in a stock exchange where a business person buys stocks with
the intention of accruing the highest possible financial gain. In this case,
buying a large quantity of certain stocks can lead to higher prices and vice
versa. In an investment partnership, where a financier lends money to an
entrepreneur or a merchant to invest or trade in, the partners agree on how
the profit will be shared among themselves. If the entrepreneur makes a
profit, then both benefit, but if there is a loss, the lender loses part or all of
his money, while the entrepreneur loses his effort and time.

   For *mudarabah* to be legitimate, certain conditions must be met (Asaf,
1987, p. 308). These are:

1. The profit must be shared between the entrepreneur and financier.
2. The share of profit for each must be specified and known to each other. If the profit amount is determined in advance or the share for both or one of the parties of the profit is unknown, then the transaction is considered invalid.
3. The transaction must not be valid for a specific time.
4. Both partners must agree freely on the conditions of the deal and the capital must be known and available to the entrepreneur.
5. The partnership must not include a condition that is contrary to its objective. There may be certain conditions that either the entrepreneur or the financer has introduced, but these should be consistent with the spirit and objective of the partnership.

However, *mudarabah* dissolves if one of the following conditions exists (Asaf, 1987): in the absence of one of the prerequisites for its validity, the borrower or entrepreneur does not keep their promises, negligence in maintaining the capital, intentionally violating the objectives of the contract, and if one of the investment partners dies. The existence of any of these conditions puts an end to the agreement and each has full right to that which is their due.

Musharaka

This can be either an equity financing arrangement or a partnership that leads to ownership. According to Ibn Hazm (died 1064), if partners contribute an equal share, profit and loss must be divided equally between them. This is a type of investment that will be dissolved if partners or a partner dies. Though there is no need for a specified day for the partnership break-up, it is up to one or both of the partners to determine a time for ending the partnership.

A partnership that ends up in ownership is different. In this case, if a partnership is in need of raising capital through loans from a bank of investors, profit sharing will be divided in accordance with the agreement on how profits are shared between the investors and the partners. This is done with an understanding that the investors or the bank will sell their shares to the partners and the latter buy these shares either immediately or in stages.

Ijarah or Leasing

This is a leasing contract where a bank or a financial institute purchases an item for a client and then leases it to him for a specific time. The financier makes a profit by charging the client rental fees. The rental contract specifies the duration and the amount of the rental fees. This is agreed upon in advance between the entrepreneur and the lender.

Deferred-Delivery Sales ('Salam) Contract

A deferred-delivery sale is a contract in which delivery of the product is in the future, in exchange for payment on the spot. That is, a company pays workers or entrepreneurs in advance the amount that they will produce for the company. The 'in advance' payment is made in order to allow small entrepreneurs to buy needed raw materials and to make payments for ongoing operations. The amount the entrepreneurs receive in advance is assumed to cover their costs and predicted profits.

For a *'salam* contract to be valid, certain conditions must be met (Asaf, 1987). These are:

1. On the spot payment of the contract amount to the entrepreneurs.
2. The payment amount must be agreed on in advance between the parties of the contract.
3. The item to be delivered must be known in terms of its specifications, such as type, nature, and quality, in addition to other aspects depending on the item to be delivered.
4. The item is to be delivered on the agreed upon date.
5. The entrepreneurs must be able to deliver the agreed on item by the due date.
6. There should be no defect that makes it difficult to deliver the agreed on item on time.

EMERGING GROWTH AND CHALLENGES

In the report, *World Islamic Banking Competitiveness Report 2013–2014*, Ernst & Young reported that Islamic banking assets are forecasted to grow beyond the milestone of $3.4 trillion by 2018. The report stated, "Islamic banking continues to be an exciting growth story characterized by robust macro outlook of core Islamic finance markets and increasing share of system assets." Though the major top six markets are found in Qatar, Indonesia, Saudi Arabia, Malaysia, UAE, and Turkey, the prospect for growth in other parts of the world should not be overlooked. In countries like the US, UK, France, Singapore, India, Nigeria, and South Africa, Islamic banking services have taken root and are expected to grow.

As we indicated earlier, the growth of Islamic banking is driven by several factors, including a demographic shift where Muslim communities in the West have established their own niche market and demand certain services in line with their religious beliefs, and the rise of middle class Muslim communities with tremendous wealth, especially in the Arab Gulf area. The bulk of growth, in recent years, has been found in the six countries mentioned above. These countries, according to Ernst & Young, accounted for 78 per cent of the international Islamic banking assets in 2012. This evidences that at present there is a concentration of Islamic banks in just a few countries which either rely on oil and gas (e.g., Qatar, Saudi Arabia, UAE) or have experienced a rise in Islamic sentiments (e.g., Malaysia and Turkey). However, in the foreseeable future, a robust growth in Islamic banking is a matter of fact. This is particularly true as there is a segment of the population, be it in the West or in countries with Muslim majorities that is attracted to Islamic banking for religious reasons. This segment, irrespective of economic changes, will be committed to these banks.

What do Islamic banks offer that make them attractive? Islamic banking offers a range of services that are assumed to be in accordance with Islamic prescriptions and law. These services include different variations of loans, deposits, investments, consultations, and other services that are deemed necessary and beneficial to the community. What is special about Islamic financial institutions is their orientation and intention. They are institutions that in their aim and scope attempt to provide their clients with a sense of certainty, in terms of operations, that they are in compliance with religious law (*Sharia*) and they are not in the business of exploitation. Both of these assurances are potent factors that shape the attitude of clients and sustain the continuity of these institutions. These, along with the other aspects, situate Islamic financial institutions apart from conventional banks. Among these major aspects are:

1. Islamic institutions, more than conventional banks, rely on equity rather than debt.
2. Islamic institutions maintain a considerably high liquidity. This gives them the needed cushion to survive economic crises.
3. Islamic institutions prefer direct investment rather than personal loans (e.g., engaging in *mudarabah* or *musharakah*).
4. Islamic institutions are more cautious in their investment selection and devise strategies that are not as aggressive as those found in conventional banks.
5. Islamic institutions are assumed to seek advancement of the public interest.

Though the prospect for continuing growth is considerably high, Islamic financial institutions do not expect to offer a solution to the ills of the market economy nor do they guarantee the safe, secure, and growing deposits of their clients. Nevertheless, the promise and potential of Islamic financial institutions are economically attractive and socially appealing, making these institutions a potent force in the global economy. However, there is a danger that success will lead to a diversion from the basic premises upon which these institutions were conceived. In fact, as these institutions grow and expand globally, the chances that the instability and crises that govern conventional banks may spread to Islamic banks are a high possibility. This is particularly true as consulting corporations advise these institutions to expand into conventional banking. For example, Ernst & Young (2013, p. 33) recommended that for Islamic financial institutions to improve their profits they should be "mainstream, look beyond the core *Shari'a* customers." This, however, constitutes a departure from the original purpose and spirit of establishing Islamic financial institutions.

There are certain challenges ahead that Islamic financial institutions face and have to confront. These challenges are not confined to obtaining lower profits but range from structuring to operational and strategic issues. Some of these issues are industry specific, while others are organizational based. The first is general and at times might seem elusive. The second is more specific and thus differs across industry and countries. The reason for this is that some countries like Malaysia have regulations that are outlined in detail. Other countries lack specific regulations, leaving each financial institution to take action in line with its interpretation of the religious law or *Sharia* and its priorities. It is possible to group these challenges into three general categories: moral and strategic vision (lack of commitment to moral transactions, lack of strategic vision, lack of clarity in issues related to the *Sharia* group or board); regularity and standardization; and misunderstanding of the nature and mission of each institution (imitating conventional banking and placing an emphasis on profit, and difficulties in coping with changing market demands). These are outlined below:

1. **Lack of commitment to moral transactions.** In the search to gain as much return as possible on their operations, some banks resort to practices that are inconsistent with the intent of the religious law. Yousef (2011a) presented some examples which violate religious law as an Islamic institution, such as borrowing money from conventional banks, depositing money with interest in conventional banks, and/ or partial dealings with assets that are religiously prohibited. Some banks do not honor contracts with clients if later on it is found that these contracts do not optimize their interests. Yousef (2012) pro-

vided a description of situations where some banks lack transparency in dealing with their clients and some have forced their clients to pay interest to banks ahead of the payment of principal. The Saudi newspaper *Asharq Al-Awsat* (2010) reported that "The financial institution's interest, whatever that may be, is not a justification for the institution, which claims to be Islamic, to contest the legitimacy of a contract that it itself had drawn up the terms and conditions of and had it approved by its Sharia body."

2. **Lack of strategic vision.** Rapid growth in Islamic banks and the passivity of most clients encourage executives to ignore changes in the industry and the need to plan ahead. This unfortunate situation may lead to inappropriate use of resources and suboptimal delivery of service to customers. For example, many Islamic banks, especially in the Gulf, focus primarily on real estate and this ultimately augments their risk (Asharq Al-Awsat, 2010). Furthermore, some executives of these banks lack strategic vision and are unable to take advantage of economic trends (see Yousef, 2011b).

3. **Lack of clarity in issues related to the *Sharia* board.** The majority of Islamic institutions have a board of religious scholars to determine whether or not their operations are in accordance with Islamic teaching and to certify that their offerings are religiously sound. However, there is no guidance and consistent procedures for selecting such experts in terms of numbers on the board, qualifications, maximum tenures, and who should appoint them and to whom they should report. Likewise, there is no guidance relative to how many boards these scholars are allowed to serve on. Many bankers have indicated that these scholars serve on many boards and, at the same time, serve on The Accounting and Auditing Organization for Islamic Financial Institutions (AAOIFI). The latter is responsible for suggesting reforms for Islamic institutions and "will likely fall short of expectations as scholars governing themselves are unlikely to cut into their own source of income, unless central banks force them to do so" (Richter, 2010). Leaders of AAOIFI object to limiting how many boards a *Sharia* scholar serves on. A leader of AAOIFI compared himself and other *Sharia* scholars to accounting and law firms asking, "why should [*Sharia* scholars] not be treated like other professionals in the field?" (Richter, 2010). There is a high possibility, too, that members of a *Sharia* board may become passive actors, approving schemes designed by those who appoint them. Likewise, when one line of thinking dominates the industry, irrespective of the dictates of the faith and changing customers' needs, innovative solutions and the introduction of new products may diminish over time.

4. **Lack of regulatory clarity.** Confusion exists with regard to how the operations of Islamic financial institutions should be regulated. Many financial institutions take advantage of this lack of regulation by not disclosing some losses (Y-Sing and Kasolowsky, 2009). Ernst & Young (2013) reported that in countries where the regulator has understood the unique aspects of Islamic finance in contrast to conventional banking and accordingly created a separate regulatory framework, the industry has experienced growth and an increase in market share. Malaysia and Oman have undertaken strict regulatory measures that have put an end to much of the confusion that engulfs Islamic banking.

5. **Lack of standardization.** Lack of standard financial reporting, investment evaluation, managing risk, and other operational aspects, such as designing contracts and what each offering entails and the degree of fit with religious instructions, hinders progress and healthy expansion. Likewise, such lack of standardization leaves customers unaware of their responsibilities and obligations regarding transactions that are supposed to observe *Sharia* rules.

6. **Imitating conventional banking and placing an emphasis on profit.** As reported in *Ernst & Young* (2013) and in the Saudi-based newspaper *Asharq Al-Awsat* (2009), Islamic banking has increasingly begun imitating conventional banking. This constitutes a departure from the intent of Islamic banking and the purpose of avoiding interest-based operations. The report in *Asharq Al-Awsat* stated, "Islamic banking has already strayed from the theoretical foundation it was based upon, namely that of joint-risk ventures. . . . [In] reality, Islamic banking has turned towards buying and selling loans. The bulk of transactions today are based on the *Tawarruq* and *Murabaha* financial structures." This particular challenge, if not dealt with adequately, is destined to derail Islamic financial institutions from their original objectives perceived by early pioneers—to avoid *riba* in commercial transactions and serve society guided by the principles of the faith.

7. **Shortage of expertise and difficulties in coping with changing market demands.** As Islamic banking experiences growth and demand increases for its products and services, one of the most significant challenges that Islamic banks will deal with is the shortage of experts on Islamic banking. Lack of experts and foresight often produce contradictory judgments. For example, when Malaysia first introduced Islamic bonds, the Arab Gulf states rejected them as not Islamic. Once these bonds turned out to be a success story, these same states invested in them and have started to issue similar ones. Expertise in the field is important for accelerating growth, enhancing innovation that is in

line with the *Sharia*, and enabling the industry to broaden product and service offerings. The latter takes on an added value as conventional banks have started to compete head on with Islamic financial institutions.

THE CHALLENGE OF RECENT FINANCIAL DEVELOPMENTS

In recent years, there have been certain investments and banking transactions that have found acceptance in the marketplace but might not be acceptable under Islamic ethics. These are either found to be excessively risky, violate principles set by the Prophet, or ambiguous. Though some Islamic scholars have found some of them acceptable (e.g., derivatives), other scholars have raised some concerns, warning against blind acceptance of the premise and/or pressure of today's capitalism. For the sake of practicality, three categories are identified: transactions involving commodities that one does not own or see; investing or transacting in items that are prohibited; and transaction in items where ambiguity is high.

1. **Transactions involving commodities that one does not see or own.** That is, the items of the transaction should be known to each partner (Asaf, 1987; Glaachi, 2000). They must understand exactly what they are embarking on. In buying financial instruments, the items must be clear and recognized by the purchaser. The Prophet instructs, "He who bought something without having seen it has the option to reject it after seeing it" (quoted in Asaf, p. 230). Likewise, the items of transactions must be deliverable. Many of today's financial instrument transactions exchange hands and some of those involved have no clue of what is transacted. The Prophet instructs, "Do not sell that which you do not have" (quoted in Glaachi, p. 108).
2. **Investing or transacting in items that are prohibited.** In Islamic thought, certain items are thought to harm people and, therefore, are outlawed. The transactions of items such as alcohol, drugs, and gambling are prohibited. Therefore, investing in them is not allowed. Many individual investors in today's markets do not have knowledge of where their money is invested. This is especially true concerning mutual funds where individuals have no precise knowledge of whether or not their money is being invested in lawful operations.
3. **Transaction in items where ambiguity is high.** Early jurists advised that when one is in doubt of whether the area of transaction is lawful or not, it is much better to avoid it (Al-Maki, 1995; Al-Mawardi, 2002).

Al-Maki (1995, p. 551) stated, "A good deed is when you are certain that what you earned is perfectly permissible. The bad thing is a doubtful one."

CONCLUSION

Islamic banking and financial services since the early 1970s have witnessed rapid growth and in recent years have become a preferred choice for a growing segment of the world's population. In this chapter, we discussed the roots of Islamic banking with an emphasis on debt, interest, and investment. Likewise, classical and emerging instruments of Islamic finance that constitute an alternative to conventional banking instruments were identified.

What should be kept in mind is that while success and rapid growth may underscore the necessity for Islamic banking and reflect a demand for such services, this neither automatically makes these services the ultimate solution for economic and financial woes in the world nor does it signify an absence of formidable challenges. On the contrary, this successful and rapid growth has generated monumental challenges that have unearthed deep minefields that can either impede Islamic banking institutions from making progress or divert them from their original vision.

Ethical conduct, therefore, is important. And in no area other than in Islamic banking has testing Islamic instruments and prescriptions become more relevant, producing immediate and tangible results. Indeed, as the market is dominated by giant commercial banks and as capitalism appears to be espoused by most countries with Muslim majorities, Islamic financial institutions face the real test of whether or not they are able to hold on to or compromise their ethical and moral guidelines.

7. Organization and work

Though work can take place in any setting, it is in an organization that it thrives. Performing work in a planned and organized way eases economic transformation, progress, efficiency, and creativity. Indeed, scholars have credited organizations and their executives for the development that has taken place in countries that have experienced economic growth. Organizations and work, therefore, have never been separated in business and economic studies. These studies have underscored the interrelationship between organization and work, between work ethic and progress, and between progress and the well-being of individuals and communities. Studies on work and organizations have flourished in the West. In fact, the ethics of work is widely studied and is presented as the primary reason for the phenomenal economic progress that the West has made for at least two centuries.

In Islamic tradition, and relative to the early centuries of Judaism and Christianity, work and its ethics have been underscored. Islamic prescriptions set the boundaries for what is considered ethical and unethical and have held work and engaging in economic activities in the highest regard. Thus, at times these prescriptions have profoundly changed how people have viewed work and business. This, however, is often ignored by researchers. This might be attributed to the economic stagnation that countries with Muslim majorities have experienced for centuries, especially after the destruction of Baghdad, the center of the Abbasid Empire, at the hands of Mongols in 1258. In this chapter, relationships between organization and work are examined from Islamic perspectives. In addition, the chapter seeks to answer questions related to the meaning of work, work ethic in the context of Islam, and to contrast Islamic Work Ethic (IWE) with that of Christianity's and Judaism's. Highlighting these issues, in the context of ethics, uncovers the unique contributions of early Islamic thinkers. Driven by Quranic prescriptions and the framework set by the Prophet, these scholars asserted the necessity of organizations in strengthening the state and optimizing benefits to society. They also drew boundaries for ethical work and activities. By doing so, these scholars made the connection between knowledge, work, public interests, and ethics.

THE ESSENCE OF ORGANIZATION

Though businesses at the inception of Islam were small-scale or family-run organizations, those who were established found, in the new religion, both incentives and limitations. Incentives revolved around praising those who contributed to economic activities, situating them in highly respected social groups, rewarding them, in this life and the hereafter, for what they had contributed to society, and obligating the state to facilitate their activities without imposing burdens on them. The limitations were aimed at avoiding exploitation, lending money at high interests, and engaging in producing and marketing commodities that may harm society.

Underscoring the significance of business activities, therefore, led at that time to thriving businesses and a positive view and respect for those who took risks to make commodities available in the market. While recent management and organization scholars in countries with Muslim majorities have outlined several organizational elements, the emphasis in this chapter is on the ethical dimensions of certain elements and their implications in the marketplace. Some of these have had a powerful influence on the faithful, especially in terms of commitment to just and ethical actions.

Al-Mawardi (2002, p. 216) argued that to achieve improvement in life and to organize affairs, six elements must exist. These are: internalized faith, a feared and loved ruler, comprehensive justice, prevalent safety, prosperity, and ample possibilities. Below is a brief summary of each element.

Internalized Faith

The strength of faith is a powerful factor that constrains desires and softens the heart so that secret bad intentions are overpowered, consciousness is alerted, and the soul is guarded and advises it during hard times. Al-Mawardi believed that internalized faith is the most powerful force for enhancing life conditions and the most beneficial factor in safeguarding and organizing affairs.

Feared and Loved Ruler

Because of their differences in goals and strategies and in the relentless competition for rank and wealth, people are in need of competent leaders who focus their attention on achieving overriding goals, minimizing rivalry, and compelling the unruly to observe law and order. The Prophet stated, "The best of your leaders are those who you like and who like you and the worse are those who dislike you and who you loathe" (quoted in Al-Mawardi, 2002, p. 223). When a ruler is a just one, as indicated in Chapter 5, subordinates avoid being corrupt or abusive. More importantly, rulers, in order to gain the approval of their constituencies, need to focus on preventing harm and optimizing benefits to the public. Accordingly, it is based on the constituency's approval that God grants His endorsement of a ruler. This dialectic relation is captured by the second Caliph, Omer's, statement to one of his deputies: "If you like to know where you stand in the eyes of God, know what people think of you" (quoted in Al-Mawardi, p. 223).

Comprehensive Justice

The existence of justice motivates people to cooperate, encourages obedience, speeds development, improves wealth, ensures population growth, and enhances the stability of governments. In contrast, oppression increases rapid economic downturns and corruption. This is because oppression has neither boundaries nor noble ends. Imam Ali, the fourth Caliph, argued that justice "is the mainstay of a nation." Without justice there would be no economic development and prosperity, safety and security of citizens, and the continuity of a community would be impossible to guarantee.

Al-Mawardi (p. 226) asserted that enhancing justice can be realized by avoiding greed and fearing God. And since justice is an essential pillar for having an orderly and functional life, it must encompass two types: justice for self and for others. According to Al-Mawardi, justice for self is doing what is good and avoiding engaging in what is despised by others. Individuals have to look at themselves and decide whether they exceed their limits (capacities) in undertaking an activity. Burdening oneself more than can bear leads to hardship, while overlooking one's own potential for self-oppression and leads to lack of consideration for others.

On the other hand, justice for others takes on three forms: justice for subordinates, justice for supervisors or those who are above you in rank, and justice for peers. Below is a brief summary of each:

- **Justice for subordinates.** Doing justice to subordinates is manifested in avoiding imposing tasks that overwhelm them, avoiding abuse of power, and behaving in a righteous manner. Thus, good relationships with subordinates will be sustained and respect, performance, and success ensured.
- **Justice for the supervisor.** This is reflected in sincere obedience, providing support, and sincere loyalty. If these do not exist, the result will be an absence of comprehensive order and development.
- **Justice for peers.** This, too, involves three things: avoiding arrogance, avoiding behaving in a spoiled manner, and preventing harm to others.

Prevalent Safety

In a situation where safety exists in the land and fear and insecurity are uncommon, initiatives and entrepreneurial activities thrive, the innocent feel their rights are not violated, and the weak find happiness. According to Al-Mawardi (2002, p. 230), "safety is a pleasant living and justice is the most powerful army, because fear hinders people from engaging in their profession and activities, obstructs their performance and initiatives, and prevents them from obtaining that what is necessary for their living and an orderly functioning of society." Therefore, safety is an important part of ethical conduct and the responsibility of the state. Without strong feelings of safety, neither development nor ethics thrive.

Prosperity

With prosperity comes opportunities; people experience optimism and those who have plenty and those who have little share what is available. Thus, jealousy is minimized and people feel less antagonism, while all take advantage of opportunities and intensify their connectivity and assistance to each other. Al-Mawardi categorized prosperity as that which comes from engaging in earning activities and which results from the availability of natural resources.

Ample Possibilities

In a state of hopefulness and optimism, people may be able to obtain what could otherwise be difficult to realize in life and be motivated to establish what could be impossible to build. The Prophet stated, "Without hopefulness, no person will plant trees and no mother feed a baby" (quoted in Al-Mawardi, 2002, p. 2002).

UNDERPINNING ELEMENTS FOR MANAGING ORGANIZATIONS

The above organizing elements are generally applicable for ensuring a functional society and set the groundwork for building organizations that are run in an orderly fashion. In his attempt to set the stage for ethical conduct, Al-Mawardi articulated these elements based on general instructions found in the faith. However, the organizational underpinnings are illustrated in the Quran and the Prophet's sayings. These underpinnings offer opportunities to understand the linkage between organization and work beliefs and enable those responsible for managing organizations to run their institutions ethically. Those responsible for managing institutions must have the skills and knowledge required not only to efficiently run their organizations but also to comprehend religious instructions and make the necessary connections with the basic foundations identified in Chapter 1 (public interest, moderation, and *ehsan*). What follows is a brief introduction to these underpinnings: vision, goals, resolve, structuring, adequate allocation of resources, and assessment and self-accountability.

Vision

Before initiating any activity, the Quran instructs that one must have vision. The Quran (17:36) states, "And pursue not that of which thou hast no knowledge." This is because those who ponder an issue get the insight needed for carrying out the project. The Quran (16:69) indicates that "Verily in this is a sign for those who give thought" and (74:18) "For he thought and he determined." An old Islamic saying succinctly captures the essence of vision: "Vision benefits, though desire is fun" (quoted in Al-Mawardi, p. 40). Thus, vision must be given priority when setting goals and in analyzing the challenges and opportunities that lie ahead. Since vision is a positive element and generates benefits, it serves public interest and further advances the welfare of society. While Adam Smith insisted that in pursuing their own interests an owner or an entrepreneur "frequently promotes that of the society more effectually than when he really intends to promote it," since for a faithful business owner, serving public interest is assumed to be part of any action he takes.

Goals

Once a vision is articulated, there is a need to identify goals. The Quran (2:148) instructs, "To each is a goal to which God turns him; then strive together [as in a race] toward all that is good." Goals, among people and institutions, differ. Therefore, Islamic instructions underscore an important fact that differences are a natural order of the universe and that conceiving goals under different circumstances is a sign of novelty and commitment to change. Al-Andelesy (1996, died 985) argued that goals must be carried out according to their importance and familiarity with their requirements. Ethical goals "are those which combine the benefits of serving this life and the hereafter" (Al-Mawardi, 2002, p. 139). That is, goals must observe the ethical foundations, public interest, moderation, and *ehsan*. While both public interest and *ehsan* motivate the faithful to have goals that serve this life and the hereafter, moderation constrains extreme tendencies. Al-Mawardi (2002, p. 163) argued that one should not undertake that which is either easy or impossible. Rather, goals should be possible to achieve. However, Al-Sabi (2003, died 1056) argued that higher aspirations elevate one to prestigious positions. This can be applied to individuals, groups, and organizations, as Al-Sabi was discussing government aspects and the role of a chief minister. Nevertheless, like other early Islamic scholars, Al-Sabi made a powerful argument that without justice and *ehsan*, organizations and individuals cannot survive and they are destined to failure. No matter the immediate outcomes, if intention is not driven by virtue and the intent to serve people in a just and ethical way, irrespective of their gender or type, in the end nothing can be sustained. This is because ethics are the ultimate safeguard for the achievement of goals. Al-Sabi (p. 6) asserted that "undertaking difficult tasks is much easier than acquiring good ethics and enduring hardship is less of a burden than cultivating ethics."

Resolve

This is the end result of the interplay of ethics and reason. Once these two exist, determination takes root and flourishes (Al-Sabi, 2003). Determination takes on four forms: acting on what was decided (translate thought into reality-product), avoidance of delaying action, discipline, and persistence. The first is reflected in the Prophet's saying, "Once you make up your mind, then go ahead." Likewise, Al-Mawardi (2002, p. 166) stated that "An Ignorant relies on his wish, the Wise man relies on his work." In terms of delaying action, Muslim scholars have asserted that failure to carry out work on a timely basis is disservice to self and faith. Thus, they gave timely performance a spiritual dimension. The second Caliph, Omer, stated, "Don't delay today's work until tomorrow." Likewise, the jurist Abu Yusuf (n.d., died 767, p. 97) stated, "Don't delay today's work until tomorrow; if you do, you squander." While discipline is intertwined with avoidance of postponing action, it also demonstrates that a person is not willing to compromise his ethics and, thus, that a person is committed to meeting deadlines and task specifications. The Prophet highlighted the significance of discipline when he stated, "O People, you have an end, so attain your end" (quoted in Al-Mawardi, 2002, p. 197). The instruction of the Quran (53:39), "That man can have nothing but what he strives for," accentuates the necessity of discipline. Indeed, as Al-Mawardi stated (p. 503), "Tirelessness is a sign of seriousness." The concept and practice of persistence was also sanctioned in the early centuries of Islam, as it was viewed as an avenue to broaden that which is good, prevent dependency, and create opportunities. The Quran (37:61) instructs, "Let all strive, who wish to strive." And the Prophet advises, "let each continue his activity" (quoted in Al-Barai and Abdeen, 1987, p. 243), while Imam Ali, the fourth Caliph, stated, "Carelessness is the key to misery. And laziness and reliance on others create shortages and destruction. He who is not persistent in his efforts, gets not what he desires" (quoted in Al-Pashehi, 2004, p. 418). Salman Al-Farsi (died 654) stated, "Moderation and persistence situates you as a forerunner in generosity' (quoted in Al-Deinori, 1999, p. 377).

Structuring

Structuring of activities was essential in building the emerging Islamic state. Whether in personal life or organizational affairs, structuring is a needed activity. Without it, goals are difficult to achieve optimally. The Quran (43:32) instructs, "And We raise some of them above others in ranks, so that some may command work from others" and (6:165) "He hath raised you in ranks, some above others, that He may try you." In these instructions, the Islamic faith seeks to create an efficient mechanism to accomplish this and to judge whether or not those who are in charge are able to shoulder responsibility. Furthermore, the Quran indicates that it is based on performance that people are rewarded. It states (46:19), "And to all are [assigned] degrees according to the deeds which they [have done] and in order that [God] may recompense their deeds."

Traditionally, structuring was sought to achieve four objectives: smooth operation, cooperation, enhancing understanding, and avoidance of conflict. Abu 'Abd Al-Rahman Al-Sulami (1908, died 1021) in his book, *Categories of Sufis*, quoted the Muslim scholar, Ali Ben Sahel Al-Isbahanni, stating, "If you do not refine your organizational principles, you will not be safe from damaging consequences." The Quran (5:2) orders cooperation: "Help ye one another in righteousness and piety, but help ye not one another in sin and rancour." Al-Mawardi (2002) considered cooperation an ingredient for better performance, while Ibn Khaldun viewed it as an important component for cohesiveness and civilization. He stated, "It is well known and proved that a person, independently, cannot meet all his needs. Human beings must cooperate among themselves to that end. What is obtained through cooperation meets the needs of a much larger number" (2006, p. 284). Thus, cooperation is not only an instrument for getting things done efficiently, but also for achieving prosperity and advancing civilization.

Likewise, structuring enhances understanding. The Prophet, in his attempt to establish a functional community and expand his state, created a mechanism for social associations to replace blood or tribal relations. This new bonding was called *muakhat* (two Muslims were paired together and declared brothers) to ease understanding, improve relations, and share resources. In the context of avoidance of conflict, the Quran (8:46) instructs, "And fall into no disputes, lest ye lose heart and your power depart." The ethical objective is to conduct affairs that lead to the thriving of the community and organization and to strengthen a culture where norms and beliefs are known and widely shared. In structuring activities or organizations, the primary principle should be maintaining and safeguarding moderation. Indeed, moderation eventually ensures flexibility and a better response to changing markets and social factors.

Adequate Allocation of Resources

Securing and deploying resources become necessary steps to guaranteeing that goals are met in an appropriate and effective way. It demonstrates the organizational capabilities of the leadership team. The allocation of resources encompasses human and material resources. The Quran (8:60) underscores the need to make resources available from the start in order to make progress, instructing "against them [enemies] make ready your strength to the utmost of your power." Also, the Quran states that rivals, before they initiate any action, have to organize and deploy resources. It states (9:46), "If they [the rivals] had intended to come out, they would certainly have made some preparation." Ibn Khaldun accentuated that building cities and towns to defend against enemies. However, he asserted that the needed resources for superior defense and achieving stability are "power and group support." The first is essential for organizing people and obtaining resources and the second is a must for achieving cohesiveness and acquiring direction essential for optimal utilization of resources.

Allocating resources wisely and ethically in running an organization is no less important than deploying resources to defend it. Though Al-Sabi, Al-Mawardi, Abu Yusuf, and Al-Asqalani addressed the allocation of resources primarily in terms of the state and government activities, their treatises also provided useful reflection on conducting business affairs. They put great emphasis on alleviating oppression and improving conditions for constituencies. In their view, just allocation of resources motivates people to work hard and enables communities to thrive. Al-Sabi, for example, reported (2003, p. 281) that when justice and generosity were widespread in a city, people from other regions resided in it and businesses in that city flourished. Ibn Khaldun (2006, p. 223) asserted that the absence of justice forces people to abandon their businesses and removes the "motive for acquiring and gaining property."

Assessment and Self-Accountability

While evaluation and control in modern organizations is a major function within an enterprise and is performed by a team or special department/unit, in Islamic thinking, control, first and foremost, resides within self. The Prophet underscored this when he stated, "Hold yourself accountable before you are held responsible" (quoted in Al-Ghazali, 2004, p. 168). Al-Mawardi (2002, p. 189) further elaborated on this when he said, "He who holds himself accountable, benefits." Al-Mawardi specified four types of outcome that a person may reach after rethinking his performance: objective is realized; mistakes take place when some things are not placed in the right position; things are not produced according to specifications; or more things are produced than what was planned.

The Quran (75:14) states, "Nay, man will be evidence against himself" and (59:18) "O you who have believed, fear Allah. And let every soul look to what it has put forth for tomorrow." The wisdom of these two instructions is that when people take their responsibilities seriously and seek to perform them accordingly, intrinsically they do what is good and avoid engaging in activities that might harm others. More importantly, they make certain that in whatever they engage in, they attempt to do their best. The Prophet said, "Verily, God loves that if any of you does a job, he does it with *perfection*" (quoted in Al-Maki, 1995, p. 507). The fourth Caliph, Imam Ali (1990, p. 768), instructed, "Failure to perfect your work when you are certain of the reward is injustice to yourself." The ethics of self-accountability, however, goes beyond perfection of work. It further reduces organizational expenses (e.g., control is the responsibility of all staff, minimizing customers' complaints and defective work), and strengthens a company's market position.

After state affairs became complex, as was the case during the Abbasid era, there were various units or departments that were responsible for control and evaluation. For example, there was the market supervisor who was responsible for preventing fraud, deception, and corruption, in addition to other primary responsibilities like monitoring market prices and the quality and availability of goods. A letter by Tahir Ben Al-Hussain, a chief administrator during the era of Caliph Al-Mamun (813–33), to his son, Abdullah, when he was appointed governor (quoted in Ibn Khaldun, 2006, p. 243), stated:

> And appoint in each district of your territory a trustworthy monitor who will provide you with reports about your deputies and write to you about their behavior and performance. This will allow you to be up to date with the affairs of these deputies as if you yourself were observing their conduct. If you intend

to order your deputies to execute a matter, review it beforehand and weigh the possible consequences. If you expect good and safe results, then go ahead. Otherwise, consult those with vision and knowledge and then deploy your resources.

In terms of control and assessment, two things stand out: self-accountability and a trustworthy supervisor. In terms of self-accountability, it was stated, "You should evaluate yourself knowing that you, in the end, are held responsible for what you have done and are rewarded for the good things you produced." Regarding supervisors, the letter states, "Have in each locality in the land under your responsibility a trustworthy supervisor who accurately informs you about the work and behavior of your deputies as if you were monitoring each deputy in person." The objectives are to spread justice, accelerate development, generate wealth, and gain the trust and love of the constituency.

THE MEANING OF WORK

The meaning of work is much broader than that of work ethic. It usually incorporates two issues: work centrality and work ethic. Both concepts are interrelated and often used interchangeably (see Twenge, Campbell, Hoffman, and Lance, 2011). However, work centrality measures the degree of significance that work has in one's life at certain times, while work ethic focuses on attachment and commitment to work. A person may think that work is significant in his/her life, but, at a certain time, the same person experiences less involvement in work. In the Arab region, a study of work centrality in Saudi Arabia (see Ali and Al-Shakhis, 1989) showed that the majority of participants (94%) would continue working, even if they had enough money to live on comfortably all their lives. A recent study by the Gallup Center (2011) found that in Abu Dhabi the new Arab generation has a positive attitude toward work and there is an acknowledgement that success in life depends on hard work. However, when one compares the economic progress in the Arab region, for example, relative to that in the West or East Asia, the conclusion may not be so satisfactory. This is particularly true when Muslim generations of the 1950s and 1960s compare what they went through to the lives of the new generation. During these decades, work was physically demanding. In addition, the expectations of previous generations were high and even sometimes amounted to idealism. These expectations reflected higher standards, manifested a sense of responsibility, and contributed to the feeling that the new generation could do better with the resources available to them.

For various reasons—psychological, economic or health—a commitment to work may reach a low threshold though a person philosophically believes that work is important. Even at a societal level, this might be true. As we see later, some Muslim societies, though their faith sanctions hard work and work involvement, have for a long time witnessed apathy and economic stagnation and decline. People give meaning to work based on their social, cultural, educational, and economic experience. This means that within the realm of human interaction work flourishes and takes root.

Previous research has shown that perceptions of work vary across societies, regions, and organizational backgrounds. Across history and civilizations, people have attached different meanings to work. Such meaning illustrates not only differences among people, if any, in their attachment to work, but also their priorities and expectations in life. Anderson (1984) indicates that the Greeks and many later civilized nations held both work and workers in low esteem. In a longitudinal study of the German view of work, Katona et al. (1971) found that Germans held negative attitudes toward work in 1951 (e.g. work was a heavy burden); however, these attitudes improved significantly by 1962 owing to the rising standard of living. Similarly, Inkeles and Smith (1974) conducted a longitudinal study of people who moved from farms to factories in six countries and suggested that a positive adjustment in attitude toward work took place as people gained more experience in modern organizations. The MOW International Research Team (1981), led by George England, has carried out a comparative study of the meaning of work (MOW) for employees in eight countries and found that employees differ not only in the importance they attach to work but also in the function of work in their lives. Ali (1986) and Al-Kuwari (1985) suggest that, prior to the oil boom in the Arab Gulf societies, people valued hard work and productive efforts, but these values have given way to leisure, apathy, and contempt for manual work. However, Ali (1989) found that, unlike the general Arab population, Arab managers have fairly positive attitudes toward work and score higher than their American and Scandinavian counterparts on work ethic.

Norms about work are related to work involvement in that they define individual expectations of doing what is considered to be correct and appropriate by a society (Triandis, 1979). Norms specify actions and include specific demands and prescriptions (Ali, 1982). Individualistic societies emphasize initiative, leadership, and the pursuit of self-interest, while collective societies emphasize obligation. This, however, does not signify that individualism is the foundation of work ethic and need for achievement. Indeed, Hofstede (1980, 1987) carried out a comprehensive study and found that individualism is not necessarily the only factor that explains work involvement and attachment. This was evident by his findings that individualism was low in Japan and high in New Zealand and

Denmark, but the three countries achieved considerable high economic growth. Hofstede notes, however, that employees in individualistic societies tend to value individual achievement and to establish objective standards for evaluation. That is, societal individualism influences expectations, commitment, and the meaning of work.

Many social scientists explain motives for working based on empirical studies of various segments of societies. Work is found to provide: economic necessities and satisfaction of lower-level human needs (England 1984; Kaplan and Tausky, 1972; Morse and Weiss, 1955); a sense of independence and an opportunity to interact with various segments of society (Ali and Al-Shakhis, 1989; Wilensky and Lehbeaux, 1965); a feeling of accomplishment and self-actualization (Steers and Porter, 1983); and fulfillment of the more elusive concepts of power and prestige (Hampton, Summer, and Webber, 1982; Kaplan and Tausky, 1972).

Islamic instructions and scholars have underscored that work is a necessity in life and is complementary to the faith, stating that faith and good deeds go hand in hand. The Prophet Mohamed and Islamic scholars sanctioned work and work involvement for various reasons. These reasons underscore the role of work in one's life and in society. Therefore, from the start, faithful Muslims did not look at work as an activity independent of its social and economic value. That is, work was viewed as an instrument for:

1. **Satisfying spiritual and social needs.** The Prophet considered work a Divine duty stating, "Among the sins are sins that cannot be recompensed by prayer and fasting . . . [but are wiped out by] a commitment to earning a livelihood," "Work is a worship," "Whoever goes to bed exhausted because of hard work, he has thereby caused his sins to be absolved," and that "Work is a divine duty" (quoted in Al-Andelesy, 1996, p. 325).

2. **Enhancing self-confidence and social involvement.** The Prophet stated that "God loves a person who has a profession"(quoted in Al-Maki, 1995, p. 500) and "The best of work is that whose benefit is lasting" (quoted in Al-Pashehi, 2004, p. 416)

3. **Strengthening self-esteem.** The Prophet elaborated on this issue on different occasions to lift the spirits of the faithful. At that time, most of those who espoused the message of Islam were abused by the rich in Mecca, Arabia. He stated, "God has guards on earth and in the sky. His guards in the sky are the angels and His guards on earth are those who work for their sustenance and safeguard the interest of the people." And when people mentioned to the Prophet that there was a devout person who was with them on a trip and was spending most of

his time praying, the Prophet asked, "'Who provided him with food and needed supplies?' they said 'We did'. The Prophet said, 'All of you are more pious than he'" (quoted in Al-Andelesy, p. 325).

4. **Enhancing independence.** Economic independence was viewed by the Prophet as an effective way to energize the economy and reach prosperity. He stated, "A person who makes an effort to support himself and avoids dependency on others and asking people for help is on the path to God" and "He who earns his sustenance and does not depend on others, God will not torment him during the Day of Judgment" (quoted in Al-Pashehi, p. 417). Likewise, the second Caliph, Omer, stated, "Persist in making a living and do not be dependent on others" (quoted in Al-Andelesy, p. 325). And a noted Muslim scholar in the first century of Islam, Hassan Al-Basri, instructed, "Work and nourish yourself, as God loves those who work and feed themselves and does not like those who do not work but depend on others" (quoted in Al-Pashehi, p. 418).

5. **Sustaining a sense of self-actualization.** The Prophet not only considered work to be a fulfillment of religious duties and a means for salvation, but also essential for accomplishment and influence. He instructed the faithful: "Rise early to make a living, as hard work generates success and reward" (quoted in Al-Pashehi, p. 417).

6. **Gaining prestige.** It was reported that a person "asked the Prophet 'which action can serve as a substitute for the duty of seeking knowledge', the Prophet replied 'work'" (quoted in Al-Pashehi, p. 416). A companion of the Prophet, Said Ibn Abada argued, "There is no prestige without action, and no action without wealth" (quoted in Al-Andelesy, p. 326). Likewise, a pious Muslim scholar, Abu Al-Qasim Al-Junayd (died 910), stated, "Hard work creates decent opportunities" (quoted in Al-Sulami, 1968, p. 161).

The above instructions accentuate that work has economic, social, psychological, and organizational significance. In addition, they provide a framework for better understanding the nature of work and its role in achieving progress. The instructions are not confined to a certain time or place. The pressing question, however, is "Why do most countries with Muslims majorities witness regrettable economic stagnation?" This question does not ignore the fact that in a new economy the meaning and process of work and, more importantly, the nature of work and the work environment have undergone a profound change. Consequently, attitudes toward work and beliefs about the necessity, priority, and centrality of work in one's life may have experienced a corresponding shift.

HISTORICAL EVOLUTION OF WORK ETHIC

The concept and meaning of work ethic across centuries has evolved in
a way that has made progress and economic growth feasible. From the
early Greek civilization through to the Industrial Revolution and up to
recent history, work ethic has progressed and consequently led to qualitative changes culturally and economically. During the Greek civilization,
work was viewed as the curse of the gods and its meaning was equated
with sorrow. The Greek civilization, however, did not only disdain physical work but also mental labor (in the mechanical arts) (Tilgher, 1930).
The Romans, too, looked down on work and in fact adopted the Greek
beliefs (See Lipset, 1990). Likewise, an earlier Jewish belief viewed work as
a sinful activity: "If man does not find his food like animals and birds but
must earn it that is due to sin" (Lipset, 1990, p. 2). However, centuries later,
the Jewish view of work changed to espouse hard work and the notion
that work itself is an essential duty in life. Since then, work has been highly
valued. This shift is explored in the following sections below.

In Christianity, the emphasis was on spiritual and ritual aspects of
the religion and work was disdained. Christians, for centuries, were concerned with salvation and the afterlife, which was guaranteed not through
hard work but through devotion to worshiping God. The emergence of
Protestantism and the assertion by Martin Luther (1483–1546) that people
could serve God through their work was a turning point in Western thinking. However, Lipset (1990, p. 62) indicates that Luther "had contempt
for trade, commerce, and finance; those endeavors required no real work.
Hence, Luther did not directly pave the way for a rational, profit-oriented
economic system." The remarkable progress in the attitude toward work
and the essentiality of working hard in Western thought took place when
John Calvin (1509–64) advocated work to be a calling; a compliance with
the will of God.

In his book, *The Protestant Ethic and the Spirit of Capitalism*, Max
Weber (1905) argued that Calvin's and Luther's writings were instrumental
in advancing the capitalist system and moving away from Roman Catholic
instruction toward work. He coined the term "Protestant ethic" to underscore the role of religion in facilitating economic growth and sustaining
hard work. Indeed, he argued that the Protestant ethic created conditions in the West that led to the creation of modern capitalism and the
emergence of sound development perspectives that profoundly changed
the balance of power in the world, politically and economically. Weber,
however, appeared to overlook a stage of economic and social development: familiarity with and the internalization of faith and its relationship
to discipline and persistence in pursuing goals. A strong sense of being

destined to make a difference in life and in charge of steering the future reinforces discipline and strengthens determination. Nevertheless, Weber, in underscoring the power of the religious message in enhancing commitment to work, undeniably contributed to our understanding of the impact of religion on economic development. Rose (1985), in turn, identified four elements of the Protestant ethic: deferment of gratification, diligence, punctuality, and the primacy of the work domain.

There are two primary perspectives that emerge to justify the Protestant ethic (Hill, 1996). These are materialistic and religious views. The materialistic view advocates that the Protestant ethic arose as a result of a changing economic structure and the presence of a new social class that was different in its orientations and outlooks from the landowning class. Such changes made it imperative that a theory had to emerge to legitimize a growing population, increased unemployment rates, exploitation of workers, high prices, increased income inequality, and harsh working conditions. By considering work a calling and a means for salvation, the concept of the Protestant ethic gave needed religious justification to controlling and ensuring the conformity of the working class.

However, religious theory advances that theological beliefs about work, in fact, existed prior to changing economic conditions in Europe. The passion to work hard, for discipline in the workplace, and the desire to reinvest profits in new ventures were the outcome of Calvinistic teachings and religious commitment. Max Weber, an advocate of this approach, asserted that societies which espoused Protestantism did much better than countries where Catholicism was prevalent. Among contemporary researchers, Samuel Huntington (2004a) is famous for underscoring the role of Protestantism in bettering economic conditions. He stated (p. 31), "Would the United States be the country that it has been and that it largely remains today if it had been settled in the seventeenth and eighteenth centuries not by British Protestants but by French, Spanish, or Portuguese Catholics? The answer is clearly no. It would not be the United States; it would be Quebec, Mexico, or Brazil." He argued (2004b) that it was Protestantism that was the primary reason for the United States having a strong economy: "Protestant values . . . have shaped American attitudes toward private and public morality, economic activity, government, and public policy" (p. 10). Huntington asserted that Protestantism encourages hard work, individualism, discipline, conformity to societal norms, and a free market economy and disdains laziness and dependency. That, because of Protestantism, Western thought regarding work has experienced profound transformation; from a disdain for work to commitment and appreciation of the role of work in improving economic conditions and compliance with religiously driven ethics.

CENTRALITY OF WORK IN ISLAMIC CULTURE

Despite the assertion by American scholars that the concept of work ethic is a new development (see Barbash, 1983; Diddams and Whittington, 2003; Ferguson, 2004; Lipset, 1990), the emphasis on working hard and perfecting one's work has its roots in early Islamic civilization. There was not only an understanding of the necessity and responsibility of hard work, but also an articulation of the profound spiritual, philosophical, psychological, social, and economic dimensions of work. In Islamic teaching, work is an obligatory activity for those who are capable. The Quran (78:11) instructs that God "made the day as a means of subsistence." The Prophet asserts that "work is a religious duty," and "Making a living is a duty for every Muslim" (quoted in Al-Shaybani, 1986, died 805, p. 18), and "Among the sins are sins that cannot be recompensed by prayer and fasting . . . [but are wiped out by] a commitment to earning a livelihood" (p. 39).

Highlighting the centrality of work in the Islamic tradition is a pressing necessity, due to the need to re-educate a public that has experienced cultural discontinuity since the Mongol invasion and the destruction of the Islamic state in 1258. Indeed, rediscovering the traditional view of the Islamic attitude to work has a social and economic significance, as it can help safeguard the general security of the people and the welfare of future generations. This can be illustrated with a brief discussion of work dimensions in Islam:

1. **Spiritual dimension.** This is reflected in the intertwined and dialectic relations between work and faith and between work and the refinement of one's soul from undesirable habits. Imam Abu Omer Al Awzai (died 774) argued, "If God wished evil to people he would grant them endless arguments and direct them away from work" (quoted in Al-Mawardi, 2002, died 1058, p. 69). Abu Talib Al-Maki (1995, died 996, p. 557) stated, "If the religion of the people is corrupted, their sustenance is ruined."

2. **Social dimension.** There is an emphasis on continuity and necessity for establishing social relations in a way that facilitates prosperity, eases distress, and strengthens social interaction among people. According to an Arab saying, the work of honorable people is embedded in "permissible earning and spending on dependents." Imam Ali asserts, "The worth of each person stems from good deeds" (quoted in Al-Mawardi, p. 48). The Prophet underscored the social dimension of work when he stated, "Whomsoever it pleases that his sustenance should be made ample or his life should be lengthened, let him be kind to his relatives" (quoted in Muhammad Ali, 1977, p. 376) and "God has guards

on earth and in the sky. His guards in the sky are the angels and His guards on earth are those who work for their sustenance and safeguard the interest of the people."

3. **Philosophical dimension.** Islam asserts the centrality of intention in judging the usefulness of work: "The value of work derives from its intention" and the Prophet further asserts that, "God does not look upon either your appearance or wealth, rather God examines your intentions and actions." Islam makes it clear, however, that the outcome of work must serve the interests of society and ease the lives of the people. For this very reason, Islam links work to developments in society that do not distort the social, economic, and psychological balance. According to Al-Pashehi (2004, p. 417), Islamic instruction indicates that "Gaining sustenance leads a soul to serenity." The jurist Al-Maki (pp. 252–3) wrote that "Islam denies faith without work," asserting that the betterment of faith is possible only through knowledge and work. Furthermore, when the Prophet was asked, "What will substitute for knowledge?" his answer was "Work" (quoted in Al-Pashehi, p. 416).

4. **Psychological dimension.** This dimension takes on a special meaning, as it strengthens the identification of employees with their profession and their role as productive citizens in society. This is because work creates a feeling of economic independence and deepens social contributions, while increasing a person's confidence in his/herself and the ability for creativity and renewal. Al-Mawardi (2002, p. 297) stated that "He who works hard gets preeminence and he who multiplies his efforts experiences increasing ascendancy." The Prophet stated that "God loves a person who has work" and "The truthful, honest merchant is with the prophets and truthful ones and the martyrs." The Prophet encouraged workers to do their work and added that those who could not work due to illness would nevertheless get a reward in the hereafter: "Any worker who is working but is unable to continue due to illness, God will record him a reward for his work" (quoted in Al-Mawardi, p. 163).

5. **Economic dimension.** Unlike the Western view of work, early Islamic scholars accentuated the link between economic necessity, personal happiness, and societal interests. Work is not an end but a means to serving one's interests and improving the welfare of society. This perspective emphasizes that economic activities are sanctioned, individuals must not be driven by self-interest irrespective of those of society and the need to continuously meet the ever-emerging needs of the marketplace. The Prophet instructed believers: "Be creative in your work" (quoted in Al-Mawardi, p. 159) and "Rise early to make a

living and gain your economic needs as dedication represents benefits and success) (quoted in Al-Pashehi, 2004, p. 418). Abu Talib Al-Maki (1995, p. 500) indicated, "through transaction, selling and buying, even in just your capital, you will gain benefits and be blessed." And, due to the increasing benefits of business to society, the Prophet asserted, "Every work is blessed." The Prophet, too, highlighted the link between ethics, business, and prosperity stating, "Good ethics and being good to ones's neighbors contributes to the prosperity of cities and increases development" (quoted in Al-Mawardi, p. 383). The Quran (2:275) further instructs, "God hath permitted trade and forbidden usury."

THE MEANING OF WORK ETHIC

The meaning of work ethic, in Western civilization, has evolved from being an activity that is considered sinful and a burden to a productive activity essential for serving God. However, while this represents a qualitative development, as the *Financial Times* reported (see Hill, 2012), the primary purpose of work "remains unchanged: to earn money."

In contrast, since the early years, Islamic thinking has placed emphasis not only on hard work but on all other dimensions of work. Collectively, these dimensions lead to improving the well-being of members of society and the happiness of individuals. Accordingly, the IWE is defined as (see Ali, 1988, p. 577):

> . . . an obligatory activity and a virtue in light of the needs of man [person] and a necessity to establish equilibrium in one's individual and social life. Work enables man [person] to be independent and is a source of self respect, satisfaction, and fulfillment. Success and progress on the job depends on hard work and commitment to one's job. Commitment to work also involves a desire to improve the community and societal welfare. Society would have fewer problems if each person were committed to his work and avoided unethical methods of wealth accumulation. Creative work and cooperation are not only a source of happiness but are considered noble deeds, as well.

Accordingly, the pillars of the IWE are: effort, competition, transparency, and morally responsible conduct. Collectively, these pillars imply that conducting business with a minimum of or no restrictions and in a spirited environment will, essentially, result in higher performance and widespread prosperity. Below is a brief discussion of each pillar:

1. **Effort.** Both physical and mental engagements in work are praised in Islam. Though the latter is given more weight in the teachings, they

are treated as instruments for improving productivity and the welfare of society. The Quran (53:39) declares, "A person can have nothing but what he strives for" (18:23) and frowns on procrastination stating, "Nor say of anything, I will do it tomorrow." The second Caliph, Omar, was quoted as saying, "I would prefer dying while struggling for my sustenance and the sustenance of my children, to dying while fighting in the defense of faith" (quoted in Abdul-Rauf, 1984, p. 23). The Prophet encourages hard work asserting, "let each work up to his capacity and if they should tire, they should take a break" (quoted in Al-Barai and Abdeen, 1987, p. 143). Efforts, moreover, are linked to the desired output. The Prophet articulates this stating, "The best of work is one that generates benefits." The fourth Caliph, Imam Ali (1990, p. 715) remarked, "Do not be one of those who hope for a better end result without working for it" and "He, who does not perfect his/her work, will bring confusion to themselves" (p. 708).

2. **Competition.** Islam focuses on ethical competition in any exchange or interaction (Quran 83:26): "Let competitors compete." In an environment where people compete to do what is good, employees are motivated to put forth their best efforts and improve the quality of their work.

3. **Transparency.** This implies sincerity and truthfulness in business dealings, avoidance of manipulation, deception, concealment of truth, and dismissal of good deeds and kindness. The objective is not to give preference to self-interests at the expense of society and human needs. For this very reason, the Prophet's remark, "Those who declare things frankly will not lead to each other's destruction" (quoted in Al-Mawardi, 2002, p. 204) underlies the significance of transparency in the work environment and the need for cooperation to get jobs done.

4. **Responsible conduct.** During the early years of the Islamic state, though the market and market activities were simple, there was an understanding that optimal service to individuals and society was almost an impossible task if ethics were corrupted. Al-Jaroud, a Muslim scholar who lived in the seventh century, asserted that "work is corrupted by bad ethics" (quoted in Ibn 'Abd Rabbih Al-Andelesy, 1996, died 940, vol. 2, p. 155). The fourth Caliph underscored the necessity of ethics in business conduct stating, "He who has fine ethics, his paths will be easy" and "Oh merchants, take and give what is just and right. When you deny what is right, you will spend much more than it in wrongdoing" (quoted in Al-Maki, 1995, p. 519).

This demonstrates that the essence of work ethic in Islamic tradition has a much broader meaning than working hard and earning more money. This necessitates the importance of moving beyond the traditional Western view of work and accentuates the link between economic requirements, personal happiness, and societal interests. Work must not be treated as an end, but as a means to serving one's interests and improving the welfare of society. This perspective emphasizes that economic activities must not be driven by self-interest at the expense of society and stresses the need to meet ever emerging and changing demands of the marketplace.

THE MEANING AND DEVELOPMENT OF THE IWE

A study of concerns that pertain to IWE is not merely an intellectual exercise, but is practical both in terms of scope and scale. As mentioned before, IWE is an orientation that shapes and influences the involvement and participation of believers in the workplace. It implies that work is a virtue in light of a person's needs and is a necessity for establishing equilibrium in one's individual and social life (Nasr, 1984). IWE stands not for life denial, but for life fulfillment and holds business motives in the highest regard (Ahmad, 1976). IWE views work as a means to further self-interest economically, socially, and psychologically, to sustain social prestige, to advance societal welfare, and reaffirm faith. The concept has its origin in the Quran and the sayings and practices of the Prophet Mohamed. The centrality of work and deed in Islamic thinking is succinctly addressed in the Quran. As such, it is work and commitment that enables people to realize their intended goals (Quran 53:39): "Human beings can have nothing but what they strive for." The Quran specifically and clearly prohibits dishonesty in business dealings, be they physical, intellectual, or transactional (27:9; 2:188; 9:34, respectively): "Give a full measure when you measure out and weigh with a fair balance" "So establish weight with justice and fall not short in the balance" and "do not swallow up your property among yourselves by wrongful means, neither seek to gain access thereby to the authorities that ye may swallow up a portion of property of people wrongfully while ye know."

The Prophet Mohamed and Muslim scholars deliberately and extensively addressed issues related to work and business and set out the above instructions. The Prophet's directives were numerous and innovatively challenged the existing practices and order. While both the Quranic and the Prophet's instructions, in terms of ethics, address issues which pertain to worldly affairs and the affairs of the hereafter, they articulate that this life's concerns can be either general or specific. The latter includes business ethics, which in turn encompasses work ethic. Since the field of business ethics, in countries with Muslim majorities, is actually still in its inception stage, a confusion concerning business ethics and work ethic is common.

Work ethic, however, has to be highlighted and recognized as a significant instrument for inducing economic growth and in building the foundation for ethically responsible engagement in organizations. For this very reason, it is essential to address the aspects of work that the Prophet and Muslim scholars considered instrumental for advancing organizational and societal welfare. These are specified below:

1. **Pursuing work that serves the greatest possible number of people.** The Prophet Mohamed explicitly instructed followers that useful work is that which benefits others and society. Subsequently, those who work hard are acknowledged and are rewarded. He elevated people and their work to the highest rank if their deeds benefited people: "The best work is the one that results in benefit" and "The best of people are those who benefit others."

2. **Quality of work.** The pre-Islam Arabs lacked discipline and their commitment mostly revolved around a primary group. The Prophet understood this fact as a statesman and reformer and attempted to transform the Arab communities into a functional society. His emphasis on discipline and commitment intended not only to highlight the essence of work, but also to draw a link between faith and work and to eventually steer the Muslim community toward becoming an economically and politically viable entity. In this context, he iterated, "God blesses a person who perfects his craft [does the job right]," "God loves a person who learns precisely how to perform his work and does it right," and God rewards a person who when "He does work, uses his imagination" (quoted in Al-Ghazali, 2004, p. 394).

3. **Wages.** The Prophet Mohamed instructed Muslims to be fair and just and prompt in compensating workers. He declared, "One must give a worker his wage before his sweat dries [should be given on time]" and "your wage should be based on your effort and spending." That is, payment for wages should be timely, fair, and adequate. In fact, the Prophet considered denying a worker his/her full wage to be an immoral act. He was quoted saying that he would personally bear witness against "he who received work from a laborer and did not pay him in full." However, wages are not given arbitrarily. Al-Ghazali (2004, p. 168) stated, "If you do not do work, you receive no wages."

4. **Reliance on self.** One of the most important functions of work is that it sustains confidence and self-reliance. The Prophet stated, "No one eats better food than that which he eats out of the work of his hand" and "No earnings are better than that of one's own effort."

5. **Sincerity in work.** Al-Maki (1995, p. 310) argued that "sincerity without work is better than work without sincerity." That is, if a

worker or manager has no intention of performing his work correctly, it will harm the organization and other stakeholders. Mohamed Ibn Al-Tirmidhî (died 869) stated that "Sincerity in and improving work leads to paradise" (quoted in Al-Sulami, 1968, p. 218).

6. **Deeds and intentions.** These constitute significant pillars in IWE. They clearly differentiate IWE from the work ethics of other faiths. One of the fundamental assumptions in Islam is that intention rather than result is the criterion upon which work is evaluated in terms of benefits to the community. Any activity that is perceived to do harm, even though it results in significant wealth to those who undertake it, is considered unlawful. The Prophet Mohamed stated, "God does not look at your matters [shapes or forms] and wealth, rather God examines your intentions and actions."

7. **Transparency.** The precondition for propagating and realizing ethical conduct is transparency. It was reported that the Prophet Mohamed said, "Those who declare things frankly, will not lead to each other's destruction," which underlies the significance of transparency in any business transaction and the necessity for enhancing trust and reducing problems in the marketplace.

8. **Generosity.** Generosity is a virtue in Islam. The Prophet Mohamed stated that "There is nothing worse than avariciousness." He declared, "The generous person is closest to God, heaven, people, and far from hell" and "He who removes a distress, God blesses in this world and the hereafter."

9. **Knowledge.** Knowledge is the basis for improving and perfecting work. Al-Maki (1995, p. 253) argued that "No faith is good without work and knowledge." Al-Mawardi (2002) indicated that knowledge is important for recognizing what is appropriate from inappropriate work and for knowing what is easy and what is difficult. Sahl Al-Tustari (died 896) stated that "An appreciation of knowledge is work and an appreciation of work is enhancement of knowledge" (quoted in Al-Sulami, 1968, p. 207).

IWE IN PRACTICE

Since the late 1970s, many countries with Muslim majorities have experienced a cultural awakening. Many groups and associations have been established to advocate cultural revivalism. In particular, intellectuals and students of management and organizations have initiated programs that address the compatibility of prevailing business practices with Islamic ethics. IWE, thus, appears to attract many segments of the population, not only for cultural reasons but because IWE encourages the individual to better him/herself and to strive for economic prosperity. The cultural awakening has resulted in some degree in a sensitivity to the economic and political calamity that exists in most Muslim societies. While the merging of the economies of these societies into the Western centers of finance and economy has encouraged business people to rethink their business approaches, the spread of economic globalization, while the rise of a new sort of entrepreneur has accelerated interests in business ethics, in general, and IWE in particular.

Among growing segments of intellectuals and entrepreneurs, IWE has been viewed as an important means for revitalizing the economy and overcoming the prevailing economic calamity. This aim, however, has been obstructed in recent years by political upheavals, rises in oil revenues in some countries that have deepened dependence on imports, and the rise of counter-intellectualism movements represented by extremism.

Consequently, many professional organizations and institutes have embarked on studying and presenting work ethics in a changing world. After an extensive review of the literature and consultation with several Muslim scholars (see Ali, 1988) developed a construct for measuring IWE. The measure includes 46 statements and has been found to be reliable and valid. Subsequent empirical studies conducted in several countries evidence the validity and reliability of the measure. IWE is unique not only in its elements but also in its optimistic view that human beings are capable of positively contributing to society, while serving their interests, and that the arena for contribution has no limitations except that which is considered harmful to self and others. That is, the IWE construct captures the essence of the work ethic in Islam. It highlights that work is an obligatory activity and a virtue in light of the needs of human beings and the necessity to establish equilibrium in one's individual and social life. Work enables a person to be independent and is a source of self-respect, satisfaction, and fulfillment. Success and progress on the job depends on hard work and commitment to one's job. Commitment to work also involves a desire to improve the community and societal welfare. Society would have fewer problems if individuals were committed to their work and avoided unethical methods of wealth accumulation. Creative work and cooperation are not only sources of happiness, but are also considered noble deeds.

It should be noted that IWE is different from the Protestant Work Ethic (PWE) not only in terms of the time framework but also in regard to its core content. The principles of IWE were articulated in the seventh century, while those of PWE were articulated by Martin Luther and John Calvin in the sixteenth century. Furthermore, the core of IWE is profoundly different from PWE. Even though both of them place an emphasis on work involvement and work as a divine calling, IWE encompasses dimensions that are not explicitly addressed in PWE. In particular, IWE stresses both difficult and creative engagement. In addition, IWE places considerable emphasis on intention, rather than outcome, as a measure of morality. Engaging in monopoly, gambling, or trading in alcohol, for example, may bring fortune, but are considered harmful to self and the community and thereby treated as immoral endeavors. Serving others and the community is an integral part of IWE, but is not highlighted in PWE. Likewise, the ever-existing possibility of deceptive behavior makes it an obligation for those engaged in any transaction to be transparent. In this context, the saying "Buyer beware" is not sanctioned, as we will see in Chapter 8.

Empirical studies show that IWE is correlated with various organizational factors. Ali (1992) demonstrated a high correlation between IWE and individualism. In their studies of work ethics in the US and Canada, Ali, Falcone, and Azim (1995) found that PWE, work involvement, and work individualism measures correlated with IWE. Other researchers (see Haroon, Fakhar Zaman, and Rehman, 2012; Moayedi, 2009; Rokhman, 2010; and Yousef, 2001) studied the relationships between IWE and job satisfaction and organizational commitment and found a strong correlation between these factors. Previously, Yousef (2000) found positive high relationships between IWE and role ambiguity and locus of control scales. Abu-Saad (2003) empirically studied IWE among Arab schoolteachers in Israel and found that, unlike Western instruments of work ethics, IWE uniquely captured the importance of one's contribution to community and society and the obligations of the organization to its employees. Recently, Ali and Al-Kazemi (2006) reported that IWE is strongly related to loyalty measures, while Imam, Abbasi, and Muneer (2013) found in Pakistan that IWE can improve the performance of employees in various ways. In these and other studies, it was found that participants scored high on IWE.

The strong commitment among participants to IWE found in countries like Indonesia, Saudi Arabia, Kuwait, UAE, Pakistan, and Malaysia, among others, evidence that participants are committed to engagement and involvement in work. Even in the US, American Muslims display a much higher commitment to work ethic than the rest of the population (71 percent vs. 64 percent, respectively) (Pew Research Center, 2007). This, however, may also indicate that these participants, representing managers, employees, or students, are different from the rest of society and thus their commitment may not be matched by others; otherwise, these societies, according to Weber's thesis, which speculates that high work ethic leads to higher economic growth, would experience economic prosperity. However, there are two other possibilities: the political and personal. The political systems in most Muslim societies are authoritarian and freedom of participation and seizing economic opportunities are highly curtailed. That is, in societies where there is a freedom deficit neither entrepreneurs nor intellectuals can utilize their skills and knowledge. The second possibility revolves around personal aspirations and orientations. In these societies, people are infatuated with ideals; thus, in answering questionnaires they are not reflecting reality but are expressing their idealism.

CHANGING WORK ETHIC

Certainly, work ethic is related to social, economic, religious, and political developments in society. These changes influence ethics and subsequently affect behavior and conduct, both in the market and within organizations. In the Islamic civilization, however, there was an understanding that cultivating good work ethics was not easy. Abu'l-Hassan Hilal b. Muhassin Al-Sabi (2003, died 1056, p. 6) stated, "Overcoming difficulties is much easier than acquiring good ethics and enduring burdens is considerably simpler than cultivating ethics. . . . Efforts to reach and achieve targets differ and effectiveness in diagnosis and realization vary but aiming high minimizes difficulties, while low aspirations lead to unsatisfactory results." This, however, does not mean work ethic does not change. On the contrary, it implies ethics is subject to evolution, adaptation, and even regression.

Centuries ago, Muslim thinkers recognized that for each era there are corresponding ethics. Imam Abu Al Hassan Al-Mawardi argued that ethics change either for accidental or objective reasons. The jurist Al-Maki (died 996) mentioned that good ethics were prevalent in the first century of Islam due to the existence of followers who had a good upbringing and deep faith; they did not take that which was not theirs. But this was changed in later years as people displayed less faith and followed their desires. In his book, *Rescuing the Nation by Illuminating Darkness*, Al-Maqrizi, (1999, died 1442) recorded that government weakness, bad leadership, and the rise to power of unqualified individuals was primarily responsible for the thriving of bad ethics and deception, inflation, corruption, and economic crises.

In modern times, most Western scholars have argued that in the West there has been a deviation from hard work. Lipset (1990) indicated that several studies have documented declining work ethics. Dauten (2007) pointed out that today's generation does not have the same work ethic that distinguished previous American generations. Alderman (2010) pointed out that workers in Italy displayed low morale and were not concerned with hard work. However, in a recent study by the Pew Research Center (2012), it was found that young people in almost all countries in the study, except

Lebanon, Japan, France, and Russia, still believe in work ethic and that hard work leads to success. Likewise, a study conducted by Gallup (2013) in the US showed that most American managers and workers were inclined to engage in work (see Yu, Harter, and Agrawal, 2013). In contrast, a similar study in China found that Chinese workers, as opposed to Americans, were much less likely to engage in work (see Yu and Srinivasan, 2013).

Early Muslim scholars recognized that each era has its own people and there are different means for achieving emerging needs. It should be mentioned that Al-Mawardi, in his comments on changing ethics (2002, p. 547), specified what was needed to cope with changing ethics. He stated:

> One should know that since ethics vary according to different times and changing habits, it is impossible to comprehend and difficult to account for all changes. But each person remembers what they were taught about ethics in his own time . . . [and] the duty of the new generation is to diligently preserve the ethics that have been forgotten, gather what is scattered, then judge their usefulness according to the preferences of the new era, the habits of the current time, and record what is consistent and ignore what is conflicting. After that, one should use reason to add what is needed and beneficial. . . . For each era, there is a pattern of speaking and accepted expressions that are more influential and easily understood.

An objective understanding of what is taking place in society, changing economic structures, social needs, and work conditions can lead to a diagnosis of what must be done to confront social and economic ills. In today's world, a better understanding of work ethic is essential for coping with the dynamics of the business and political environment and for building a foundation for a sound economy. This task takes on an added value in countries with Muslim majorities. These countries have not only experienced economic stagnation, but have also suffered from the lack of vision to pull themselves away from backwardness. Though the task of achieving economic revivalism is challenging and in some cases appears to be an impossibility, channeling the spirit of work ethic effectively and diffusing it across populations might be a means by which this can be achieved.

CONCLUSION

In this chapter, issues related to organization and work have been discussed. While work, an integral part of individual life, can take place in various forms, it is within an organization that work thrives and individuals find the needed resources to reinforce their economic engagement and involvement in creative endeavors. That is, work is characteristically linked to organization. Organizations serve as institutes for facilitating, easing, and making transactions less costly, in comparison to having an individual carrying out the work independent of others.

The chapter elaborated on organizational work and the significance bestowed in the Islamic tradition on discipline, cooperation, planning, and execution of tasks and duties. Likewise, the meaning of work was discussed in terms of centrality of work and work ethic. While the two terms are often used interchangeably, highlighting the aspects of each uncovers certain elements that are essential for understanding the relationship between organization and work. Indeed, how individuals view and relate to the concept of work offers undeniable organizational opportunities for enhancing motivation, discipline, and creativity within organizations.

The concept of work was viewed in its historical evolution and in how the three monotheistic religions, Judaism, Christianity, and Islam, have looked at work since their inception. This historical framework enables researchers to identify the evolution of the meaning of work among the three religions and, thus, anchors the discussion on sound and logical foundations. Furthermore, the historical perspective gives insight into how each religion manages to cope with historical and modern challenges by espousing what is essential and necessary to enrich humanity and move forward.

IWE was discussed in detail. Its philosophical, spiritual, social, psychological, and economic dimensions were highlighted. The logic for each was explained and the theoretical justifications based on religious instructions were provided. In addition, aspects of work that place Islam apart from the other two monotheistic religions were elaborated on and the differences between IWE and PWE were highlighted, as well. It was argued that, unlike centuries ago, the welfare of self and of society had become highly interlinked and it is impossible these days to separate them. This is where IWE is instrumental in providing a new paradigm to overcome ever-emerging societal and organizational difficulties.

8. Marketing ethics and consumerism

Whether in a traditional or modern society, the marketing function plays a pivotal role in advancing societal welfare and enhancing individuals' well-being. It is marketing that makes it possible for members of society to obtain what they want and that offers the necessary commodities and/or services at the desired time and place. Marketing not only presents options, but also creates various possibilities for market actors to select from or to pursue. Indeed, among business functions, marketing is intertwined with social desires and preferences. While marketing offerings and promotional methods influence these desires, they in turn are shaped by social priorities and preferences. This is because, as Wilkie and Moore (2007) have argued, the marketing function is a "social institution that is highly adaptive to its cultural and political context." This underscores not only the nature of marketing, but also its strategic link to cultural ethics and public policy concerns.

However, cultural ethics are shaped to a large degree by religion. That is, religion remains a determining force in ethics formation and application. Indeed, each religion has its own set of values and beliefs, which in turn determine what is considered right and wrong and the standards upon which behavior/conduct is judged; in short, the application of values and beliefs to reality is ethics. Ethics affect elements of market transactions, what should be marketed and what should be avoided, how and when transactions should take place, and specifies the necessary conditions for the legitimacy of any market transaction.

One of the elements closely linked to modern marketing is consumerism. In Western societies, consumerism celebrates consumption and spending, irrespective of the financial ability of a person to repay his/her debt on a timely basis. This consumerism trend has propelled to the front concerns about ethical conduct in the marketplace, along with socio-political issues. Indeed, this type of consumerism raises the question: "Do consumers behave ethically in exercising their rights in the marketplace?" There is no straightforward answer. In fact, the existing literature provides conflicting conclusions. There are those who provide either direct or indirect relationships between ethics and consumption behavior (Doran, 2009; Muncy and Eastman, 1998; Steenhaut and Kenhove, 2006; Vitell and Paolillo, 2003).

On the other hand, some researchers have found out there is a lack of consumer concern for ethical and environmental issues (Belk, Devinney, and Eckhardt, 2005). As we will see later, consumerism has long been addressed in terms of ethical conduct by early Muslim scholars.

This chapter has several objectives: to provide insight into Islamic ethics in the marketplace; identify ways to minimize market abuses, while having confidence in market institutions and assuring their vitality and continuity; contrast Islamic marketing ethics with ethical marketing practices in Christianity and Judaism; and provide traditional insights on marketing issues, including consumerism and what marketers should learn from instruction generated during the first six centuries of Islam.

DEFINING MARKETING ETHICS

While marketing is highly adaptive to its cultural and political circumstances, its definition should be understood in the context of exchange function. This might generate different definitions in different contexts. However, the most common definition, suggested by the American Marketing Association (AMA), is "the activity, set of institutions, and processes for creating, communicating, delivering, and exchanging offerings that have value for customers, clients, partners, and society at large." This definition highlights an important aspect of marketing: creating value to stakeholders. A stakeholder can be anyone who has a stake in corporate offerings and is influenced by or concerned with its activities. Those concerns reflect, to a larger degree, those of society. However, having "value" for customers differs across cultures. Certainly, customers in a poor country expect different value in a product than those customers who live in a prosperous society: a bicycle may be used as a means to meet basic transportation needs in one country but an instrument for leisure in another country. The AMA's definition is very specific and stems primarily from the American culture. However, while there might be semi agreement on concept and process of marketing across societies, there are differences in perception, goals, and practices. This is especially true in the Islamic civilization. Two issues are illustrative. First, in Islamic marketing, faithful marketers observe the Islamic prescriptions of being generous in exchange and or lowering prices for those who are in need or who face difficulties. The second issue revolves around purposeful conduct and the fear that marketers might be inclined to fall into the trap of temptation. Al-Maki (1995, p. 505) reported that two of the Prophet's companions, as they entered a market, asked for God's mercy to avoid marketing enticements, material entrapment, and to overcome moral dilemma, as material temptations are real and powerful. Al-Maki (p. 505) argued that there are temptations in the marketplace that only knowledgeable people with strong faith are able to identify and avoid. Those marketers who do not seek virtue and do not have appropriate knowledge of the ethical require-ments are more likely to deviate from what is morally right. In contrast, the marketing definition by the AMA is a reflection of the religious belief in the US. This is illustrated by the Association's definition of marketing ethics. It states that marketing ethics is, "Standards of marketing decision making based on 'what is right' and 'what is wrong,' and emanating from our religious heritage and our traditions of social, political, and economic freedom." While the definition accentuates the role of Christianity in shaping ethics and in determining what is right and wrong in marketing practices, it leaves more room for the possibility of being influenced by political and economic systems. Moreover, American capitalism gives profit making a priority over other considerations, and self-interest and CEOs' judgments are unquestionably accepted.

As indicated in Chapter 1, Islamic ethics is broader in scope and places an emphasis on furthering public interest. Thus, marketing ethics in Islam seeks to sustain responsible marketing conduct in accordance with reli-giously sanctioned instructions, from the prevention of deception and fraudulent behavior to strengthening transparent operations, munificent behavior, and the prohibition of any transactions with marketers who are abusers or are thought to be associated with oppressors. That is, the primary concern of Islamic ethics is societal welfare. For this very reason, its precepts provide useful guidelines for marketing functions and proc-esses. These range from promotion and pricing, to packaging, distribution, storing, and delivery. For example, Islamic ethics prohibits deception in advertising and exaggerating the benefits, characteristics, or qualities of a commodity. Sellers are held responsible for any trickery or unfounded claims. Unlike prevailing market ethics in some Western countries which endorse profit maximization and cut-throat competition that can drive competitors out of business, Islamic ethics does not consent to such inten-tional and deliberate actions.

Marketing activities and socio-economic systems are an integral part of the economic system. Some of these activities are sanctioned and some not. Fisher (1988, p. 144) reiterated this when he stated, "Despite the frequent assertion that sentimentality and the pursuit of economic interests don't mix, economic systems are in fact ethical systems. Whether by law and regulation or by custom, some economic activities are sanctioned, while others are not. And what is sanctioned differs from culture to culture." Such cultural differences make the understanding of ethical priorities a must for those who are engaged in marketing activities. This is because certain societal ethics are prioritized, often widely shared, and, therefore, play a significant role in shaping marketing expectations and conduct.

Tradition and culture in countries with Muslim majorities have shown remarkable endurance despite rapid economic changes. In traditional societies, ethics and cultural norms are deeply rooted and, subsequently, changes take place at a slow pace. This has situated dominant ethics as powerful standards for judging what is right and what is wrong. These ethics and cultural norms set the boundaries for acceptable conduct and, more importantly, are broadly utilized by members of the society in the assessment of individual character and morality. Culturally, these societies are characterized by the supremacy of personal relations. This blurs the boundaries between personal and public roles and deepens the influence of ethics in all spheres of life. It helps to spread its impact to broader activities relative to societies with clearly delineated boundaries of private and public matters.

Though the ethical framework (public interest, moderation, and *ehsan*) is based on religious prescriptions and constitutes the foundation for Islamic ethics, marketing ethics, in particular, is shaped by government regulations and guidelines, along with the prevailing economic system. The interplay among the elements of these factors influences Islamic marketing ethics and what marketers should do to observe morally responsible conduct. This interplay (see Figure 8.1) is likely to induce informed Muslims to rethink their activities and ponder transactions that might provoke even a trace of doubt relative to their religious legitimacy. Religion, however, remains a determining force in ethics formation and application. During the formative period, the state was in the early stage of inception where economic and social openness were instrumental in ensuring the survival and growth of the new faith, which was facing mounting challenges from formidable adversaries. Likewise, the state was determined to build a foundation for a thriving economy to confront powerful rivals and attract new followers to the emerging faith. While the three factors specified in Figure 8.1 influenced ethics, it is Islam that was and has been the determining factor. In return, Islamic marketing ethics leave their mark on individuals, markets, and corporations. These entities take note of what society considers morally appropriate and conduct their affairs accordingly. The conditions for observing marketing ethics vary. In a society where government guidelines and Islamic ethics are articulated and coincide, marketing ethics has a noticeable influence on personal inclinations, market functions, and corporate decisions. In a situation where Islamic market ethics and government guidelines are not well articulated, market functions and transactions are primarily shaped by the prevailing economic system's norms (e.g., Lebanon, Turkey, Djibouti, Tunisia, Jordan, etc.). In these

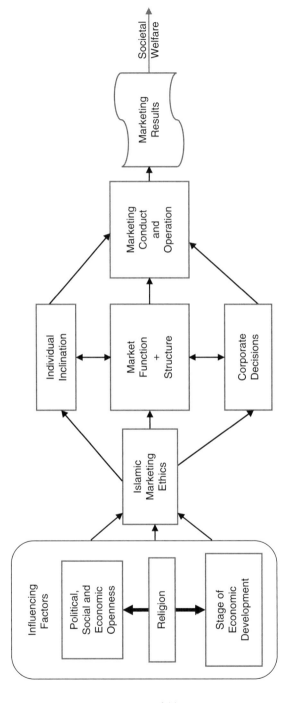

Figure 8.1   Impact of marketing ethics

countries, like many others, principles of capitalism and the quest to make a profit play major roles in market interaction.

Abu Talib Al-Maki (1995, p. 38) warned marketers not to be guided primarily by economic considerations and material benefits. He stated, "If a person engages in market transactions in order to make a living and his material gains are held to be more important than those of others, he will not be sincere in his transactions." This judgment is in line with the general Islamic instructions which obligate market actors to be generous and considerate to the economic and social needs of other actors. The Prophet makes it obligatory in the marketplace to ease the lives of those who are in distress. The Prophet stated, "May God have mercy on the man who is generous when he buys and when he sells and when he demands" and "He who deals with people without abuse, does not lie to them, and meets his promises, then he is a noble person whose justice is validated" (quoted in Al-Mawardi, 2002, p. 501).

THE SIGNIFICANCE OF MARKETING

Though marketers differ in their aims, approaches, and activities, their place in Islamic thought is governed by two seemingly contradictory categorizations: admiration and admonition. The first focuses on the importance of social, economic, religious, and political roles that marketers assume in this world. The second underscores the fact that in conducting their activities marketers are easily disposed toward market temptations at the expense of spiritual and sanctioned duties. These considerations were and are still vital in any treatment of marketing. The objective is clear: to optimize marketers' role in society, while at the same time create conditions conducive to morally driven conduct. In today's business, the second part of the objective might be difficult to achieve, though its pursuit is considered a religious duty.

Both Quranic instructions and the Prophet's sayings, along with the actions of his immediate four wise caliphs, underline the significance of marketers and the marketplace. This emphasis presents the four roles of marketers as something noble, desirable, and spiritually rewarding. In fact, the Quran (62:10) considers business activities a divine duty saying, "Disperse through the land and seek of the bounty of God." This instruction pertains to business activities, in general, and includes marketing, especially the duties of buying and selling. The (4:29) Quran further underscores the importance of marketing stating, "Eat not up your property among yourselves in vanities; but let there be amongst you trade by mutual good-will" and (2:275) "God hath permitted trade and forbidden usury."

While the Prophet Mohamed elevated marketers to the highest status, stating that "The truthful, honest merchant is with the prophets," he accentuated the significant role that marketers play in ensuring community growth and economic robustness by stating, "He who brings goods to the market is blessed and the hoarder is cursed" (quoted in Glaachi, 2000, p. 16) and "Among the sins are sins that cannot be recompensed by prayer and fasting . . . [but are wiped out by] a commitment to earning a livelihood" (p. 39).

The economic and political roles that marketers play were highlighted by Ibn Khaldun (2006). He observed that when rulers become unjust and increase taxes and or force merchants to buy goods at high prices, merchants find their funds dwindling and have no recourse except to leave the market. He pointed out that this situation caused capital funds to dwindle:

> As losses occur, profits decline and capital diminishes leaving merchants with no option but to give up their businesses. Furthermore, merchants who reside elsewhere are discouraged from coming and engaging in commercial activities in the area. The market experiences slow economic activity and stagnation and people lose their livelihood which primarily depends on trade. As the market experiences decline and people lose their sources of income, the ruler's tax revenue either decreases or worsens. . . . Since the primary source for revenue for a dynasty, in its later stage, comes from taxing commerce activities, this accelerates its demise and the collapse of the urban civilization. Usually, this takes place slowly and imperceptibly. (p. 226)

Imam Ali, the fourth Caliph (1990, pp. 637–8), in his letter to his governor in Egypt, further elaborated on the significance of marketers when he advised:

> Be responsive to the needs of the merchants and craftsmen and take good care of them, whether they are settled or travelling across countries, or working on their own to make a living. They are the creators of benefits and the dispensers of goods, which they bring from other countries, by sea or by land and through mountains and valleys, making them available to people who are in need of them. These are the people who have an interest in maintaining durable peace and understanding. Give your attention to their affairs whether in your vicinity or in remote areas of your land.

The above instruction shows how early Muslims regarded marketing functions and the guidelines they were provided with, which are relevant even in today's business world. First, the stated primary role in business is to provide protection for business activities, ensure the safety and security of trade, and remove obstacles that are detrimental to business transactions. Second, the interests of marketers serve the interest of the state, as they not only prolong stability but also enhance the function of the state. Third, marketing activities are essential for economic growth and improving societal welfare and offer several options for customers to choose from, thereby sustaining the well-being of consumers. Fourth, marketing functions make it possible to connect markets across nations, make cross-cultural understanding possible and in return boost economic activities. And fifth, commercial activities make it possible for peace among nations to take place and the sustained allegiance of citizens to their respective governments. This emphasis on the economic, political, religious, and social significance of marketing is in itself a major development. Therefore, marketing is not treated merely as an economic activity, as it is normally perceived in the West, but as a mechanism for strengthening the link between societal and political interests and the exchange function. This broadens the arena of marketing and offers implications which are useful for understanding the interplay among the economic and socio-political forces in today's world.

Therefore, marketing in Islam focuses on practical issues common in the marketplace and acknowledges that mankind, as is part of human nature, on many occasions finds it difficult either to resist temptation to engage in morally questionable behavior or to overcome a desire to accumulate wealth. Competition in the marketplace and the opportunities that emerge are powerful forces that may weaken the will to avoid temptations, deceptions, and manipulation of events. The fourth Caliph, Ali (1990, p. 475), stated, "it is difficult to wrench the human soul from temptation. It would rather persist in sin and passion." The first Caliph, Abu Baker, stated, "We used to avoid seventy opportunities of permissible trading for fear that one might be prohibited" (quoted in Al-Maki, 1995, p. 562). This is the very reason that the Prophet called for transparent market conduct stating, "Truthfulness leads to good deeds and the latter guides to heaven" (quoted in Al-Hashimi (2001, p. 209). In order to limit the spread of market abuse and manipulation, the Prophet established the position of market inspector. Those who held this office were known for their piety, sound judgment, and their ability to supervise market transactions and ensure that deception was prevented (Ali, 2005; Siddiqui, 1987).

ETHICAL MARKETING

The ethical foundations that were outlined and discussed in Chapter 1 gave rise to certain pillars of ethics. These pillars are general, pertaining to life affairs, be they political, social, or business. Marketing pillars stem from these general foundations. They are equally applicable to the exchange function. Figure 8.2 depicts the relationships between ethical foundations, pillars of marketing ethics, and expected transactional outcome.

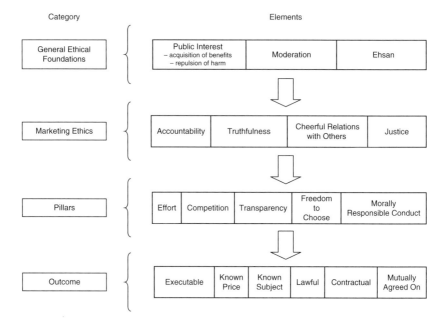

Figure 8.2   Marketing ethics and ethical outcome

Islamic ethics, in their focus on exchange, relations with others, and benefits to society, establish moral boundaries for marketing functions. These boundaries constitute the sanctioned arena where interface with organizational stakeholders takes place. The latter, be they individuals or organizations, have their own aspirations, expectations, and goals. In an environment of trust and responsible conduct, exchange is assumed to occur to the satisfaction of those who are involved. In contrast, where competing interests collide, the exchange function may not be optimally realized.

Marketing Ethics

As was discussed in previous chapters, ethics are moral standards that govern human conduct and individual relations with others. In Islam, marketing ethics is founded on four interrelated major concepts: account-ability, truthfulness, amiability (cheerful relations with others) and justice. These set the framework for ethical marketing. The first marketing ethics are accountability or responsibility. The Quran (17:15) clarifies that what a person does is solely his/her responsibility and no one should be held responsible for the mistakes of others: "No bearer of burdens should bear the burden of another." In the context of marketing, responsibility is broad and goes beyond relations with other immediate market players to include a responsibility toward community. Though general religious precepts often highlight responsibility toward God, this responsibility is expressed in terms of company, self, and community at large. The instruction "No harm and harm-doer" is intended to hold any actor responsible for whatever act might intentionally harm others, their livelihood, and their surroundings. Greed, for example, may harm markets in the exchange function if a deception is contemplated. Likewise, selling at a price higher than the current market price or hoarding can lead to harm that eventually hurts those with limited income or those who have no access to other options. Likewise, decoy shoppers (those who bid on a product to induce a potential buyer to pay a higher price and elicit interest in the item, or who intentionally lure a consumer to select a product over others) are prohibited, as evidenced in the instruction of the Prophet: "Decoying in sales is prohibited– '*La Tanajashoo*'" (quoted in Al-Asqalani, 1947, died 852, p. 167).

Accountability

Accountability toward a company focuses on doing no harm to its interest and avoiding weakening its market position. This must be done in a way that serves the interest of society and of the company. For example, the marketer must not engage in promotion that may be considered too aggressive or predatory in order to increase yearly bonuses and rewards. Likewise, a marketer should not undertake activities that mislead customers to buy certain products or bribe other members in the channel of distribution.

Accountability toward self is a manifestation of a person's ability to reason. As Al-Tirmidhi stated, "A rational person is the one who fears God and holds himself accountable" (quoted in Al-Sulami, 1968, p. 219). It should be mentioned that self-accountability is ensured when a marketer shies away from any act that compromises ethical standards and religious principles, when his material gain or interest is given priority over others. For example, Abu Talib Al-Maki (1995, pp. 91–2) recorded that a merchant, Sri Al-Sagdi, was told that a fire had swept through the market during the night and destroyed shops. As he was going to check on what had happened, people informed him that his shop was safe, but the blaze had destroyed the rest. His reply was, "Thank God." He immediately reflected on what he had said and told himself, "I said thank God for the safety of my wealth, neglecting that others have suffered devastation to their wealth." And so, he gave all his wealth to charity to eradicate his sin.

Truthfulness

This has four dimensions: spiritual, psychological, social, and economic.

- **Spiritual.** The Quran (11:119) instructs, "O ye who believe! Fear God and be with those who are truthful" and (33:35) "truthful men and truthful women . . . for them God has prepared forgiveness and a great reward." This spiritual dimension guides believers to strengthen their bonds with fellow market actors and enhances understanding. Once market actors come to appreciate that their friendly and truthful relationship with others serves the advancement of their spiritual commitment, their dedication is likely to be enforced.

- **Psychological.** The psychological dimension gives a reason for market actors to refine their involvement and boost trust in market institutions and operations. The Prophet stated, "Truthfulness is certainty and lying is suspicion" (quoted in Al-Nawawi, 2001, p. 30). The Prophet, as was previously discussed, argued that when members of the exchange function are truthful, God blesses their transactions.

- **Social.** Socially, the status of members of market exchange who are truthful is ranked much higher than those who are not. In addition, people seek their friendship and to strengthen bonds with them. The Prophet Mohamed's saying, "*Al-Din Al-maamala*" (Religion is found in the way of dealing with other people), underscores that in relations with others, truthfulness is a foundation. Al-Pashehi asserted that "Truth is a pillar of faith, the basis for ethics, and the root of moral courage" (2004, p. 416).

- **Economic.** Market actors who are known to deceive, charge higher prices, hide defects, are insincere, and always delay delivery, eventually lose their businesses or their jobs. That is, truthfulness enhances customer loyalty and helps business growth. The Quran (92:5–10) states, "He who gives (in charity) and fears God and accepts the truth, we will ease his path to success. But he who is greedy and thinks that he is self-sufficient, and denies the truth, we will ease his path to misery."

Amiable Relations with Others

While the Prophet's saying, "*Al-Din Al-maamala*," offers the spiritual driving force for having good relations with others, regardless of their background, amiability accentuates that such spirit must be exhibited so the members of the transaction feel not only comfort, but also are encouraged to be part of the team or any setting. Amiability takes on three primary forms: sincerity, appreciation, and thankfulness. The first reinforces trust among members of the exchange function and sustains fruitful relationships. The second serves as a mechanism for motivating market players and broadening the arena of exchange. The third form makes it ethically obligatory for market actors to be thankful to customers and the rest of the stakeholders. This was exemplified by the saying of the Prophet: "He who does not thank people, does not thank God." Similarly, the fourth Caliph, Imam Ali, stated, "God has situated good ethics as a mechanism for connecting people to Him" (quoted in Al-Mawardi, 2002, p. 366). In terms of marketing, the Prophet was clear that it is much better for buyers to obtain what they need from those who are amiable. He stated, "Get your market needs from those who are pleasant" (quoted in Al-Mawardi, p. 519). This saying has far reaching implications for business conduct. First, amiability implies optimism and this eventually leads to a vibrant market. Second, amiability is a kind of charity. This is best expressed by the Prophet's saying "Every good deed is charity." And since amiability in Islamic ethics is part of good deeds, it is a form of social responsibility. Third, amiability is one of the most powerful mechanisms for lifting spirits. People with good spirits are more likely to be active market actors. More importantly, lifting the spirit is an inexpensive tool for motivating and enhancing participation in the marketplace, as it can lead to less conflict and more cooperation among market actors.

Justice

Justice is a prerequisite for any responsible conduct. It is a mainstay for security and economic prosperity. Whether a person is a marketer or not, the standards of justice must be applied uniformly. The Quran (16:90) instructs, "God commands justice, the doing of good . . ." As indicated in Chapter 7, in terms of work, deepening commitment to justice is possible to realize by avoiding greed and fearing God. However, in the context of business conduct, justice is an important element of marketing ethics. Therefore, whatever market actors do, they should neither discriminate, defy ethical precepts, nor arbitrarily violate the rights of others. For example, marketers should not, as the Prophet instructed, treat others differently or deny them access to information or business opportunities. Also, giving preference to one market actor is considered a violation of morally sanctioned conduct. It is reported that an Arab women questioned the fourth Caliph, Imam Ali, because her food allowance was equal to that of a non-Arab female. He informed her, "I looked in the Quran and did not find a preference for the sons of Ismail [Arabs] over those of Isaac

[Jews]" (quoted in Glaachi, 2000, p. 39). In marketing, this implies that corporations should treat customers justly, regardless of where they reside. Companies, too, might find it advantageous to offer a variety of commodities based on different segment needs and market conditions. Most importantly, justice in marketing implies avoidance of dealing with oppressors or those who are known to be fraudulent or deceptive. Abu Talib Al-Maki (1995, p. 503) reported that a marketer should not deal with agents of oppression and if he does, according to religious law, he should be treated not as an enabler but as an oppressor. Likewise, a marketer should not lobby a government for preference to the detriment of other actors.

PILLARS OF ETHICAL MARKETING

The pillars of marketing ethics encompass five components (see Figure 8.2): effort, competition, transparency, freedom to choose, and morally responsible conduct. Collectively, these pillars provide a practical framework for guarding the interests of those who are partners in the exchange function and those who might be affected indirectly. Indeed, the first two pillars thrive only when transparent and moral conduct is observed. The meaning and marketing implications for each component are briefly discussed.

Effort

Al Pashehi (2004, p. 418) argued that "Hard work is a blessing, slothfulness is extinction, and laziness is a misfortune." In Chapter 7, it was stated that effort is a cornerstone of the IWE. Effort is seen as the necessary ingredient for acquiring social prestige and confidence, independence, and serving self and society. That is, productive involvement minimizes social and economic problems, while allowing a person to achieve success in life and gain rewards in the hereafter for taking financial care of his family and serving society at large. What is significantly important is that in Islam effort is held in the highest regard. The Quran (53:39) underscores this fact, asserting that "a person can have nothing but what he strives for." The Prophet instructed believers, "Rise early to seek your livelihood and fulfill your aspirations because the effort ensures blessing and success" (quoted in Al-Pashehi, 2004, p. 418). Imam Ali reiterated this when he declared, "Slothfulness opens the door to misery and produces scarcity leading to calamity" (quoted in Al-Pashehi, 2004, p. 418). In marketing, the message is clear: companies should introduce products on a timely basis and customers should be served efficiently. Furthermore, marketing personnel should probe and anticipate market needs, offering products/services that satisfy market demands. In their efforts to supply needed commodities, markets perform not only an economic function but also religious duties. The second Caliph, Omer, underscored the relationship between effort and divine duties when he stated, "There is no place that I prefer to die in other than a place where I engage . . . in buying and selling during my travel" (quoted in Al-Maki, 1995, p. 500). Jasim (1986) argues that whatever serves people serves God. Consequently, the purpose of marketing in Islam should be to meet societal demands and to be in line with societal goals. Serving people in the exchange function, therefore, must be driven by avoidance of deception and cheating, withholding of goods, manipulation of prices, etc.

Competition

While Islam underscores the necessity for competition in the marketplace, it calls for responsible conduct to either prevent or minimize any harm to market participants or society. The Quran (4:29) states, "Eat not up your property among yourselves in vanities, but let there be amongst you trade by mutual good-will" and (2:275) "God hath permitted trade and forbidden usury." In Islam, the whole globe is a market arena for competition and there are no limitations except on prohibited items (e.g., selling and buying alcohol, pork, gambling, etc.) and price manipulation. The Quran (45:13) states, "He [God] has also made subservient to you all that is in the heavens and the earth" and (62:10) "Disperse through the land and seek of the bounty of God." The Prophet acknowledged that through transactions benefits: "Let people transact in the marketplace as it is through transactions they make a living" (quoted in Al-Maki, p. 536).

The Quran encourages competition (*munafasa*) stating literally (83:26), "Let competitors compete." (Note: this is commonly translated as "let those aspire, who have aspirations" by Quranic experts.) Islamic instructions have certain conditions for competition. These are:

1. Competition should ease market transactions rather than lead to monopolies and concentrations of power. According to the Prophet, "Whoever withholds a commodity from the market is a sinner" and "He who brings goods to the market is blessed and the hoarder is cursed" (quoted in Mahmud, 2000, p. 158).
2. There should be no manipulation of prices. The Prophet left that to market conditions. Two sayings attributed to him on this topic are commonly accepted (see Asaf, 1987; Raghib, 1995 for details). These are: "If a buyer has an existing agreement with one seller, another

seller should not ask the buyer to cancel his original agreement, so
that he can sell him his commodities," and "Pricing belongs to God's
domain. He provides and withholds sustenance. Therefore, I shall not
determine pricing for fear that I will be questioned in the hereafter
for possible harm done to any actor in the market." The first saying
applies to a buyer who is about to buy a commodity and is approached
by a rival who offers him better goods at the same or a lower price.
This amounts to not only driving a competitor out of business, but
it is also an unethical act that threatens confidence in market norms
and operations. The second saying has far-reaching implications for
market mechanisms. Not only should the state not intervene under
normal conditions in setting market price (Asaf, 1987, p. 212), but also
the market is the best place, in its absence of manipulation and unre-
strained access, to ensure fairness and justice. That is, the price should
be left to supply and demand in order not to burden either the buyer
or the seller. Imam Ali (1990, p. 638) instructed his governor saying,
"A transaction between a buyer and seller should be one of mutual
consent . . . and the price should be fair to both buyer and seller. If
anyone engages in monopoly after you have warned against it, punish
him, but not excessively." The state, however, may intervene in price
setting in the case of a crisis or when prices skyrocket (Asaf, 1987).
Most scholars agree that any agreement among market actors to raise
prices is outlawed. Ibn Taymiyah (1900, p. 16) argued that if a group
of merchants have a gentlemen's agreement to buy specific items at a
certain price and sell them at more than market price, it is considered
an oppression toward society.

3. Competition should not be used to drive other competitors out of the
    market. It was reported that the second Caliph, Omer, noticed that a
    seller was deliberately lowering his prices and undercutting the prices
    of the rest. He told him: "Either you bring your price up, or leave
    the market" (quoted in Raghib, 1995, p. 344). Dumping, therefore, is
    treated as an act that hurts other rivals and may lead to monopolies.

4. It should serve the public interest. As the Quran (16:90) instructs,
    "God commands justice and *ehsan*" in any transaction, Muslim
    experts agree that competition should aim to enhance the welfare of
    society and set the foundation for just market operations (see Asaf,
    1987; Glaachi, 2000, Ibn Hazm, 1982). This is precisely the reason
    for outlawing hoarding. Hoarding is viewed as an obstruction of
    free market exchange and a manipulation of market function. It not
    only obstructs competition but also harms society and endangers its
    welfare. The Prophet states, "He who brings goods to the market is
    blessed and the hoarder is cursed" and "Shame on the hoarder, when

the price is low he is sad and when it is high he rejoices" (quoted in Glaachi, 2000, p. 16). Abu Talib Al-Maki (1995, died 996, p. 508) recorded that a grain merchant sent a shipment to his agent in Basra, Iraq. He told him that the commodity had to be sold on the day it arrived. The agent consulted with local merchants who told him they expected the price to go up the following Friday. The agent hoarded the shipment and sold it on the Friday, thus doubling the profit. When the agent informed his boss of his activities, the latter was angry and told his agent "You violated our order and committed sin by hoarding . . . give all the amount of the sales to the poor in Basra, as I do not like to be party to hoarding."

5. Competition should lead to improving the quality of products and services. Most Muslim scholars agree that the focus of competition should be on what is good and creates benefits. These scholars argue that "if you buy a commodity, buy the best" (quoted in Al-Maki, p. 523). In the marketplace, rivals should compete to introduce new and better quality goods or services (Asaf, 1987; Raghib, 1995). Like any other activity, competition should have an end game—serving the people.

Transparency

In the marketplace, the transparency issue is essential for marketers to act in ways that maximize benefits and minimize doubt. The Quran (17:35) instructs faithful marketers to be honest and avoid deception: "Give a full measure when you measure out and weigh with a fair balance." The instructions aim to safeguard the interests of market players and build sound foundations for market function. The Prophet and medieval Muslim scholars accentuated the need for transparent market operations, highlighting the spiritual, social, and economic significance and the benefits to the public. It was reported that the Prophet Mohamed once inspected a bin for dates and found that those that were not good were hidden underneath the fresh dates. The Prophet ordered the merchant to differentiate between the quality of the dates saying, "He who cheated us is not one of us" and if buyers and sellers "conceal and tell lies, the blessing of their transaction shall be obliterated." His saying, "Those who declare things frankly will not lead to each other's destruction," underlines the significance of transparency in any business transaction and the necessity for enhancing trust and reducing problems in the marketplace. Transparency has a moral dimension, as it manifests a commitment to the faith. It has, too, an economic dimension. This is because it is based on an understanding that faulty conduct and acts of deception obstruct justice and limit freedom of action in the marketplace. Morally based conduct is an essential precondition for sustaining a prosperous economy and a vital business community. Nasr (1984) asserts that Islam provides a climate of work within which the ethical is not separated from the economic. He argues (p. 35) that Islam bestows "an ethical dimension on all kinds of work and in extending the ethical to include even the qualitative aspect of the work in question."

Abu Talib Al-Maki (1995, p. 509) reported a story which demonstrates that for the faithful transparency in transaction is taken seriously. There was a representative to a sugar merchant who informed his boss that the sugar crop that year was infected with disease. Thus, he urged the merchant to buy a large quantity of sugar and store it. The merchant bought a huge quantity from a supplier. When the time came, the merchant sold the sugar making a 30 000 dirham profit. The next day, the merchant informed the supplier that he had committed a mistake in not revealing to the supplier the complete information before he bought the sugar; that the sugarcane for that season was infected and the price of the sugar in the market would go up. So he requested the supplier to take the whole profit, as it was lawfully his.

Al-Maki (1995, p. 517) argued that a precondition for transparency is for marketers to be selective in engaging in transactions by seeking those who are pious and fear God and that they should ask about those who prefer to deal honestly in order to avoid those who do not mind engaging in prohibited transactions or transactions which are stained with doubt. Transparency, therefore, enables markets to function in an orderly way and minimizes fraudulent operations and market mistakes.

Freedom to Choose

Though the Quran (4:29) instructs believers to engage in commercial activities by mutual consent, the Prophet made it clear that involvement in business transactions should be up to marketers and none should be forced to enter any deal without their consent. He stated, "The buyer and the seller have the option (of cancelling the contract) as long as they have not separated, then if they both speak the truth and make manifest their transaction, it shall be blessed" (quoted in Muhammad Ali, 1977, p. 295). Likewise, the Prophet outlawed any action that seeks to take what rightly belongs to others without the owner's consent stating, "Transaction has to be the result of mutual agreement" (quoted in Al-Hasiany, 2000). A chief minister during the Abbasid era, Ali Ibn Esa, reprimanded one of his officers for interfering in market activities and constraining the free access of people to opportunities. He stated, "It is not permissible for you to prevent them [constituents] from that which they own; do not deny them that which they bought unless they choose to dissolve the buying contract" (quoted in Al-Sabi, 2003, p. 364). Furthermore, Ibn Taymiyah (1900, p. 28) indicated that marketers must not be forced to engage in any transaction, as this represents oppression and transgression. He stated, in the context of selling, "Forcing marketers to sell ... or denying them what is permissible is oppression." The freedom to participate in commercial transactions results in the following: it encourages marketers to engage in business activities to sustain growth, enhances ethical marketing and business ethics, motivates business people to venture outside their territory, safeguards the interests of marketers and the rest of stakeholders, especially in preventing prices from rapid increase, and ensures stability and trust in market functions. Ibn Khaldun (1989), Al-Sabi (2003), and Al-Maqrizi (1999) documented, for example, that when rulers forced merchants to buy goods at higher than market price, the public was harmed and inflation and scarcity of goods became common.

Morally Responsible Conduct

Earlier scholars on Islamic thought made a powerful argument that good ethics leads to prosperity and the fortunes of marketers who are driven by sound ethics multiply. The Prophet stated, "He who is forbearing prospers" (quoted in Al-Mawardi, p. 397) and "God blesses a person who is benevolent when selling and buying" (Al-Qurni, 1987, p. 120). The aforementioned pillars of competition, effort, freedom to choose, and transparency may produce benefits to self and others in the short term. However, their durability without morally guided action is questionable in the long term and may lead to disastrous results. Islamic ethics sharply differ from Protestant ethics in that they do not sanction wealth which is generated through gambling, *riba*, excessive prices, etc.

The ethical dimension of conduct is exemplified in the Islamic view of pricing and profit. While Islam, generally, sanctions prices that are determined freely in the marketplace, under emergency conditions (e.g., food crisis, price manipulation, etc.) and price rocketing, the state is permitted to intervene to temporarily limit prices. There are two considerations, however, that should be kept in mind. The first is related to the quality of product, risk involved in distribution, and distance (Ibn Khaldun, 1989). If the risk is high, the sellers are permitted to charge higher prices to compensate for losses. Likewise, if the country of origin is far, the merchants may find it appropriate to charge a higher price for a product than if it were sold in the home country or nearby cities. As was argued before, Ibn Khaldun made a strong argument that it is more advantageous and more profitable for merchants to bring goods from countries that are far away but it is risky to transport them. This allows merchants to charge higher prices for rare and not commonly available goods. Similarly, the highest quality of any type of goods is demanded by wealthy people who are very few in number. Therefore, the price is normally high relative to the goods which are of "medium quality" and suit the majority of the people.

The second consideration in pricing is related to the logic of *ehsan* and the degree of the seller's observance of the faith. In some cases, even though the competitive market may permit a higher price, a seller, guided by *ehsan*, may consider the state of customers and opt to charge them a price that they can handle. Recently, the *Washington Post* (see Bahrampour, 2010) reported on a Muslim farmer in Virginia who, in raising animals and in setting his prices, was motivated by his faith. The *Post* indicated that the market price for organic non-halal goat meat is anything between $12 and $14 a pound. But the Muslim farmer sold his meat for $3.75 to $4.75 a pound, just like any commercially produced non-organic goat meat. The farmer was quoted saying, "Philosophically speaking, the whole concept is, as social beings we have some responsibility—it's not just cutthroat I'll-make-as-much-as-I can."

The practice of selling goods to the poor and needy at prices lower than current market price was common in many countries with Muslim majorities. This was done before the advent of Western capitalism and the rise of big corporations. However, personal relationships between buyers and sellers and the familiarity of business people with the status of their customers has since rapidly deteriorated. Even in smaller establishments, those who run them are either national citizens or foreign employees who are unfamiliar with the economic status of their buyers and do not have the authority to lower prices when the customer is poor.

As stated in Chapter 4, there is an agreement among scholars that the concept of profit maximization is inconsistent with Islamic ethics (e.g., see Ali, Al-Aali and Al-Owaihan, 2013; Ali, 2005; Raghib, 1995). Imam Ali urged, "Do not discard the low profit margin, so you will not be deprived of more profit" (quoted in Ibn Al-Josie (1995, died 1177). Likewise, a Sufi Muslim, Maruf Al-Karkhi (died 815), called for doing business transactions with little or no profit stating that "Capital grows through transactions (like pastures)" (quoted in Jasim, 1990, p. 83). Moreover, Abu Talib Al-Maki (1995, died 996, p. 500), an Islamic jurist and scholar, stated, "God will bless your wealth though you engage in trade and commerce even without making a profit." Islamic thinking views a moderate profit positively. Ibn Khaldun (2006) suggested that making a little profit per item enables marketers to sell a large volume and, thus, generate a large sum of profit. The preference for a moderate profit in Islamic ethics may stem from two reasons: Islam precepts reflect an abhorrence of greed and a belief that maximization of profit harms society and obstructs the efficiency of the exchange system. The Quran (92:8–11) states, "But he who is a greedy miser and thinks himself self-sufficient . . . [w]e will indeed make smooth for him the path to misery; nor will his wealth profit him when he falls headlong [into the pit]." Greed may harm society when a member of the transaction aspires to charge higher prices or withhold commodities, hoping to accumulate wealth at the expense of others. It leads to injustice and adversely impacts market function. Such action, therefore, violates market trust and ethical principles. Actions inspired by greed weaken trust in business relationships and market institutions. More importantly, as Rice (1999) argued, an obsession with material wealth can obscure the ultimate objective of enriching human lives.

ETHICAL OUTCOMES

It is without doubt that early Muslim scholars thought ethical outcomes in marketing must be those that coincide with the intentions of religious law. The outcomes, however, are not independent of the marketers. Marketers immersed in the general foundations of marketing ethics and the prevailing conditions of morally driven marketing are essential for ethical marketing. It was made clear in the previous chapters that merchants' roles in society are perceived in Islamic teachings as favorable. The merchants were held in esteem as long as they were unwavering in their commitment to safeguarding human interests. Indeed, the teachings of these scholars were decisive in their commitment to safeguarding human interests. The Prophet elaborated on good ethics and generosity in a statement succinctly articulated by Al-Mawardi (2002, p. 384) that can be applied to marketers: "A person with good ethics is one who is tolerant, lenient, of cheerful countenance, patient and can converse courteously." These characteristics, if they are exhibited in the marketplace, undoubtedly lead to desired results.

Marketers who exhibit these characteristics show a commitment to safeguarding human interests. These marketers understand that everything on earth revolves around facilitating the interests and services to mankind and minimizing its burdens. The Quran (67:15) states, "It is He Who has made the earth manageable for you, so traverse ye through its tracts and enjoy of the sustenance which He furnishes" (70:24–5) and "for those with wealth, they have an obligation with that wealth to the petitioner and the deprived"; and (57:7) ". . . spend [in charity] out of [substance] whereof He has made you heirs." According to the Prophet Mohamed, "The best of people are those who benefit others." Similarly, Imam Ali stated, "Do not shy from giving only a little; deprivation is worse" (1990, p. 694).

These are clear instructions with specific implications for the exchange process and marketing functions in particular. Furthermore, safeguarding human interests implies, in Islamic teaching, that mankind are custodians of their surrounding environment. As such, individuals and their organizations must not only be responsible for its well-being but also show an understanding of the linkage between their welfare and the protection of nature—be it earth or atmosphere. Nature is the whole of which people and corporations are a part. Therefore, protecting it is part of the process that furthers people's interests and that of their society.

The aforementioned aspects, along with the pillars of Islamic ethics, set the boundaries for morally accepted transactions and result in contracts which have the following qualities:

1. **Mutual agreement.** There should be no coercion in the transaction. The Quran (4:29) specifies that it must be an outcome of mutual agreement, free of any deception or coercion: "Let there be amongst you trade by mutual good-will."
2. **Contractual.** Contractual agreements are intended so that neither party's rights or duties are overlooked and promises are fulfilled without serious misunderstandings or disagreements. The Quran (2:282) instructs, "To write [your contract] for a future period, whether it be small or big, it is more just in the sight of God, more suitable as evidence, and more convenient to avoid doubts among yourself. But if it be a transaction which ye carry out on the spot among yourselves, there is no blame on you if you reduce it not to writing. But have witnesses whenever ye make a commercial contract and let neither scribe nor witness suffer harm."
3. **Lawful.** The subject of transaction must be lawful (e.g., distributing alcohol, drugs, and gambling are prohibited.). Furthermore, any contract that involves usury is prohibited. The Quran (2:275) states, "Those who devour usury will not stand except as one whom Satan by his touch hath driven to madness. . . . God hath permitted trade and forbidden usury."
4. **Items of the transaction are known to each partner** (Asaf, 1987; Glaachi, 2000). That is, the party to the contract must know exactly what they are embarking on. In the case of purchasing, the Prophet instructs, "He who bought something without having seen it, has the option to reject it after seeing it" (quoted in Asaf, p. 230).
5. **Known and agreed upon price.** The amount of the transaction item should be known to each party. Though under certain conditions the price is left to experts to appraise, the party to the contract has the right to dissolve the contract (see Asaf for detail).

6. **Execution.** The subject of the transaction is deliverable. In the case of selling, the Prophet instructs, "Do not sell that which you do not have" (quoted in Glaachi, 2000, p. 108).

TYPOLOGY OF MARKETERS

Marketers differ not only in their disposition but also in terms of their knowledge of and commitment to marketing ethics, as outlined in the faith. This combined with the existence of powerful temptations in the marketplace make marketing practices vary in terms of their benefits to society and how closely they match religious instructions. Abu Talib Al-Maki (1995, pp. 562–3), using the analogy of pearl divers, grouped marketers into five types. A description of each and the commitment to ethical marketing are outlined below:

1. **One who dives and obtains good quality pearls** (Spiritually Driven Marketer). Those are the blessed marketers who are committed to serving others and observe the prescriptions of their faith. Therefore, they are happy in this life and are blessed in the hereafter. This type of marketer seeks optimizing interactions with other marketers and behaves morally in the marketplace.
2. **One who dives but instead finds stones** (Materialistically Driven Marketers). Those are driven by the interests of this world and are obsessed with material gains rather than spiritual benefits. They might focus on their task but show no concern for ethical standards. Therefore, their activities are likely to offer nothing useful to society. Marketers in this category seek cooperation with other market actors, as long as such activities lead to personal gain and strengthens their position within the company.
3. **One who dives but instead obtains fish** (Thrift Driven Marketers). Those are the marketers who are thrifty. They are not driven by furthering the interests of others and, at the same time, do not purposefully seek to do harm. They are driven by saving as much as they can and helping other marketers or contributing to society is not on their list of priorities.
4. **One who dives deep and drowns** (Ego Driven Marketers). Those are the marketers who are overwhelmed by the interests or the desires of this world. In their work, they seek to reach goals at any expense and are driven by satisfying their desires regardless of consequences. The chance for rethinking their activities and doing good, given their psychological stance, is nil.

Table 8.1   Typology of marketers and differences in selected approaches

Typology	Approach
Spiritually Driven Marketers	Shun greed and personal gains. They seek to optimize relations with the rest of market actors and create an environment of trust and sharing, enjoyment and enthusiasm, while underscoring the essence of cooperation and serving overarching goals.
Materialistically Driven Marketers	Seek cooperation with other market actors and engage in activities if these are thought to lead to material gains and enhance their economic role.
Thrift Driven Marketers	Seek to maintain modesty in spending and engage in cooperation and alliances with other actors if this results in economic savings and avoidance of risky decisions.
Ego Driven Marketers	Seek cooperation and attempt to serve others if these activities put them in the spotlight.
Redemption Driven Marketers	People at this level are sensitive to moral and ethical standards, aware of their weak tendencies, and seek to resist selfish pursuits. They foster cooperation and providing benefits to customers in hope of redemption and spiritual satisfaction.

5. **One who moves up and down on the sea waves** (Redemption Driven Marketers). Those are marketers who seek to do good things; goodness raises them, but old habits of desire toward material gains pulls them back down. They are always in a constant struggle between engaging in good deeds and meeting their desires. Their willingness to observe ethical standards and ask for forgiveness evidences their intention to engage in activities that generate benefits to others.

The above typology illustrates that marketers are different in their orientations and desires and consequently they adopt various approaches in their marketing conduct. Table 8.1 presents such differences. This, however, does not convey that, under different circumstances, these marketers may find themselves contributing differently or their attitudes toward life and others may profoundly change.

CONSUMERISM

Is consumerism sanctioned ethically? Does consumerism serve Islamic marketing and the emphasis on balanced conduct in life and the marketplace? These questions are on the minds of practitioners and researchers. But the answers to these and other related issues are not complex. The rapid rise of consumerism in countries with Muslim majorities has been fueled by globalization, materialism, and the spread of Western ideologies, along with the willingness of new generations to express themselves through conspicuous consumption. Consumerism constitutes a threat to modesty in conduct and in spending. This trend is powerful and attracts consumers from different backgrounds and, thus, the possibility that it will diminish is slim. For example, a study found, in 2006, that the UAE's private consumption by individuals and families on goods and services totaled $84 billion. This represents $19 761 per individual on consumer goods (Glass, 2008). A report by *Aljazeera Net* (2013) documented that in Qatar and the UAE an individual's monthly spending on luxury good exceeds $5000 a month.

Whether consumerism is antithetical to Islamic ethics is a matter that will be debated for years to come. What is certain, however, is that consumerism has already taken root in many countries with Muslim majorities. In many of these countries, not only the oil rich ones, consumerism has attracted various segments of society and has become a means to show social status, acceptance, modernity, and independence among other reasons. Some governments have raised concerns about increasing consumerism. In the UAE, Abu Dhabi's government issued condemnations of corporations for fueling excessive spending stating, "The combination of easy loans in addition to advertising and media propaganda have all combined to plunge consumers into a quagmire of spending sprees" (quoted in Bowmen, 2008). But simply blaming corporations for encouraging consumerism is shortsighted. This is because government policies, the nature of a free market economy, and increasing awareness of market offerings and world connectivity all contribute to enhancing the trend of consumerism.

One of the best policies toward limiting the negative impact of consumerism is to channel consumers' energy and enthusiasm toward consumption that furthers societal interest, individual welfare, and economic development. To achieve a positive outcome, this should be addressed in schools, in homes, and through government direction with reference to Islamic teachings that pertain to avoiding excessive spending, focusing on social issues, and investment in areas that further societal welfare. In Islamic thinking, consumerism takes two forms: conspicuous consumption and buying more than what is needed. Though the difference between the two may seem to be a matter of semantics, in marketing behavior it is not. Conspicuous consumption goes beyond buying more than what is needed. That is, conspicuous consumption is primarily for show and attracting attention. In this context, the individual is either extravagant or buys things that are not needed. In the first case, the individual behaves like an irresponsible market actor and may do more significant harm when squandering wealth than those who buy more than what they need. The latter action might be the result of bad calculation or habit. Indeed, Islamic prescriptions in the Quran and the sayings of the Prophet may be used as reminders and as motivation to participate in activities and functions that lead to enhancing what is good for the society at different stages of development. For example, the Quran (25:67) instructs, "Those who, when they spend, are not extravagant and not niggardly, but hold a just [balance] between those [extreme]" and (7:31) "Waste not by excess, for God loveth not the wasters." These instructions, broadly, outline the moral justifications for prudent spending and responsible market conduct.

Furthermore, the Prophet and early Muslim scholars have articulated the harm of consumerism and the essence of development and investment. The Prophet stated that "He who is prudent in spending will not be dependent on others," while a companion of the Prophet, Abu Al-Drada (died 652) commented, "Proper spending is better than half of your earnings" (quoted in Al-Deinori, 1999, p. 381 and p. 382, respectively). Likewise, Al-Jahiz (1998, p. 26) quoted a Muslim scholar saying, "If you wish to know where a person gets his wealth, look at what he spends his money on, as squanderers engage in excess spending [consumerism]." Al-Maki (1995, p. 382), on the other hand, stated, "He who buys what he does not need, sells what he does need." This means that those who do not give careful consideration to what they should have, end up losing what is important. These sayings, along with the Quranic instructions, articulate that consumerism, as a lifestyle and practice, can harm society and therefore it is considered to be an obstacle for sound economic development. That is, consumerism contradicts responsible conduct and sanctioned behavior in the marketplace.

UNACCEPTABLE MARKETING CONDUCT

There are certain transactions that are outlawed (e.g., trade in alcoholic and pork, gambling, *riba*). These are usually known by marketers and, to a large degree, some of these transactions have been addressed extensively by policy makers, religious scholars, and researchers. There are two types: prohibited and erroneous (Al-Qurni, 1987, p. 103). The first must not take place at all (e.g., trade in alcohol or pork). The second violates certain conditions of the transaction.

Moreover, there are some marketing conducts and practices that have been considered inappropriate, deceptive, or exploitative and thus are prohibited by the Prophet. Some of these are expressed in the examples below:

1. **Deception and or cheating.** The Prophet stated that "He who cheats us is not one of us" and "The buyer and seller have the option (of cancelling the contract) as long as they have not separated. . . . If they conceal and tell lies, the blessing of their transaction shall be obliterated."
2. **Taking of oaths.** The Prophet asserted, "The taking of oaths makes the commodities sell, but it obliterates the blessing."
3. **Approaching suppliers to buy commodities before they get to market.** This applies when suppliers do not have accurate information about either market conditions or current prices. However, it is permissible for individuals to purchase for their immediate needs rather than for reselling (Al-Qurni, 1987).
4. **Selling items which are not yet available.** The Prophet stated, "Whoever buys food shall not sell until he receives them." This requirement is set to avoid conflicts among parties regarding conditions, quality, size, etc. of the commodity and also to prevent speculation.
5. **Hoarding.** The Prophet and his companions instructed marketers not to resort to or engage in hoarding. Hoarding commodities may hurt those who are in need of them or increase prices and manipulate market functions.
6. **False bidding.** That is, a person offers a higher price for an item without a sincere intention to buy but to induce the present buyer to buy the same item, probably at a higher price.
7. **Inducing a buyer to return goods to the seller and to buy the same from someone else.** For example, a seller asking a buyer to return what he bought from another seller, so he can buy his goods.
8. **Transactions that involve uncertainty.** This is called the *Al-Gharar* or something that is uncertain or a risky transaction. For example, selling fish that is not yet caught or fruit that is not yet ripe or in a condition to be consumed.
9. **Performing two transactions in one.** That is, for a seller to say, "I sell you this for $3000 and you sell me what you have for $3000, too" (Al-Qurni, 1987). However, if the sale is deferred or payment is prompt and the parties of the transaction agree on the price and the object, then the transaction is valid.
10. **Selling a debt for a debt.** This prohibition stems from the fact that speculation takes place and one or both parties to the transaction may bear a risk.

11. **Dealing with counterfeit.** Al-Maki (1995, p. 512) argued that spending one counterfeit dirham is more threatening than stealing 100 dirham. The reason is that counterfeit money will circulate for years, while stealing a few dirhams is a one-off illegitimate act.
12. **Transactions that have some elements of doubt.** This is any transaction whose legitimacy might be in doubt. That is, the seller might have stolen the goods, taken bribes, charged *riba*, dealt with oppressors, etc. The doubted area is any area of transaction that lies between what is legitimate and what is prohibited.

The prevalence of the aforementioned examples can be minimized. Muslim scholars have suggested two conditions to reduce engaging in activities that might be considered inappropriate or harmful. These are: marketers must be knowledgeable and an office of market inspector should be established. Each is briefly discussed below.

Knowledgeable Marketer

While Al-Shaybani (1986, p. 41) placed great emphasis on the importance of knowledge in the marketplace to avoid activities that involve *riba* or which are considered false or invalid, Al-Maki elaborated on the significance of market knowledge for marketers. He insisted that market knowledge is important for three reasons: to avoid work that might be contaminated by *riba*, to avoid being trapped into activities that faith, in general, has prohibited, and market knowledge as a foundation for economic development.

Market Inspector (Ombudsman or Muhtasib)

As was discussed in Chapter 3, the Abbasid Caliph, Al-Mustershid, instructed his chief justice regarding the role of the market supervisor, the *Muhtasib*, stating, "give adequate consideration to the function of market supervision, as it represents the greater public interest by offering wider comprehensive benefits to the people: protecting their wealth, organizing their affairs in an orderly manner, and swiftly dealing with sources of corruption." Thus, the job of *Muhtasib* constitutes a significant one for ensuring social and economic justice and furthering the interests of citizens. Ibn Taymiyah (1900) argued that the role of a *Muhtasib* is much broader than simply supervising market activities, which includes anything under "Promotion of Virtue and the Prevention of Vice." This argument, nevertheless, can be misused in practice, as it goes beyond the marketplace to include personal and worldly affairs.

APPLICATIONS AND IMPLICATIONS

One of the primary concerns of Islamic business ethics, including marketing, is societal welfare. Indeed business ethics provides a useful framework that guides marketers in their market engagements and thus acts as a safeguard for market functions and processes. While marketing ethics prohibits deception and cheating, it highlights that those who are committed to principled conduct are blessed in their activities and rewarded in the hereafter. Marketing ethics prohibits deception in advertising and exaggerating benefits, characteristics, or qualities of a commodity. The sellers are held responsible for any trickery or unfounded claims. Unlike prevailing market ethics in some Western countries, which endorse profit maximization and drive competitors out of business, Islamic ethics do not condone such intentional and deliberate actions. Transparent and cooperative operations are encouraged and harm done to any market actor is considered to be immoral conduct.

According to business ethics, firms are primarily social and economic actors that gain their legitimacy from optimally serving societal interests and evolving needs. It is this legitimacy that allows organizations to compete, create value, and grow. In fact, adhering to general instructions of avoiding deception, cheating, and manipulating the public situates firms as responsible players in the marketplace and the society. That is, from an Islamic perspective, firms have obligations toward society and meeting these obligations enhances their reputation and ultimately strengthens their survival and competitive position. Indeed, as firms shun deception and are transparent, they not only minimize their overall transaction cost but also engage their suppliers, customers, and even competitors in matters that have both organizational and societal benefits.

Business ethics has a wide range of implications in the marketplace. Some of these implications are presented in Table 8.2. In presenting these implications, the intention is to underscore what is relevant and common. In particular, we cover issues which have either specific marketing implications (e.g., usury, bribery, consumerism, profit margin, etc.) or those which are general in their meaning but have far-reaching impact on the position of the firm in the marketplace (e.g., transparency, competition, cheating, truthfulness, etc.).

The listed selected ethical dimensions and their implications underscore the fact that the marketing function and process are an integral part of an organization and its goal for enhancing survival and growth, while serving societal goals and meeting emerging needs. That is, ethical conduct sends a clear message to stakeholders that societal goals and priorities are a strategic concern for their company. More importantly, commitment to ethical conduct manifests a moral stance where a company views its employees

Table 8.2   Selected ethical issues and their marketing implications

Category	Implications
Profit Margin	A moderate profit benefits the company and does not inflict harm on society; excessive profit manifests greed and limits its market.
Usury	Avoid issues related to imposing interest in any transaction; alternatives exist and should be discussed with experts before selecting any of them.
Consumerism	A drive to maintain balanced tendencies; maintain modesty in spending, according to Quranic instructions, and direct spending in areas which have the greatest value to the greatest number of people.
Bribes	Prohibited religiously; avoidance is a virtue.
Dealing in Counterfeit	A menace to society's well-being and a squandering of the national wealth.
Generosity	Products should be marketed in different variations to satisfy customers with varying income levels, utilize discount policies, and offer free samples and lower prices to those who are less fortunate.
Deception	Fraudulent activities weaken confidence in market institutions and may result in market turmoil.
Transparency	Openness and truthfulness enhances customer loyalty and marketers' reputation. More importantly, transparency strengthens confidence in market institutions.
Promises	Fulfilling obligations or promises in the marketplace on a timely basis eases market function, trust among marketers, strengthens formal and informal networks, and increases confidence in market institution transactions.
Competition	Avoid destructive approaches and those which drive rivals out of business; cooperative competition serves as a protective mechanism for market function.
Efforts	Commitment to contractual agreements, meeting promotional promises, and reciprocating offers.
Moral Responsibility	Commitment to the welfare of the society is not divorced from commitment to safeguarding the environment and the welfare of the company.

and customers equally as citizens, and their desires and aspirations are considered in marketing planning and execution.

Table 8.3 presents the implications for specific marketing issues and other related elements. The implications of these issues highlight that *ehsan* is a philosophy which is assumed to permeate all organizational activities.

Table 8.3   Selected marketing elements and their implications

Elements	Implications
Price	Should take into consideration the risk involved, geographic distance, season, and quality. Executives should consider the welfare of the community and market conditions in setting prices.
Hoarding	He should avoid it, as it is not looked on favorably; hoarding for personal use is permitted.
Product	Avoid dealing with a prohibited product. Quality should be satisfactory to a wide range of the population.
Transaction in Stolen or Confiscated Commodities	Encourages violation of property rights, legitimizes unlawful operations, and spreads confusion and doubt.
Buyer beware	A deceptive approach that burdens customers and society; marketers should avoid it, as it increases mistrust among market players and weakens market institutions.
Value creation	Delivering new products, finding new applications, improving quality, etc. all serve as instruments for positioning a firm competitively.
Promotion	Avoid exaggeration or claims that are difficult to prove.
Place	Transactions should take place in the market and be documented.

For example, pricing policies may differ due to various factors but should not hurt either the seller or the buyer. Ibn Taymiyah (1900, died 1328, p. 14) stated, "Forcing sellers, without sound reason, to sell at an unfavorable price or prohibiting them from that which God has made permissible is religiously unacceptable." This applies, too, to marketing confiscated or stolen commodities. Not only are the rights of owners violated but also such actions increase risk and uncertainty among marketers. In Islamic ethics, marketers must make sure that items of transaction are within the permissible boundaries. This, therefore, requires from them additional resources or collected information to prevent any wrongdoing and avoid doubt. The same can be said regarding transactions in counterfeit items, as deception in marketing is prohibited and the negative consequences will linger over many years. More importantly, these examples deny the rights of marketers the fruits of their efforts and make free transactions and mutual agreements an impossible task. Not only are public interests ignored, but *ehsan* and commitment to the well-being of members of society are neglected.

While pricing policies are set independent of the government and according to market mechanisms, such policies must be set to further the interests of society and must not have any element of exploitation. Sellers and buyers must mutually agree on prices without manipulation of market function or any marketers. Likewise, promotion should revolve around upholding the truth, while advancing the corporate goals in the marketplace. In other words, in line with Quranic (2:83) instructions, "Speak fair to the people," marketers in their advertising, sales promotions, and packaging activities should neither make false claims nor should they inflate the quality or the safety standard of their products. They should, too, give buyers the opportunity to make their own minds up without undue pressure.

One common marketing concept and practice in Western society that is sanctioned by Christianity and Judaism is "buyer beware". This concept was prohibited as a practice by the Quran and the Prophet was clear in outlawing it. The concept does not fit within the Islamic business ethics framework and with general instructions in life which condemn deception, cheating, and lack of transparency. Four reasons exist for this. First, the underlying assumption of buyer beware implies that deception is not only a possibility, but a normalcy of market operation. Second, the prohibition of this concept stems primarily from the fact that it shifts the responsibility of inspection from the producer or supplier to the buyer or customer. That is, acting on this concept leads to a hidden cost and essentially creates formidable obstacles to free and fair market practice. In fact, the concept implies that a competitive environment is inclined toward corruption and abuse. Third, dubious activities are considered obstructive for fruitful trade and legitimate business. Four, the practice of the concept is situated in the prohibited doubtful arena. Any doubtful transaction of this kind implies deception and lack of sincerity and has an element of the "unknown," and is, therefore, prohibited. Thus, marketers must have the knowledge required to differentiate between the permissible and the prohibited. This necessitates that they must be more careful than other social actors to avoid any hint of doubt in transactions.

Other important dimensions identified both in Tables 8.2 and 8.3, such as profit margins, generosity, consumerism, and competition, set Islamic ethics apart from what prevails in some Western countries. Profit maximization is not sought. Rather, a modest profit is thought better to serve self and society. Likewise, generosity implies that parties to a contract should go beyond what is specified in the contract to ensure *ehsan* and harmonious relations. For example, in the service contract the provider often performs additional services free of charge. The Quran (64:16) declares, "And those saved from the covetousness of their own souls—they are the ones who achieve prosperity." In recent years, some Christian and Jewish scholars have reached the conclusion that excessive profit or profit maximization may not fit well with the principles of the two religions. Unfortunately, such thinking is not yet widely accepted.

Traditionally, the marketplace has been a designated public arena where exchange functions are performed and or sales are set up. However, modern developments in technology now make virtual markets not only a possibility but also a necessity. In fact, the flourishing of e-marketing in the world, including in countries with Muslim majorities, has opened new avenues for marketers. Marketers, however, should still observe the aforementioned morally accepted transaction elements. That is, whether on the Internet or in a designated open area, market transactions should be carried out according to sanctioned ethical norms.

While Islamic ethics sanctions free market principles, they place limitations on behaviors which are perceived to be destructive both to market actors and society at large. Competition in the Quran is treated as an instrument to inspire and energize rather than frustrate and destroy. Likewise, marketers have to take note that in Muslim societies, customers react favorably to messages and advertisements that underscore societal norms and the contributions of corporations to the community. This, along with the perception that firms create value to society, constitutes a social capital essential for positioning the company strategically.

CONCLUSION

In this chapter, Islamic marketing ethics and precepts are examined. First, the chapter addresses general issues that marketers should be familiar with. It covers the nature of marketing and defines marketing ethics. In order to present a concise and practical, yet conceptual, understanding of marketing ethics, a framework is developed. This framework not only identifies the foundations, but also specifies elements of ethical marketing and its pillars.

The chapter provides a detailed reflection on early Islamic scholars' treatment of marketing and marketers' responsibilities. This reflection not only addresses how marketers should behave, but also what is expected of them in the marketplace. The significance of marketing, therefore, is articulated.

This chapter also underscores the linkage between cultural ethics and marketing. Indeed, marketing functions are characteristically linked and associated with prevailing cultural norms and values. The more widely and deeply held these values and norms are (e.g., elements of *ehsan*, prohibition of usury, etc.), the more they shape marketing expectations and conduct. As members of a society become more aware and sensitive to their cultural values and identity with them, the more they expect organizations to market goods and services that conform to their beliefs.

In the previous discussion, it was stated that the marketplace is full of temptations and that marketers may easily be enticed and trapped. The chapter identified such risks and discussed how marketers should avoid such pitfalls. In addition, this chapter categorized marketers into four groups: Spiritually Driven, Materialistically Driven, Thrift Driven, Ego Driven, and Redemption Driven Marketers. Implications for such groups were provided. Furthermore, elements of marketing were identified and implications were illustrated. Most importantly, the chapter discussed the several aspects of marketing that are relevant to today's practices, including counterfeiting and buyer beware. These are contrasted with contemporary practices, especially in the West.

In conclusion, this chapter presents the argument that Islamic ethics provides a practical framework for guarding the interests of those who are partners in the exchange function and those who might be indirectly affected. It elaborates on issues that are essential for the welfare of society and for economic progress, while underscoring the need for morally driven conduct by marketers to do their best to serve their organization and society.

9. Ethics and human resource management in modern organizations

Whether in traditional or contemporary societies, human resource (HR) issues have topped the list of decision makers' priorities. In the early years of Islam, these concerns centered on building a vital state, informing the public of their duties and rights, and responding to the needs of a growing constituency. As the state expanded and covered new geographical areas, the emphasis was on selecting qualified people and cultivating their skills to perform their duties, act ethically, and promote social and economic justice. In selecting subordinates, the second Caliph, Omer, instructed them to be fair to the people: "Judge among them according to what is right and divide wealth among people justly . . . and do not deny them their rights" (quoted in Al-Mawardi, 1986, p. 353). The fourth Caliph, Imam Ali (1990, p. 625), advised one of his deputies not to listen to a subordinate who is "a miser who attempts to prevent you from spending what is beneficial to others . . ., nor [to] a coward who is never decisive, nor [to] a greedy man who presents injustice as a necessity." During these years, rules governing HR issues were either informal or were found in treatises written for rulers or merchants.

The advent of the Industrial Revolution and the dominant role that the private sector has since played in the world economy has shaped HR policies and practices. This development has engulfed all countries, including those with Muslim majorities. In almost all countries, the scarcity or abundance of skilled resources, along with the nature of market structure and competition, has highlighted the necessity of competing effectively in the marketplace. The issue of organizational survival and growth has been closely linked to effective HR management. Indeed, the interweaving of HR policies with organizational strategic initiatives has been reinforced as market competition has intensified at national and global levels. Capitalistic driven HR issues have challenged traditional organizational concepts and practices in countries which were, for many decades, not a part of the global capitalism system. In particular, traditional societies, since the middle of the twentieth century, have experienced increasing

economic pressures to accelerate their adaptation to the pillars of capitalism and thus organizations in these nations have had to reshape their goals
and priorities in line with the Western system.

Among these nations, countries with Muslim majorities have faced the
challenge of adaptation to Western management practices, while attempting to observe and maintain religious prescriptions and norms. In particular, the challenge has been exemplified in terms of HR practices. In the
Western world, scientific management practices set the foundations for a
work sphere where boundaries are clearly defined with articulated tasks
and rules. Only very recently have some corporations begun to reconsider
the spiritual dimension of work. This is not the case in many countries
with Muslim majorities (CMM) where, according to religious instruction,
spiritual guidelines are the foundations for personal and organizational
conduct. Since the majority of CMM societies have adopted the capitalism
system, a conflict between economic reality and religious instruction has
been brought forth.

In this chapter, HR issues in the context of Islamic prescriptions are
delineated with an extensive reference to the Quran and the teachings of
the Prophet Mohamed and early Muslim philosophers. The application
by and implications for modern organizations are specified and possible
contradictions are highlighted. As in previous chapters, references to two
other monotheistic religions—Christianity and Judaism—are made. This
is because the three religions share a common root and commercial interaction among their respective communities has intensified in recent decades
making it imperative to highlight their business prescriptions. Likewise,
contemporary HR theory and practices have their roots in countries where
Christianity is the dominant religion. Accordingly, the perspective of other
religions on HR is needed as business becomes highly globalized. The
chapter addresses, too, whether or not Islamic HR norms are relevant to
modern organizations. Most importantly, the chapter challenges researchers and practitioners to rethink their existing perceptions of HR and offers
insights necessary for safeguarding human dignity without compromising
the concerns of organizations and societies.

Primarily, the chapter surveys Islamic texts and treatises and compares
certain elements with Christian and Jewish instructions. Furthermore, the
chapter surveys HR practices in certain Muslim countries and examines
them in terms of Islamic prescriptions. Along with the introduction and
conclusion, the content of this chapter is viewed in terms of the ethical
framework presented in Chapter 1.

ISLAMIC LOGIC AND HR PRACTICES

In Chapter 7, the logic and dimensions of work were addressed. The spiritual, social, and economic dimensions of work stress that able individuals should engage in work and have an occupation. The emphasis on the divine aspect of work situates HR policies as central to motivating workers/employees and enhancing their engagement in productive economic activities. This is because, in Islam, work and knowledge are preconditions for true faith (Al-Maki, 1995). Furthermore, HR policies must be based on the two logics, *ehsan* and moderation. The first, *ehsan*, as shown in this chapter, ensures that policies are designed to advance the well-being of employees, while attempting to effectively meet the desired organizational goals. The underpinning of *ehsan* is that everything in the universe derives its legitimacy from facilitating the interaction and growth of human beings. The latter sets the stage for understanding the nature of labor relations and interaction at work.

In the workplace, the second logic or moderation involves three primary aspects. First, it seeks to have policies that are free of oppression and that contain motivational elements that lift the spirit of employees and reinforce their commitment to the organization. That is, moderation conveys the interweaving responsibilities of employers and employees. Employers have responsibilities toward their employees, while employees should act with sincere effort to meet their obligations toward achieving organizational goals. Second, moderation implies that both employers and employees are transparent in their interactions and relationships. The Prophet Mohamed's saying: "*Al-Din Al-maamala*," (Religion is found in the way of dealing with other people), though the meaning is broad, has far-reaching implications for setting HR policies. And, third, moderation assumes that efforts are made not to waste or squander resources.

Labor issues are an integral part of human relations and, by necessity, manifest prevailing cultural and societal norms. In CMM countries, cultural values and beliefs have been profoundly shaped by Islamic teachings and principles. Due to the presence of strong traditions and a commonality in uttering Quranic verses and the Prophet's sayings in public, individuals have developed, since early childhood, an awareness of and sensitivity to what is socially and religiously sanctioned. In the workplace, therefore, both *ehsan* and moderation are taken for granted. However, in most cases, efforts are made by corporations to give the impression that these pillars are not consciously and intentionally violated. This is especially prevalent among those who have no intention of applying their faith principles. For example, in Qatar, Amnesty International (2013) reported that "many migrant workers are being ruthlessly exploited, deprived of their pay and left struggling to survive."

In the workplace, these relationships and interactions are primarily personal, inclusive, span class and race considerations, and are expected to be flexible and broad in their application. The Quran (49:13) states, "The noblest of you in the sight of God is the best of you in conduct." The Prophet Mohamed underscored this when he defined the obligation of the faithful in terms of their relationship to others and as a responsibility to "feed [the poor] and offer salutation to whom thou knowest and whom thou dost not know." Human considerations, therefore, in the workplace, take priority in matters related to recruitment, treatment of employees, and conditions in the workplace. The latter brings to mind the work conditions in the garment industry in Bangladesh. The collapse of the Rana Plaza factory building in 2013, which led to the death of more than 1100 workers, demonstrates that those in positions of power neither follow religious prescriptions nor do they have policies that correspond to the HR policies that prevail in some Western countries.

Furthermore, Islamic teaching prohibits discrimination among people. In the marketplace, this is translated as inclusiveness and equal treatment of all, regardless of their backgrounds. The Quran (49:13) explains, "O mankind! We created you from a single [pair], male and female, and made you into nations and tribes that you might know each other." And the Prophet in his last sermon reminded people: "An Arab has no superiority over a non-Arab nor a non-Arab any superiority over an Arab; also a white has no superiority over a black nor a black any superiority over white, except by piety and good action." The fourth Caliph, Imam Ali (1990, p. 622), succinctly stated the essence of equality when he wrote, "They [people] are either brothers in religion or equals in creation," and they (p. 639) "have equal rights irrespective of where they reside, whether in your vicinity or far away." These prescriptions are normative, but their application in the workplace may vary considerably. Nevertheless, their observation could make the application of diversity easier and ensure that work relationships are governed by fair access to power and authority.

One of the most important aspects of *ehsan* is generosity at work. In this context, *ehsan* takes on the meaning of *sedakah*; commonly referred to as charity but signifying any sincere or beneficial deed, making it much broader than charity. The term is a derivative of *sedak* (truth) or righteousness. As in Judaism, in the general context of *sedakah*, it is assumed that employers and employees will treat each other with kindness, sincerity, and responsibility beyond what is specified in the contract and the boundaries of work. This means that either party, but mostly those who are in charge, should go beyond the letter of the religious law in their generosity and in providing assistance to employees. While both Islam and Judaism place considerable emphasis on *sedakah*, in Islam it has two forms—obligatory and voluntary. The two forms of *sedakah* are specified in the Quran (9:60): "Charity is only for the poor and the needy, the collectors appointed for its collection, those whose hearts incline to truth, the ransoming of a captive, those in debt, and for the way of God and for the wayfarer; a duty ordained by God." In regard to the obligatory monetary aspect, only people who can afford it are expected to contribute.

The broader meaning of *sedakah*, as outlined in Chapter 4, was articulated by the Prophet Mohamed. This broader meaning emphasizes that *sedakah* is obligatory for every Muslim, whether in monetary or non-monetary terms, and is morally binding.

While *sedakah*, in a monetary sense, can be a form of obligatory legal duty collected by a government official, this is not part of the domain of this chapter. It is the morally binding form which is applicable to HR management (for details see Chapter 10) that concerns us. Without overlooking the fact that a person's commitment to the moral form of *sedakah* is a matter of personal choice and that people differ in their inclinations and behavior, this form, in a broader application, has wide-ranging implications for HR practices and organizational activities. Doing good deeds in the performance of duties, lifting the spirits of co-workers, providing training to those who are in need, and avoiding any harmful act either toward the organization or fellow workers represents broader guidelines which, if observed, could transform organizational culture into a strong one and considerably ease understanding between management and employees, thereby setting the stage for a productive and safe workplace.

ETHICAL CONSIDERATIONS IN HR

As stated above, developing nations including CMM societies have experienced profound economic, technological, and political changes and, with no exception, these countries have espoused, in varying degrees, the capitalistic system. Likewise, at the socio-cultural level, these countries have exhibited collectivistic orientations or values. These values change more slowly than business ideology—economic, political, and technological (Ali, 2005; Ralston, 2008). In developing countries, in general, socio-cultural and business ideological influences may be in conflict with one another, resulting in the development of new and unique value systems among individuals (Ralston, 2008). Ralston labeled this perspective *crossvergence*. This perspective postulates that as countries espouse a form of capitalism, depending on their specific experiences, business related values change more rapidly than core social values and a contradiction between socio-cultural orientations and business related ideology takes place. The depth of such conflict varies among CMM societies. For example, Saudi Arabia has been successful in adopting global capitalism but, so far, has managed to keep the demands of capitalism and social values in check. On the other hand, the political upheaval in Tunisia, in 2011, manifested a failure of the political system to align the requirements of capitalism with social values and beliefs. This led to the resentment of the youth, who objected to the increasing inequality gaps between rich and poor.

In the remainder of this chapter, issues of recruitment, selection, compensation, performance evaluation, and training and development are addressed. Though these issues are covered from a normative or prescriptive aspect, a reference is made to prevailing HR practices. The objective is to demonstrate whether or not HR practices correspond to Islamic instructions. Many CMM countries have merged in the global capitalism system. Nevertheless, their exposure and adaptation of Western HRM differ. This is because many of them have purposefully sought to project modernity (adoption of Western business) and religiosity in their affairs. Accordingly, CMM societies have espoused various HRM models and these models have evolved to reflect not only their own unique evolution but also their relations and experience with the colonial powers. That is, these models reflect the distinct historical contexts within which they have developed (Budhwar and Mellahi, 2006) and appear to confirm the crossvergence perspective. Furthermore, even in countries like Malaysia, which have purposely attempted to reinvigorate an Islamic approach in the conduct of business and government, many employees are not sure about Islamic HRM (Hashim, 2009), while Western HRM practices are widely adopted in varying degrees in that country (Chew, 2005). The diversity and plethora of HR models makes it difficult to thoroughly and adequately investigate them in light of Islamic prescriptions and condoned actions. However, since most CMM societies claim to follow Islamic prescriptions, a look at HRM issues from an Islamic perspective provides insight into their claims and the ethics that govern their HR practices.

There are four issues that should be pointed out: labor theory of value, labor contract, a supervisor's responsibility toward actions committed by subordinates, and work as a moral obligation. Unlike Judaism, which does not have a labor theory of value (Van Burns, 1999, p. 337), or Christianity, which initially did not address it, Islamic thinkers developed their own theory of labor. Building on Islamic instructions, Ibn Khaldun (1332–1406), the medieval Arab sociologist, argued (1989, p. 238), "Civilization and its well-being, as well as business prosperity, depends on productivity and people's efforts in all aspects for their own interest and profit. When people no longer do business in order to make a living, and when they cease all gainful activity, the business of civilization slumps and everything decays." He asserted that labor is the source of value, stating (2006, pp. 225–6):

> One of the greatest injustices and contributors to the destruction of civilization is coercing subjects to perform against their will and compelling them into forced labor. . . . This is because labor is the factor that generates sustenance and wealth. Their efforts and economic activities generate capital and the means to make a living; indeed these are a way for them to obtain wealth. Those subjects who have skills essential for development, their income is the outcome of their labor. Thus, if they are compelled to perform activities unrelated to their professions and are used as forced labor, they are denied the rights to make a profit and are deprived of the value of their labor, which is their capital, thus, inflicting on them unbearable harm.

The above quotation demonstrates how early Islamic thinking situated workers at the center of economic activities and acknowledged that without them there would be no value or wealth creation and the prosperity of the society would be jeopardized. The quotation, too, highlights the issue of the labor contract in its emphasis that workers must not be forced to carry out duties against their wishes. The contract, however, does not need to be detailed. That is, the contract may be brief and often it will not cover all elements of entitlements and obligations. Nevertheless, Islam makes it obligatory that economic relationships and market engagement are written down so that neither party's rights or duties are overlooked and promises are fulfilled without serious misunderstandings or disagreements. The Quran (2:282) instructs, "To write [your contract] for a future period, whether it be small or big, it is more just in the sight of God, more suitable as evidence, and more convenient for avoiding doubts among yourself. But if it be a transaction which ye carry out on the spot among yourselves, there is no blame on you if you reduce it not to writing. But have witnesses whenever ye make a commercial contract and let neither scribe nor witness suffer harm." Therefore, it is preferable to put into writing any commercial contract, irrespective of its amount or significance. In contractual matters which are undertaken spontaneously, witnesses may be sufficient. Nevertheless, the Quran instructs that, in either case, the parties involved must act on their promises. The Quran (2:177) orders the faithful, "Fulfill the contracts which ye have made." As stated in Chapter 3, there are four qualities for any contract: easy to execute, articulated content that minimizes hesitation, free of ill feelings that may result in backbiting, and free of deception and cunning.

The requirements for labor contracts and the expectations of both the employees and employers, though generally governed by *ehsan*, are outlined in different treatises and commentaries. Nevertheless, there are three preconditions for any labor contract to be valid: the legal contracting age, consent, and contract subject (type of work) must not violate Islamic law (e.g., no gambling, production of alcohol, etc.). The obligations of the employer (see Asaf, 1987) include the advance agreement of the wage and pay schedule, showing goodness to workers and treating them with dignity, enabling workers to perform their tasks without undue burden, and providing adequate instruction. Many organizations in the Muslim world, especially in the public sector, are officially obliged to meet such guidelines. However, in the case of subcontractors performing work for a government and in the private sector, there is often widespread deviation. For example, in Qatar, Amnesty International (2013) reported, "Behind the often complex contractual chains linked to employment in Qatar lie the widespread and routine abuse of migrant workers—in some cases amounting to forced labour." Likewise, the Human Rights Watch (2013) reported that in the Arab Gulf region "Migrant workers in these countries typically have their passports confiscated and are forced to work under the highly exploitative *kafala* system of sponsorship-based employment, which prevents them from leaving employers. Employers are rarely, if ever, prosecuted for violations of labor law. As a result, migrant workers in the Gulf frequently experience hazardous working conditions, long hours, unpaid wages, and cramped and unsanitary housing."

Most Muslim policy makers and philosophers in the first six centuries of Islam placed strong emphasis on employees' obligations toward their superiors or employers. The emphasis primarily focused on giving advice, sincerity in performing duties, defending their superiors and not revealing their secrets. The second Caliph, Omer, stated, "The closest person to me is the one who pointed out to me my weaknesses" (quoted in Al-Suyuti, 1996, p. 110). Al-Mawardi (2002, p. 227) underscored three duties toward the superior: sincere obedience, unwavering support, and loyalty. These obligations were formulated in the language of that period and were no different from other terminologies found in other societies, be they governed by Christianity, Hinduism, Judaism, etc. What makes the difference in a society with a Muslim majority is that the concept of *ehsan* should govern the relationship between employers and employees and, thus, constitutes a foundation for action and behavior.

In an organizational setting, a superior cannot abandon responsibility for the wrongdoings of his/her subordinates. This aspect is important for enhancing the bond between stakeholders and a superior. It motivates a superior to take the necessary steps to ensure that corruption and unethical conduct are not tolerated. Most importantly, it induces a superior to be careful in selecting individuals who are known for their decency, foresight, and qualifications. The second Caliph, Omer, stated, "If any deputy committed injustice against someone and I learned about it and did not reverse it, then it is me who committed the oppression" (quoted in Ibn Al-Josie, 1995, vol. 4, p. 138). The fourth Caliph, Imam Ali (1990, p. 637), in his instructions to his governor in Egypt stated, "Put in charge of each division of your government a person who is highly qualified, willing to confront difficult issues and is not intimidated by a diversity of tasks. Any misdeed committed by your employees which you ignore, that fault is your own responsibility."

The fourth aspect, work as a moral obligation, implies that employees have to take their responsibilities seriously. They have a commitment not only toward their organizations, but also to society. This moral obligation includes, among many others, avoiding fraudulent activities, receiving gifts, or abusing public property.

Since the avoidance of corruption is dealt with extensively in this book, the issue of employees receiving gifts deserves some attention. Employees are not allowed to receive gifts for carrying out duties that they are hired to perform. The ethical reasoning for this prohibition is the fear that receiving gifts may corrupt employees, who receive gifts because of their positions, and lead to employees ignoring their normal duties. Most importantly, only able and rich people can easily give gifts. This may result in the affairs of the poor being ignored; thus, injustice will thrive. Therefore, gifts should be treated as part of public wealth or treasure. Ibn Al-Jawzi (vol. 4, p. 139) indicated that when Omer's wife received gifts from the Roman Palace he turned them over to the public treasury. Likewise, Caliph Omer stated, "Beware of Gifts" (quoted in Al-Deinori, 1999, p. 94). In terms of public wealth, the first two Caliphs and the fourth one were careful not to take anything from the public treasury or give access to members of their families to public wealth. The first Caliph, Abu Baker, asked the senior Muslims to give him wages that would meet the bare necessities of life. The second Caliph, Omer, was given only two dirhams a day (see Al-Andelesy, 1996, vol. 4, p. 257). The fourth Caliph, Ali, not only lived like a very poor person, but used to light only two candles at night when receiving people. If a visit related to state matters, then he lit the state candle. But if the conversation turned into personal affairs, he lit his own indicating that he would not use public funds for personal matters.

Despite the prohibition on giving gifts to expedite business processes, in most MCC societies gifts are customarily given. Likewise, in some MCC societies, rulers have difficulties in differentiating between their own wealth and that of the state's. Even in the private sector, where some corporations are no longer family businesses, senior executives behave as if the corporation is their own property. This is mostly attributed to the personalism (see Chapter 5) aspect that governs relationships among people, be it in their personal or business interactions. MNCs working in MCC societies should have certain policies in place to minimize the abuse of organizational property and the habit of gift giving. This has been made possible in recent years, as many governments have started to view gift giving as a form of bribery.

SELECTED HR FUNCTIONS

In Table 9.1, some issues pertaining to HR are outlined. However, a more detailed discussion of selected issues is provided below. The discussion focuses on ethical conduct in the context of the major functions of HR management. These functions are addressed with specific emphasis on the normative or religious prescriptions and their practice in or relevancy to today's organizations. Two aspects are highlighted: the ethical dimension and practical implications for HR management.

Recruitment

The process of identifying and attracting qualified personnel in early Islamic teaching was not articulated in detail. Rather, like any general function at the time, it was addressed in a broad framework where freedom of discretion and exercising of judgment were emphasized. The Prophet Mohamed's statement, "We do not or shall not employ a person who desires to be so appointed" (Muhammad Ali, 1977) served as a guideline for HR practice under his administration. It implies that people should be recruited not just because they asked for a job but rather there should be a recruitment pool from which vacant jobs are filled. More importantly, recruitment, during his administration, was marked by diversity, as reflected in the Prophet Mohamed appointing officers from those who had joined his movement earlier (emigrants) and those who supported him at a later stage (*ansar*).

In modern organizations, the recruitment process is highly complex. In Saudi Arabia, despite the fact that there are certain jobs that are reserved for a specific group by birthright (e.g., all governors of the 13 administrative regions must come from the Al-Saudi clan; senior jobs in most business firms are reserved for family members), there is a law which regulates recruitment. For example, the Labor Law of 2005, Article 25 mandates that firms must send to the labor office:

1.   A statement of vacancies and new jobs, their types, locations, wages, and required qualifications within 15 days of the date of vacancy or creation of a job to a government labor office.
2.   A notice of steps taken to employ nationals suggested by the employment unit within seven days of receiving the nomination letter.

Table 9.1   Human resources issues and their organizational meanings

HR Issue	Organizational Prescriptions
Recruitment	Organizations should identify and attract qualified personnel; there should be a recruitment pool from which vacant jobs are filled; and diversity is a virtue.
Selection	Should be based on competency, experience, shouldering of responsibility, organizational fit, and reputation within the community.
Diversity	Making sure that religious prescriptions against discrimination are observed and that employees are hired based on their qualifications.
Compensation	Must be based on contractual agreement, differ according to expertise and situation, be determined in advance, and wages must be given immediately once work is completed, this can be either cash and/or in kind, should be increased according to circumstances, sufficient to provide a decent living, prevent corruption, and maintain safety and security.
Rewards	Must be linked to performance and behavior, reinforce good deeds, be ethically driven, can be either monetary or non-monetary or both, and should not generate ill feelings among subordinates.
Benefits	These should be provided to provide protection to employees, such as insurance, pension, vacation time, etc.
Training and Development	A morally anchored and performance-based evaluation aims to allow employees to consider their performance in line with their contribution to their organizations and society; individuals are endowed with varying capacities to learn and develop; knowledge and experiences are essential for individual growth and utilization of potential.
Performance Evaluation	Should be driven by the logic of *ehsan* and based on what was done rather than claimed. The latter should be investigated and fraudulent activities dealt with on a timely basis.
Cultivation and Retention of Talent	Essential policies for attracting and rewarding talent to further the interests of an organization and create an environment of professional growth and development.

3. A list of names, jobs, professions, wages, nationalities of workers, numbers and dates of work permits for non-citizens and other related information required by the law.
4. A report on the status, conditions, and nature of work, and the anticipated increase or decrease in jobs during the year following the date of the report.

The Law specifies, too, that firms must have prior approval and a valid license before engaging in recruitment. This applies both to the recruitment of citizens and of foreign personnel. Furthermore, the Law outlines requirements for recruiting nationals and the steps that must be taken to obtain work permits for non-citizens. In terms of recruitment, both government agencies and private firms utilize various means, including media advertising—newspapers and TV—employment agencies, recruitment agencies, colleges, word of mouth, the Internet, and referrals. Employment agencies specialize in finding jobs primarily for citizens. On the other hand, recruitment agencies specialize in recruiting workers from abroad. The latter is a huge and thriving business where these agencies obtain licenses from the government for arranging work for employees from Asia and many other countries. Similarly, word of mouth is utilized by citizens and non-citizens. Because of the nature of tribal relations and the fact that most expatriates live in housing complexes, word of mouth has been an effective method for attracting employees to work for organizations. In recent years, online recruitment has become a favorite means of recruiting employees, especially from abroad.

The rise of complex recruitment mechanisms, including the persistence of sponsorship programs for expatriates, reflects the dramatic increase in demand for foreign labor in a region where there are more than seven million expatriates. The complexity of recruitment mechanisms stems from companies' persistent needs for skilled and less costly foreign labor, concerns for security, and the government's attempt to force companies to hire citizens as part of the Saudization of workforce initiative. These mechanisms, however, have encouraged fraud and corruption and have facilitated the abuse of workers. The *Arab News* (2008) quoted the head of the National Commission for Recruitment as stating that the Kingdom is relaxing the enforcement of the new recruitment rules, as some labor supply agents have resorted to swindling and forgery of documents related to recruiting. Previously, the same officers praised the new rules as a means to "eliminate the malpractices of the past and put an end to most problems, especially those of absconding housemaids and drivers" (Al Hakeem, 2008).

Selection

Islamic instruction and traditions set five conditions for selecting employees (competency, experience, shouldering responsibility, organizational fit, and reputation within the community) and orders the faithful not to follow their desires. The Quran (28:26) advises, "Truly, the best people for thee to employ are ones who are competent and trustworthy." Furthermore, the Prophet Mohamed asserted that "He who is in a leadership position and knowingly appoints a person who is not qualified to manage others, then he violates the command of God and His messenger," and "When a person assumes an authority over people and promotes one of them because of personal preferences, God will curse him forever." Similarly, the second Caliph, Omer, emphasized behavioral and moral aspects along with performance potential in selecting employees for jobs. He is reported to have said, "When a person is in charge of Muslim affairs and appointed for reasons of favoritism or kinship relationship [nepotism], then he cheats God, the Prophet, and the community" (quoted in Asaf, 1987, p 346). Furthermore, in the Islamic tradition, it is a virtue to test individuals before showering them with praise. As Al-Andelesy (vol. 3, p. 28) stated, "Do not exalt before assessment."

Early Muslim policy makers and scholars placed an emphasis on the social reputation, experience, and decency of those to be selected. These scholars understood that reputation and decency are prerequisites for selection. This is because individuals with those qualities are less inclined to engage in fraudulent activities. However, these policy makers and scholars recognized that decency and honesty are not enough to effectively carry out responsibilities. When a trusted companion of the Prophet, Abu Zur, asked to be given a job, the answer was, "Oh Abu Zur you are a weak person and the job is one of trust. On the Day of Judgment there is a sorrow and regret [if it is not carried out correctly]." That is, capability and shouldering responsibility are essential elements for carrying out duties diligently. According to Al-Andelesy (1996, vol. 3, p. 121), when a Caliph asked a Muslim scholar how to carry out affairs fairly, he was informed, "Affairs should be given to those who are qualified." Indeed, the philosophy of linking the prerequisite to the knowledge of the job was espoused in the first six centuries of Islam. For example, the fourth Caliph, Imam Ali, in a letter to his governor in Egypt (the Al-Asthar document), underscored the significance of the selection function and its importance to the welfare of the society. He stated that selection of employees "should not be based solely on your intuition. . . . Rather, you should scrutinize their record of service with good rulers before you and select those who have left the best impression on the people and who have a reputation for honesty. . . . Put in charge of each service a person who is not afraid to shoulder responsibility" (p. 329). Imam Ali underscored the need to go beyond experience and what candidates say about themselves. Specifically, he emphasized the importance of the interview in observing and evaluating how candidates react to certain questions and what they say. Such information has to be assessed in line with feedback received from members of the community regarding the candidate's moral standing and effectiveness. Imam Ali held those who are in charge, the governor in this case, fully responsible for bad selections arguing that "any fault of your employees which you overlook is your own responsibility."

Organizational fit, also, is to be given priority in selection. Situational aspects and specific job requirements may dictate that priority is given to those who can meet a special challenge. For example, in selecting governors, the Prophet Mohamed gave considerable attention to task requirements and job specifications. Most of his appointees were known for their determination and foresight and were mostly from the influential clans. The reason underlying this is that, at that time, Arabian communities appreciated personnel who were known for their bravery, assertiveness, and noble social affiliations. In selecting market administrators, those who were appointed were known to be pious and kind to their fellow men. Market administrators dealt with issues that demanded empathy and sensitivity to and identification with immediate daily problems. This situational aspect in selection influenced Muslim thinkers even during the era of decline. For example, Ibn Taimiya (1263–1328) argued that in selecting an employee, task requirements should be taken into consideration. In a situation where the primary job involves maintaining wealth or the treasury, then the appointed person must be trustworthy. In the case of generating and maintaining wealth, both competency and trustworthy attributes are prerequisites. This is applied, too, in the case of war or national instability; a decisive rather than pious leader is recommended. Competency, however, is seen as instrumental for establishing a functional organization and for advancing prosperity and justice. In the context of the government, Al-Mawardi (1986, p. 558) indicated that a ruler cannot discard competency, competency cannot be detached from generosity, generosity cannot be separated from wealth, and wealth cannot be divorced from justice.

Much of the selection of personnel in modern organizations in Muslim societies does not nearly resemble what is outlined or sanctioned by the faith. Nevertheless, in selection and other related functions, there is a common phenomenon called "unity of contradictions" (Ali, 2008b). This situation arises when managers repeatedly utter Islamic sayings which prohibit nepotism and sanction competency, however, in practice, preference is given to those who are relatives recommended by friends irrespective of their qualifications (see Abdalla, 2006; Namazi and Tayeb, 2006). This inconsistency is conspicuous and is an integral part of organizational normalcy. In the Gulf Cooperation Council (GCC) countries, the contradictions find fertile ground. The selection is often an outcome of the interplay of several factors. These factors range from scarcity of qualified personnel, nepotism, bureaucracy, and political considerations, to rapid growth in the number of private and state enterprises which have thrived since the early 1970s. The most important factors that render the selection process subjective and sometimes worthless are personalized relationships or personalism—kinship, regional favoritism—as well as the presence of a large number of guest workers and employees. In particular, personalism undermines objectivity and sanctioned procedures. In practice, for both interview and selection procedures, especially for non-citizens, various forms and lengthy procedures must be followed. Nevertheless, actual selection is often done subjectively and arbitrarily.

The presence of guest workers and employees also constitutes an obstacle to objective recruitment and selection. Companies have at their disposal a large number of workers from other countries from which to select. These workers, by law, do not have or are not qualified for permanent residency and work permits are normally only issued for a specific occupation or employer. This makes it easier for employers to employ those who are willing to work for the lowest possible wages and, most likely, under conditions that would not be tolerated by national workers. A case in point is the tendency of many highly qualified foreigners who seek employment in Saudi Arabia to state in official documents that they are laborers in order to qualify for work visas, as restrictions are eased for manual and low-paid jobs (Fakkar, 2008).

Compensation and Reward

Unlike other issues in HR, compensation in the early days of Islam was, relatively speaking, given special attention. While the subject of equality was important, the nature of work and the family and task responsibilities were highlighted in wage differentiation. Furthermore, compensation was contingent upon work. As Al-Ghazali (2004, p. 1680) asserted, "No wages without work." Compensation in the early years of the Muslim State was governed by specific guidelines. These are outlined below:

1. **Employment is a contractual agreement.** The fulfillment of such a contract is a moral and ethical obligation and involved parties must avoid any attempt to circumvent it. The Quran (7:85) instructs, "Nor withhold from the people the things that are their due."
2. **Compensation differs according to expertise and the situation.** The Quran (46:19) states, "And to all are ranked according to their deeds" and (39:9) "Say: 'Are those equal, those who know and those who do not know?'" Kurd Ali (1934) reported that the second Caliph, Omer, used to arrange wages for his subordinates and deputies according to hardship, living standard in a region, nature of the task, and needs of subordinates (e.g., family size).

3. **Compensation must be determined in advance and wages must to be given immediately once work is completed.** The Prophet Mohamed asserted that "if one hires an employee, he must inform him of his wage" and "the employee must get his wage promptly after the work is done" (quoted in Asaf, 1987, p 362).
4. **Compensation can be either cash and/or in kind depending on the contract and mutual agreement.**
5. **Wages should be increased according to circumstances.** It was reported that the first Caliph, Abu Baker, followed equity principles as the state's resources were scarce. However, during the era of the second Caliph, Omer, the state expanded and resources increased. Therefore, he differentiated in compensations among senior members of his groups; those who were close to the Prophet and those who were the first to espouse the faith were given more than others.
6. **Wages and compensation should be sufficient to provide a decent living.** This point was clearly illustrated in the Al-Asthar document which stated (p. 50), "Give them [subordinates] decent remuneration. That will give them the power to resist temptation and make them less susceptible to abuse what they are entrusted with."

In today's practice, government and business organizations have adopted pay and compensation systems similar to those found in Western countries. Most companies use a mixture of base salary, incentives, and benefits. In fact, it is common to have a base salary, cost of living allowances, special bonuses, and benefits in almost all business and government institutions. However, since most countries with Muslim majorities were once under colonial rule, primarily British or French, HR practice is influenced by civil service laws. In countries like Iraq, Algeria, Kuwait, Malaysia, etc. the colonial power, at the time, gave considerable attention to building government cadres and institutionalized a system that thought to optimize operations. The HR system which emerged and later evolved, in terms of compensation, places a priority on seniority rather than performance and qualifications. Though most civil service laws incorporate elements of Islamic law, the application, in most cases, is limited. It is possible that equity issues and a just compensation system that was highly cherished in the early years of the Muslim State are often violated. For example, in Saudi Arabia, the *Arab News* (2008) reported that "After negotiations between the NCR [National Commission for Recruitment] and authorities in various labor-supplying countries, salaries for housemaids have been fixed at SR500 per month for Nepalese, SR650 for Sri Lankans, SR750 for Vietnamese and SR800 for Indonesians and SR1500 for Filipinos." This difference in scale demonstrates that there is no minimum wage and that discrimination in wages for the same job does exist based on ethnicity or national origin. In fact, according to the Minister of Labor, a minimum wage is under consideration but only for Saudi nationals (*Saudi Gazette*, 2008). As a result of outside pressures from non-government organizations and governments of labor-exporting countries, the Ministry of Labor in the UAE issued Decree No. 788 in, 2009, requiring companies to pay wages according to specific schedules.

In terms of rewards, in the early Islamic state, the practices differed according to circumstances, especially availability of resources. Two general philosophies governed rewards: egalitarian and elitist approaches. The first and the fourth Caliphs, Abu Baker and Ali, respectively, followed the egalitarian approach. The second Caliph, Omer, however, witnessing a rapid expansion of the state and a sudden increase in resources, was an adamant adherent of the preferential philosophy, in terms of reward. He adopted an elitist approach and those who were pioneers in their faith were given preference (see Glaachi, 2000; Kurd Ali, 1934). The dynastic states which emerged after 661, without exception, showed a preference for the elitism principle. In recent years, both in public and private business enterprises, approaches to rewards have been similar to those which exist in Western countries. Nevertheless, Islam sets the following guidelines for rewards (see Ali, 2005):

1. **The reward must be linked to performance and behavior.** The Quran (27:90) admonishes, "Can you expect any recompense other than what you deserve for your deeds?" and (37:131) "Thus, indeed we reward those who do right."
2. **The reward must reinforce the good deeds.** The Quran (6:160) states, "He that doeth good shall have ten times as much to his credit: He that doeth evil shall only be recompensed according to his evil."
3. **The reward must be ethically driven.** In administrative documents written during Caliph Al-Mamun's time (813–33), reward was described "as an ethical obligation and as a philosophy and practice. . . . Decent remuneration should be given as such that God made it easy for them [subordinates] to overcome their urgent material needs and strengthen them, thus they will be more obedient and loyal to you."
4. **The reward can be either monetary or non-monetary or both.** In the case of non-monetary reward, the leader must show recognition and appreciation. Imam Ali elaborated on this matter in the Al-Asthar document stating (p. 319), "Show recognition of their [subordinates'] good deeds. Repeat your appreciation of the achievements of those who do well. That will encourage the valorous and entice the reluctant."

5. **The reward should not generate ill feeling among subordinates.** That is, it should be based on objective measures and be given to those who deserve it. Imam Ali made this point when he stated (1990, p. 631), "Give them [subordinates] hope, always recognize those who do well, and take notice of their achievements. This will motivate achievers to perform well and encourage the careless to make more effort."

As in the case of compensation, reward in Islam underscores the importance of performance and seeks to achieve three objectives: enforcing good behavior and avoidance of apathy, ensuring commitment and loyalty to broader societal goals, and encouraging employees to do their best, while observing spiritual norms.

Performance Evaluation

Performance assessment has been given extensive attention and is clarified in the Quran, the Prophet's sayings, and those of his immediate four successors. The first two provide the normative standard, while the last translates the normative into workable guidance. The normative realm is revealed in Quranic instructions and can be grouped into three categories: contractual arrangement, self-responsibility and control, and the Almighty's assessment of performance. In terms of contractual aspects, Islam views the employment of a person as a reaffirmation of an obligatory relationship between the organization and the employee. That is, the company and the employees have expectations that must simultaneously be fully met. The Quran (17:34) instructs Muslims that any promise or engagement is a contract that must be met by participants: "And fulfill the engagement [promise], for the engagement will be enquired into." Indeed, the Quran (5:1) presents the fulfillment of obligations as a command: "Fulfill all contracts."

Under self-responsibility, the Quran clarifies that what a person does is solely his/her responsibility and no one should be held responsible for the mistakes of others. While the normative responsibility is clearly specified (74:38), "Every soul will be held in pledge for its deeds," the Quran (75:14) articulates that individuals are aware of their deeds and are, therefore, capable of initiating corrections, "Nay, man is a witness against himself." Morally, employees have a duty to monitor their performance. Since both contractual arrangement and self-assessment are verified in the hereafter, faithful employees and employers should observe their obligations and entitlements. The Quran (11:112) is specific, "For He seeth well all that ye do" and (16:91) "Indeed you have made God your surety; for God knoweth all that you do." Therefore, the normative aspects make the assessment of performance first and foremost a responsibility of the employee. This responsibility is transcended to the hereafter, when a person is presented with a record of his/her performance in the world (17:14), "Sufficient is thy soul this day [of judgment] to make out an account against thee." As the Quran (2:234) states, "God is well acquainted with what ye do," a faithful employee takes performance and self-evaluation seriously making the relationship between performance and evaluation an interactive process. The advantage of self-evaluation is exemplified in the saying of a senior Muslim scholar, Hassan Al-Basri: "He who evaluates himself obtains benefit and he who avoids evaluation loses. He who considers consequences succeeds" (quoted in Al-Andelesy, vol. 3, p. 111).

In line with the normative standard, the Prophet's immediate four successors outlined, depending on conditions, how the performance evaluation should be carried out. The second Caliph, Omer, used three approaches to monitor performance: directly reviewing public complaints and asking subordinates for accountability, sending monitors to assess the performance of public officers, and giving assessment and feedback to governors and subordinates during the season of pilgrimage. In the Al-Asthar document, the fourth Caliph specified that evaluation of subordinates must be strictly based on deed and behavior toward the public. There were direct and indirect approaches. The direct approach was practiced by the Caliph himself in regard to those who were working around him or those who were asked to bring their records with them to be evaluated. The second was practiced by sending monitors to far regions to evaluate governors and other employees. The document (p. 325) states: "Monitor their [subordinates'] performance and use for this purpose people who are known for their truthfulness and loyalty. Your discreet monitoring of their work will ensure that they remain honest and considerate of their subjects. Beware of your close assistants. If you have reliable information from your agents that one of them has committed treachery, then that should be sufficient evidence to impose punishment." In his letter to his son, who was a governor of a region, Tahir Ben Al-Hussain wrote that evaluation should not be based on suspicion or what others have claimed stating, "Do not suspect anyone who works for you of misdeeds until you verify what he has done" (quoted in Ibn Khaldun, 2006, p. 240).

In both normative and practical guidelines, Islamic perspectives set a framework for a morally anchored and performance-based evaluation. More importantly, it appears that such a framework is aimed at allowing employees to consider their performance in light of their contribution to their organization and society. It is in this context that employees may have the opportunity to broaden their perspectives and improve their involvement. It is not clear from today's practices in CMMs whether or not organizations or governments follow Islamic perspectives on performance evaluation. What is certain, however, is that in almost all countries and in medium to large-sized organizations, one form or another of performance evaluation is used. The literature, however, reveals that performance evaluation lacks seriousness and objectivity (see Abdalla, 2006; Ahmed, 2006; Aycan, 2006; Namazie and Tayeb, 2006).

Training and Development

In Islamic thinking, both the theoretical and practical dimensions of training and development fit within the broad concept of human existence and the capability of a human being to make a difference, assume responsibility, and provide value to society. According to the Quranic teachings, a person does not exist independent of the group or society, and a person is endowed with the faculties to shoulder responsibility and evolve according to circumstances and prevailing conditions. Without overlooking these conditions, the Quran (13:11) states, "God does not change the condition of people unless they change what is in their heart." However, the Prophet acknowledged that people are different in their capacities and abilities to process information stating, "They shall be burdened only with what they can bear," he asserted that learning leads to development: "Knowledge is obtained through studying" (quoted in Muhammad Ali, 1977, p. 38). The dialectic relationship between learned individuals, knowledge, and work is captured in the Prophet's saying, "Learned people, knowledge, and work are blessed. When those who have knowledge do not act upon it, they are not blessed; but work and knowledge are always blessed." Notwithstanding Islam's explicit acknowledgment that differences in capabilities exist, unlike in Judaism and Christianity, it does not place limitations on the development and capacity to do "good" in life and work. According to both Judaism and Christian theology, human beings are inherently inclined to engage in evil activities. Berkovits (1964, p. 187) made this clear when he accentuated the importance of evil desire and asserted that it is a "necessary ingredient of life itself." Rabbi Harold Kushner (2001, p. 55) agreed: "God has planted in each of us something called the *yetzer ha-ra*," or "the evil impulse." That is, the evil impulse is essential for the existence of human beings because any attempt to "amputate the part of a person that leads him or her to be selfish and aggressive . . . would be a disaster. What we'd be left with would be less than a whole human being."

Similar to Judaism, Christianity strongly believes that the human "capacity for evil is not only a fact, but a shocking fact" (Lowry, 1998, p. 2). Though the belief is that a person is created in the "image of God," the propensity to evil is strong and perhaps though it is not ultimately the stronger, it is by far the more obvious. According to Lowry, "the evil tendency is like a mighty king who lays siege to a city, says the Talmud, and the good inclination is like a meek man inside the besieged city" (Lowry, 1998, p. 3). More importantly, the Christian tradition "affirms that the perfection of human beings is unattainable in history and that it is sinful to even try to attain it" (Hanson, 1999). Indeed, Hanson suggests that in the Christian tradition a human being has his/her limits and "is unaware of the limits of . . . possibilities." In Christianity, and in the Protestant perspective in particular, therefore, "all aspects of human existence," to a certain degree, are defective. Consequently, any treatment or technique to improve human abilities and motivate people "must be approached with suspicion" (Hanson, 1999, p. 127).

In Islam, mankind is situated between two extreme possibilities: perfection (God's spirit) and lowliness (clay). Therefore, according to Islamic teaching, human beings have infinite choices to make in life. Shariati (1979, p. 92) argues that a human being is in an "infinite direction," either toward clay or toward God. There are endless possibilities and, depending on their psychological level of existence, individuals make their own choices. Therefore, a person is "compelled to be always in motion. His own self is the stage for a battle between two forces that results in a continuous evolution toward perfection." Consequently, attaining perfection in Islam is a virtue. Islam recognizes that people have different desires and have under their disposal various means to achieve their goals. The Quran (92:4) instructs, "Verily, [the ends] ye strive for are diverse" and (53:39) "Man can have only what he strives for."

In terms of the practical dimension of training and development, early Islamic teaching highlighted two aspects: probationary appointment and apprenticeship. The second Caliph, Omer, is reported to have said to one of his subordinates, "I appointed you to test you. If you do well, I will promote you; but if you do not, then I will dismiss you" (quoted in Abu-Doleh and Ayoun, 2001). Similarly, the fourth Caliph, Imam Ali, wrote, "Monitor the performance of your subordinates and employ them only after probation" (1990, p. 633). In the latter stage of the Islamic state, and especially during the Abbasid era (749–1258), the state bureaucracy was well established. Thus, there was a heavy reliance on professionally trained individuals who, in turn, evolved into a professional class that was carried within families from generation to generation (e.g., *al-Khadi*, judge; *al-Jabi*, collector of taxes; *al-Khazin*, warehouse director; *al-Katib*, scribe). During that era, Tahir Ben Al-Hussain suggested that evaluation can be an instrument for training. He stated that fair evaluation ensures the support of subordinates and is a vehicle for training them. In the business sector, however, apprenticeship was the norm. Perhaps the flourishing of apprenticeships and the growth in the economy, during the first six centuries of Islam, was what gave rise to flourishing industries and an associated professional class (*al-Saag*, jeweler; *al-Waraq*, producer of book notes; *al-Najar*, carpenter, etc.).

In addition to a probationary appointment and apprenticeship, in the early era of the Islamic state, seminars were conducted and pre-job oral instructions were provided. In today's business, whether in the public or private sector, organizations espouse various forms of training and development and spend considerable amounts of resources on such activities. In fact, the GCC countries, especially Saudi Arabia and UAE, have attracted consultants from all over the world and major training corporations have established offices in these countries. In many Muslim countries, large companies have their own training centers. Likewise, both on and off job training are pursued. Senior level managers and those who need special skills are sent to outside institutes to acquire knowledge and expertise. Onsite training is mostly reserved for operational and technical aspects. This type of training is either carried out by internal staff or by contracted professional consultants and experts. The latter are drawn from foreign firms, mostly American and British.

PRACTICAL HR CHALLENGES

In CMM societies, applying Western management principles has been a pressing concern. Not only because this application obstructs the development of indigenous knowledge but also because there is a belief that adopting Western theories, without serious reflection, impedes organizational development (for more detail see Ul-Haq and Westwood, 2012). Hofstede (1980) asserted that it was impractical to literally apply American management principles in foreign cultures. This is especially true in CMM societies where tradition is deeply rooted and change is taking place rather slowly. For example, Leat and El-Kot (2007) have indicated that in the Middle East HR policies are influenced to a great degree by Western management. While rules and policies are designed with a Western framework in mind, the practices are still culture specific (see Al-Hamadi, Budhwar, and Shipton, 2007; Mellahi, 2003). This particular situation raises two issues in terms of HR practices in Muslim countries. The first revolves around the cultural specificity of management theories and subsequently that of HR. Most Muslim countries, especially the GCC states, have been economically linked to the centers of global capitalism (the US, UK, etc.) and are integrated into the world economy. Many of these countries are left teetering between global capitalism and the dictates of their own cultural traditions. The second issue centers around the degree of religious influence on the practice of HR. Islam does not separate between the sacred and secular spheres of life. This makes it obligatory for the faithful to behave ethically and observe Islamic instructions in their business dealings and management. However, in their quest for a quick and easy profit, managers in these countries are faced with two contradictory directions: religious dictates and the logic of global capitalism. Each has its own prescriptions and demands.

What should be kept in mind is that the Quranic text and the sayings of the Prophet are ever present. They are cited on a regular basis and are continuously read, studied, and promoted. As such, it is possible that the intensity of their citations and pronouncements has created a situation where a deviation from the written word is not consciously processed and, when faced with contrary evidence, those who deviate in practice do not see a problem. The latter may validate and give credibility to a "unity of contradictions." This particular phenomenon is culturally idiosyncratic and it may shed light not only on the personality of Muslims (intense pride in religious identity and simultaneous self-condemnation for not following religion) but also on the practice of HR management where the interplay of tribal, political, religious, colonial legacy and economic factors takes place. This interplay, combined with what Ali (1995) called cultural discontinuity, makes it possible for many Muslims to treat foreign elements and practices as their own. The inconsistency between business ideology and cultural values can be viewed in the context of crossvergence perspectives. In their adoption of capitalism, CMM societies have experienced rapid changes in business, technological, and political spheres. However, a shift in their socio-cultural core will take years if not decades to take shape. Thus, the appearance gap between HR practices and Islamic prescriptions is part of a values evolution resulting from integration in the world economy and the subsequent, albeit slow, adoption of individualistic values inherent in the capitalism system.

From socio-cultural perspectives, Islam offers useful prescriptions for HR practitioners. Indeed, as was shown in the previous sections, while Islamic normative guidelines for selection and compensation, for example, were envisioned more than 1400 years ago, their message and content are in line with contemporary and probably futuristic thinking. Nevertheless, Islamic prescriptions for HR, especially with their emphasis on human dignity, kindness in dealings, and concern for the welfare of society, may not fare well with secular Western HR policies and practices. Most HR policies are based on American individualism and Protestant-capitalism. Under both philosophies, the pillars of *ehsan* have no place. Employees, and especially workers, are viewed solely in terms of their economic contribution to the firm. Moreover, Islamic views of HR focus on communal relationships and the concerns of the community. That is, the firm has a specific role to play in society, well beyond its economic role. Though Islam underscores individual rights and dignity, these are regarded within the context of the community and its interests.

Most importantly, in its emphasis on morality in conduct, Islam expects that both employers' and employees' obligations be grounded in ethics. While in Protestant–capitalism there are no restrictions as employers have the right to hire and fire employees, these two tasks are highly restricted in Islamic teachings. In fact, the concept of morally responsible business conduct, including HR, constitutes a powerful force that guards against abuses and prejudices in the workplace (see Ali, 2005 for details) and, in essence, places moral limitations on the employer's rights to dismiss employees and the treatment of employees in the workplace. For example, firing employees without good reason is injustice. Those who do so commit sin. The philosophy of *ehsan* in the workplace emphasizes that there are no inconsistencies between business and moral obligations, making it obligatory for HR policies to be built on transparency, accountability, justice, and generosity. That is, the prosperity of workers and employers is intertwined. Ibn Khaldun argued (2006, p. 284) that "Prosperity comes to those who produce these things [items that are essential for cultural development and affluence] by utilizing their skills." Centuries later, Protestantism, and subsequently capitalism, reaffirms the same. The difference, among others, is that *ehsan* is the foundation upon which prosperity is sustained. As Ibn Khaldun asserted (2006, p. 224), the growth of any enterprise is contingent on justice and "People can maintain their dignity through the help of wealth. The only way to wealth is through persistence. The only way to persistence is through justice. Justice is a balance set up among people."

Six primary challenges stand out. The first is for HR to treat the interests of labor as complementary to that of employers and vice versa. Unfortunately, in contemporary business, the application of this proposition, be it in Western or Muslim countries, is a far-reaching possibility. Economic pressures and the urge to maximize profits and accumulate wealth by any means make it difficult to apply Islamic HR prescriptions on a wide scale, even in Muslim countries. In Muslim countries, however, the adoption of Western HR policies, while asserting the claim of observing Islamic prescriptions, may seriously impede sound economic and social development. This is not only because these principles are culturally bound, but also because false claims deepen confusion and enlarge the gap between the ideal and reality.

The second challenge revolves around the term *sedakah* and the duties of faithful business people to go beyond the letter of the law and what is specified in the contract in helping employees and alleviating their suffering or preventing any potential harm to them. In Muslim societies, where various forms of capitalism are adopted, to go beyond what is agreed on may not sound like good business practice, leaving those who believe in *sedakah* in a dilemma. Furthermore, as shown in Chapter 10, Islam recommends that *sedakah* should be given discreetly or preferably anonymously. This might be problematic, too, where a firm's contribution and its record of social responsibility has been touted as a marketing tool.

The third challenge concerns talent cultivation. This is an issue that is critical for human capital formation and a company's competitiveness and market positioning. Both at the corporate level and in the government, the prevailing environment, in general, places an emphasis on maintaining and securing those traditional autocrats who are in power. Even new executives in the private business sector cling to the old cliché that they know better than the rest. These executives along with their governments fear indigenous talent. Therefore, they create an environment which does not attract, cultivate, or unlock the energy of existing HR. For example, in its study of human resource capabilities in the Gulf region, Aon Hewitt (2012) concluded that the "engagement and advancement of national talent is without doubt the single biggest HR issue." The study found that employees' confidence in the most senior leaders of their organizations was low and that levels of engagement among women and national talent were considerably low.

Inclusion and diversity stand out as serious challenges in HR practice. While diversity in the workforce is common in CMM societies to a large degree, the inclusion in decision making is not guaranteed. For example, in its survey of global diversity and inclusion, the Society for Human Resource Management (2009) found that companies in mostly Muslim societies (Middle East and South Asia) scored below the world average, with Pakistan and Saudi Arabia at the bottom. Inclusion is essential for increasing productivity, loyalty, and cultivation of necessary talent. This challenge demands a profound change in outlook and a commitment to ethical conduct that underscores the significance of inclusion in cultivating human talent.

Fifth, as a spiritual guiding principle, *ehsan* asserts justice, abhors exploitation, and underscores the importance of social relations and priorities in conduct (e.g., the employer has to give due consideration to firings or layoffs beyond economic calculations). In an economic system where competition pressures and profit maximization dictate how labor relations should be managed, the application of *ehsan* is impossible. Even when senior managers believe in *ehsan*, they might find it necessary to overlook its prescriptions in the short term. Once this becomes habitual, it might be difficult to reverse. Ibn Al-Samak, a Muslim scholar, was quoted saying, "A good deed is a light in the heart and strength in work" (quoted in Al-Andelesy, vol. 3, p. 111).

The last challenge is how to maintain kindness and forgiveness in the workplace. This is related to the above point and is characteristically linked to firing and punishment. In an environment governed solely by market considerations, both kindness and forgiveness might be overlooked. The Quran (42:43) instructs, "But indeed if any show patience and forgive, that would truly be an affair of great resolution." And the Prophet stated, "He who does not display kindness, denies all that what is good" (quoted in Al-Nawawi, 2001, p. 172). For instance, firing employees in close-knit communities is certainly bad publicity which in the end tarnishes a company's reputation. More importantly, firing employees, just for the sake of cost cutting, is considered morally unacceptable. It inflicts distress upon those who are subject of the punishment and it violates principles set by the Prophet, "None of you has faith unless he loves for his brother what he loves for himself."

CONCLUSION

This chapter articulated three points. First, that normative aspects and ideals pertaining to HR can be a powerful force in the workplace. Second, labor theory in Islam, though advanced in the medieval era, is still valid and its application safeguards the interests of employers and employees. Third, ethical conduct is possible only in an environment where principles are upheld. Thus, it was argued in this chapter that Islamic HR prescriptions are relevant to today's business organizations. Since the emphasis in Islam is on optimally serving human beings, and the validity of any act is judged in terms of its benefit to society, Islamic HR policies can be factors that enhance the survival and growth of organizations. Throughout this chapter we underscored two facts. First, in most Muslim countries there is an official commitment to Islamic teachings. Nevertheless, this commitment, in the organizational context, is questionable. This is because the applications of HR often deviate from Islamic prescriptions. Secondly, though in most Muslim countries modern organizations appear to follow HR policies, which are driven by Western principles of management and organization, their practice is shaped by various factors including tribal, religious, colonial legacies, and political norms. Therefore, these organizations often, intentionally or unintentionally, have contradictory priorities and goals. This makes designing HR policies that reflect the spirit of cultural priorities and norms an urgent task.

Likewise, the chapter briefly highlighted the inherent contradictions between Western HR management and Islamic instructions. It was argued that the latter elevates communal concerns over individuals and characteristically links the interest of the organization to that of the society. In other words, in morally guided HR policies, Islamic teachings are vital and a rich source for designing HR policies, which optimally serve the broader interest of the society and enhance the contribution of organizations to the general welfare of the society.

The core message in the chapter is that that while Islamic HR prescriptions are vital for ensuring a balance between employer and employee interests, in the current quest for speedy integration in the world economy, HR practices often deviate from the ideal. Market pressures to make a profit, accumulate wealth, and gain power may induce both individuals and organizations to tolerate deviation from societal sanctioned norms. In recent years, this attitude has become common in almost all organizations, be they state, local, or MNCs. Therefore, HR managers, CEOs, policy makers, or legislators may find it useful to consult professional HR experts who are familiar with the religious prescriptions and their applications in a dynamic and competitive business environment. The challenge might be monumental, but it is worth confronting to effectively minimize possible deception and fraud.

One has to acknowledge that shortcomings always exist in any HR policy and that even an astute HR specialist may not have an accurate understanding of the spirit and the applicability of certain religious prescriptions. Specifying boundaries of religious instructions in terms of business practices is not only an impossible task but may lead to curtailing an individual's best judgment. In this chapter, we relied on authentic instructions formulated by early Muslim philosophers and policy makers in addition to Quranic instructions and the Prophet's sayings. These instructions were intended to answer concerns regarding events in a different time. Today's countries with Muslim majorities vary in their cultural, political, and economic experiences. This makes the study of HR issues from an Islamic perspective a difficult task. However, the fact that the best HR practices are ones that are responsive to the needs of employees and organizations cannot be overlooked. These needs have to be judged in terms of their benefits to the greatest number of people and to society as a whole.

10. Social responsibility and sustainability

For the last six decades, in the Western world, social responsibility (SR) has become a dominant topic of ethics in the discourse on business and organizations. However, irrespective of the rising secular emphasis on social responsibility, the topic has its roots in the religious and philosophical discourse which took place centuries ago. While religions across centuries have underscored individuals' obligations toward their primary groups and societies, these obligations have not been clearly articulated in any form and their relevance and implications to the modern business world have often, until recently, been overlooked. In this chapter, the issue of social responsibility in the context of Islamic thinking is addressed. In particular, we intend to highlight how Islamic prescriptions and the teachings of early scholars have set the boundaries for ethical conduct and how observing responsibilities toward individuals and society at large have been viewed as instrumental in establishing a healthy and economically functional and stable society. In this regard, social responsibility is viewed on three levels: the individual, the corporation, and government.

Before addressing the topic from Islamic perspectives, it is important to outline, at the corporate level, the evolution of the concept in the Western world. There are many scholars who have argued that corporate social responsibility (CSR) is a Western concept (Idemudia 2011; Ip, 2008; Muller and Kolk, 2009; UNIDO, 2007). Furthermore, others believe that interest in CSR is a recent phenomenon and is actually a product of the past half century (Carroll and Shabana, 2010). This assertion, however, does not take into consideration that certain individual executives and scholars in the past have addressed the issue but their message may not have received wide acceptance. Therefore, we can say that the discourse on CSR has gone through four stages. The initial stage (late 1920s to early 1950s), represented an attempt by a few scholars and practitioners to link corporate actions and future endeavors to societal issues. This development, however, was never transformed into a well-organized campaign promoting CSR. One of the active pioneers in this endeavor was E. Merrick Dodd (1932, p. 1154), of Harvard University, who argued that corporations had responsibilities beyond stockholders. He made a powerful argument that a corporation "shall not only do its business honestly and properly, but, further, that it shall meet its public obligations and perform its public duties—in a word, vast as it is, that it should be a good citizen." The 1960s to early 1980s constituted the beginnings of a wider acceptance of CSR and the emergence of a keen awareness of the impact of corporations on the environment and the health and welfare of communities. This particular development was boosted by resentment of the Vietnam War and the rise of student revolutions in most of the Western world, especially in the US. This changed not only the landscape of the debate but also enlarged the arena of CSR to focus not only on moral commitment but also on environmental and health issues.

The third stage (1990s–2010s) witnessed a much wider acceptance of CSR between both executives and the general public. At this stage, the debate on what constitutes CSR became much more sophisticated. Several theories were advanced and those who supported CSR were confronted by rivals who used classical economic theory and other notions to discredit CSR. This stage paved the way for the fourth stage (2010s onwards) and the start of a wider acceptance of CSR among practitioners and senior executives. These executives not only accept the tenets of CSR but also see it as a strategic tool to differentiate their companies from rivals and a means to gain a competitive advantage. This has constituted the beginning of the institutionalization of CSR and placed CSR as an integral component in strategy formulation and execution by many corporations across the globe.

CENTRALITY OF SOCIAL RESPONSIBILITY

Most of the debate in the West has focused on legitimizing and validating involvement in societal affairs. In societies where individuals or corporations are assumed to have their own identity and are primarily responsible for their own interests, independent of the society, this debate may make sense. The debate, too, is appropriate in countries with Muslim majorities where two conditions are prevalent: adoption of Western thinking and practices regarding business conduct and where jurists or *fagiha* issue religious decrees to comply with the preferences of a ruler. People may blindly follow these decrees irrespective of their purpose and impact. In this case, as Islamic thinker Burhan Ghalioun (1991, p. 326) has argued, a person "becomes a citizen without deep religious consciousness and without any feeling of solidarity with the collective of the believers as brothers. . . . This means constraining of faith and limiting the development of human relations outside the boundaries of politics and the state; making the collective just a legal group and denying it its spiritual depth. This obstructs the development of the ethics of brotherhood that was advanced by Islam." Unfortunately, these two conditions are common in most CMM societies, making the gap between the claim and reality an ever increasing one.

Nevertheless, a look at the framework of Islamic ethics (see Chapter 1) reveals that social responsibility is an integral component under each element of the framework. To demonstrate this significance, a brief discussion of each element in terms of centrality of social responsibility is provided below.

Public Interest (Acquisition of Benefits and Repulsion of Harm)

Any action that individuals, corporations, and governments undertake is judged by whether or not it generates benefit to the public. While this captures the essence of social responsibility in general, Islamic thought underscores two premises. First, the intention must be to do good and should not be used as a means to seek advancement for personal benefit (e.g., showing off, touting social responsibility as a marketing tool or as a mechanism to gain access to those in positions of influence, etc.). Second, the act must be directed toward minimizing, if not avoiding, any possible harm to others or society at large, now or in the future.

Moderation

Under the logic of moderation, avoidance of extreme action is considered a virtue. In terms of social responsibility, the logic conveys a commitment to utilizing resources without waste or harm to nature, sustaining the environment, and avoiding charging high prices. It implies, too, that employees are treated fairly and that their dignity is not encroached upon.

Ehsan

Like advancing public interest, social responsibility under *ehsan* means that in any activity, market actors seek to enhance and strengthen relationships with employees, customers, suppliers, and even competitors. Furthermore, it implies that market actors should go beyond the terms of their contracts and legal obligations by being generous, forgiving, and tolerant. In *ehsan*, not only is doing harm avoided but attempting to ease the lives of those who face difficulties or are under stress is considered a virtue.

SEDAKAH AS SOCIAL RESPONSIBILITY

As in Judaism, in Islam *sedakah* is considered a virtue. The word *sedakah* is commonly translated as charity, though its meaning may go far beyond charity. As indicated in Chapter 9, *sedakah* is either voluntary or obligatory. The two forms, however, in practice, are difficult to separate as both may be given simultaneously. Likewise it is also difficult to distinguish between them when a person who engages in the act of *sedakah* gives an amount that exceeds what is required. This is often carried out for spiritual reasons or to avoid uncertainty (fearing that what is required may not be enough or does not amount to generosity). Practically, *sedakah* is viewed in terms of righteousness (*ber*). According to Al-Mawardi (2002, pp. 295–6), righteousness takes on two forms: reaching out to others (*sela*) and enjoining what is good—or as an act of kindness (*ma'ruf*). The first form primarily involves donating money for specific activities or areas without expecting any return. The act of kindness (*ma'ruf*) consists of two types: word and deed. The first is to communicate in the best way possible, meet others with a cheerful countenance, and approach them politely. The Prophet instructs, "If you do not help people with your wealth, you can help them by being cheerful, and behaving ethically" (quoted in Al-Mawardi, p. 322). The second type or deed is direct help and assistance to others who experience certain difficulties. Thus, the meaning of *sedakah* is broader in terms of its application than merely donating money. The Prophet asserted this notion when he stated, "Each good deed is *sedakah*." He further explained that giving *sedakah* helps to smooth activities and generate rewards. He pointed out, "Engaging in an act of kindness prevents bad events." Furthermore, he stated, "O God, increase the wealth of the generous and obliterate the wealth of those who are covetous" (quoted in Al-Mawardi, 2002, p. 323). In this context, *sedakah* is treated as an instrument that not only helps the subjects who are receiving it, but also those who give it. Whether in business or personal affairs, *sedakah* serves as a motivational tool for both spiritual salvation and economic progress. The Quran (92:5–10) instructs, "He who gives [in charity] and fears God and accepts the truth, we will ease his path to success. But he who is greedy and thinks that he is self-sufficient, and denies the truth, we will ease his path to misery."

Even though *sedakah* might be given openly under certain conditions, the consensus is that this should not be the first option. The Prophet and early Muslim scholars guided by the Quran set conditions for *sedakah*. These conditions seek to maintain the dignity of those who receive it and prevent those who give it using it as a tool to gain fame or influence. These conditions are:

1. It must be secret. The Quran (2:264) states, "O you who believe, do not invalidate your charities with reminders or injury as does one who spends his wealth [only] to be seen by the people." The purpose of this condition is to set a foundation for responsible conduct so personal desires or passion may not blind believers to doing that is good. The Prophet commented, "There is a man who gives *sedakah* and who conceals it so well so that his left hand does not know what his right hand spends." This statement is similar to the Christian teaching in the Bible which states (Matthew 6:1–4), "Beware of practicing your righteousness before other people in order to be seen by them, for then you will have no reward from your Father who is in heaven. Thus, when you give to the needy, sound no trumpet before you, as the hypocrites do in the synagogues and in the streets, that they may be praised by others. Truly, I say to you, they have received their reward. But when you give to the needy, do not let your left hand know what your right hand is doing, so that your giving may be in secret."

2. It must generate benefit to those who receive it. The Quran (2:267) instructs, "O ye who believe! Give of good things which ye have [honorably] earned and of the fruits of the earth which we have produced for you and do not aim at anything which is bad." Al Pashehi (2004, p. 221) stated that "The best of charity is that which is given to those who are in need." Likewise, Abu Sulayman Al-Darani, eighth to ninth century scholar, argued that "The best *sedakah* is the one that fits the need" (quoted in Al-Sulami, p. 77).

3. The contributor of *sedakah* must be kind and considerate to those who benefit from it. Imam Al-Ghazali (2006, p. 409) asserted that a person who gives *sedakah* must never "talk about it, and be kind to the beggar or the needy." There are two ethical justifications for this. First, kindness in giving and contributions enhances solidarity and trust among members of a community. Second, those who receive *sedakah* have their own reasons for needing it and, thus, treating them with kindness may ease their distress and may serve as motivation for them, if they are able, to overcome their difficulties and participate in economic activities.

4. The contributor of *sedakah* should always view it, irrespective of how large it is, as a minor thing and must execute it on time (Al-Maki, p. 215). These two conditions seek to relieve distress and address certain problems on a timely basis.

5. *Sedakah* must aim, too, at reducing income inequalities without inflicting a heavy burden on those who give. The Prophet instructed that God has "made charity, which is taken from the wealthy among them and given to the poor, obligatory." Imam Ali, the fourth Caliph, indicated (1989, p. 694) that "God Almighty has made it obligatory

for the wealthy to feed the poor." The objectives are to reduce social resentment, enable those in need to maintain a decent living, and provide them with the means to take care of themselves.

6. Obligatory *sedakah* must be collected with complete willingness from those who give it. Caliph Ali instructed his deputies to approach people who give *sedakah* "with empathy and dignity . . . [to] salute them kindly" (1990, p. 560).

7. *Sedakah* is not necessarily monetary and can take any form as long as its intention is to benefit people. It ranges from removing harmful objects from a road, to being cheerful in interaction with others, or providing assistance to the elderly. The Prophet instructed, "Give *sedakah* to your brother by providing knowledge to guide him and an idea to enhance his vision" (quoted in Al-Mawardi, 2002, p. 127).

Though *sedakah* appears to focus on individuals and groups, it does not exclude either corporations or the state from obligation. Corporations, in their active role as economic actors, are involved in social and political affairs that make them potent actors on the community and world stage. It is in these roles—economic, social and political—that corporations can contribute significantly to social responsibility and sustainable development. Economically, corporations make goods and services available to customers and if they are driven to contribute to social and market needs, without exploitation or abuse, they are indeed providing *sedakah*. The same can be said in their quest for advancing discovery (e.g., research and development) and hiring activities and in their quest to reach remote markets, build schools, roads, museums, etc. These activities enhance overall economic development and sustainability. Socially, corporate contributions to skill development, arts, spiritual, and social causes further corporations' engagements in social affairs. Politically, defending human rights and lobbying politicians against war, minimizing social and political instability, and removing harm to individuals or societies are also considered part of *sedakah*.

State roles in SR are sanctioned in the Quran and the sayings of the Prophet. The aims are to provide a decent living for those who do not have adequate resources and the means to engage in vital economic activities. As we mentioned in previous chapters, the Prophet made it clear that any person is entitled to three rights: food to strengthen existence, clothing to cover oneself, and a house for shelter. Indeed, most Muslim scholars (see Ahmad, 1995; Glaachi, 2000; Al-Sadr, 1983) consider safeguarding the welfare of the needy and the poor to be an important social function of the state. The Quran (59:7) states, "Whatever God grants to His Messenger [out of the property] of the people of the towns, belongs to

God, the Messenger, the kinfolk, the orphans, the destitute and to those who may become needy while on a journey, so that it will not only circulate in the hands of the rich ones among them" and (93: 5–10) ". . . soon will thy Guardian-Lord give thee [that wherewith] thou shalt be well-pleased. Did He not find thee an orphan and give thee shelter [and care]? And He found thee wandering, and He gave thee guidance. And He found thee in need, and made thee independent. Therefore, treat not the orphan with harshness nor repulse the petitioner." These injunctions make it obligatory for the government to offer a welfare system to those who are in need. This was expressed in a letter sent by the fourth Caliph, Imam Ali (1990, p. 668), to his governor in Mecca, Qath'am Ibn al-Abbas, stating "Look at the revenues God has placed at your disposal and disburse them among the needy, especially those with many dependents and those who are deprived, in order to eradicate poverty and despair." Tahir Ben Al-Hussain, in his letter to his son when he was appointed a regional governor, went a bit further when he made it a responsibility of the state to build hospitals for the ill who could not afford to take care of themselves and to provide medical doctors to treat them (for details, see Ibn Khaldun, 2006, p. 243).

In performing certain SR activities, the state aims to protect the environment and encourage economic initiatives that ensure sustainable development. The money spent on these activities is considered an investment in the future and in areas essential for improving the well-being of citizens. This was made clear in the letter that was sent by the fourth Caliph (1989, p. 327) to his governor in Egypt. The instructions emphasized that he should be kind and affectionate to constituents and he indicated that undertaking SR activities are worthy and rewarding endeavors: "Any shortage of revenue as a result of relief measures is not a real loss. It is rather an investment that will have good returns in terms of more productive land and a more prosperous country." That is, early Muslim scholars and policy makers linked SR to sustainable development and to the welfare of citizens. Indeed, Muslim scholars like Al-Maki, Al-Mawardi, and Ibn Khaldun thought that prosperity is contingent on the behavior of those in power and on the state's willingness to take care of its needy citizens and facilitate economic activities by having an efficient infrastructure.

The preceding discussion demonstrates that social responsibility is not independent of Islamic ethics. Rather, the whole subject of ethics focuses on promoting, practicing, and broadening the application of SR. Indeed, Islamic ethics is built on three interrelated premises: "Everything on earth is created to serve people," "The best people are those who benefit others," and "He who does not thank people, does not thank God." These premises constitute the reason for serving others, advancing societal interests, and preventing any harm that might arise from business and non-business

conduct. This constitutes the essence of SR in Islamic thought and, therefore, should not be divorced from the socio-political perspectives that
govern people's relationships with corporations, governments, and the
natural environment.

Typology of Those who Give Charity

Islamic scholars and philosophers have held those who sincerely give
sedakah in great respect. They are ranked according to their intention and
action. Typologies pertaining to those who give *sedakah* were identified by
Al-Pashehi (2004, p. 221). They are:

1. **Those who share part of their wealth with others (Generous).** These
    individuals literally observe religious instructions and view SR as a
    necessary activity. Nevertheless, they do not like to burden themselves.
    They think that they should retain adequate means to take care of the
    welfare of their dependents. Probably, these individuals are motivated
    by the belief that maintaining a balance in life will serve their material
    and spiritual interests.
2. **Those who give a large part of their wealth to others (Bountiful).** The
    bountiful assume that charity should be grounded on *ehsan* and the
    more he/she gives the better the reward will be in this life and the here-
    after. These individuals value spiritual rewards and believe that life has
    meaning when those who are in need are adequately served.
3. **Those who put others' needs before their own (Altruistic).** These people
    are motivated primarily by the rewards in the hereafter and are content
    with what they have. Their satisfaction in life is driven primarily by
    serving society. They experience happiness when the lives of others are
    improved and the community is generally prosperous.

In the context of corporations, these three types resemble, to a degree,
models identified by Kanter (2002): good corporate citizens, social innova-
tors, and heroes/martyrs. Those who give charity as articulated in the above
typologies though they believe in SR differ in the amount of resources
committed and the approaches they utilize. To gain a better understanding
of each model in terms of a business context, a brief discussion of each is
provided below and implications appear in Table 10.1.

Generous corporations
These corporations uphold the law and strictly follow religious instructions. However, companies, in their quest to meet the literal meaning of
religious law, though they have not violated any, may fall short over time

Table 10.1　Typology of corporations and SR implications

Corporation	Implications
Generous Corporations	Meet legal, social, and literal religious instructions. Spending on SR activities that are common and are expected. They seek to maintain a healthy economic position, while contributing to SR within well-defined boundaries.
Bountiful Corporations	Go beyond what is required legally, expected socially, and the literal requirements of the faith. They invest sizeable resources in SR to prevent social and economic ills and invest in areas with future consequences. These corporations consider that investing in SR leads to competitive positions and like generous corporations they prefer not to brag about their SR involvements.
Altruistic Corporations	They avoid showing off or being in the public spotlight relative to their SR activities. They freely invest resources on issues that prevent social and political ills, lobby aggressively to confront social and political abuse and to safeguard human dignity, sustainability, and the interests of future generations.

of meeting social expectations. This is especially true as these corporations avoid pressing social and political issues or calling for profound changes to existing political and economic conditions regarding people and their surrounding natural environment.

Bountiful corporations
Bountiful corporations attempt to be attentive in meeting social expectations relative to SR and, thus, they are involved in activities that are dedicated to serving what has to be done now and in the future to optimally serve changing social interests. Corporations, too, seek to maintain a healthy economic position in the marketplace so that they can always contribute to improving social welfare. These corporations accept the logic of *ehsan* and the principle of preventing harm.

Altruistic corporations
These corporations often take a stand on social, ecological, and political issues at the expense of profits. They invest resources not only to eradicate social and political ills but also to prevent the occurrences of these ills and take a responsive position in anticipating what might take place. They invest the needed resources, therefore, in futuristic issues that they hope will improve the welfare of future generations. Unlike bountiful corporations, they assume the role of social activists in aggressively confronting

what they perceive as a threat to social safety and societal interests. That is, their commitment to *ehsan* and the principle of repulsion of harm is deeply and widely accepted and vigorously pursued.

THE ETHICS OF ENGAGING IN SR

In the preceding discussion, the conditions for giving *sedakah*, a form of SR, were specified. These have various implications for corporations in today's world. The discussion, however, does not dismiss the fact that in today's business environment there are numerous corporations and individuals who contribute to SR. Each has different motives and expectations for pursuing SR. All types of corporations specified in Table 10.1 are driven in their engagement in SR by serving society and furthering the well-being of individuals. However, other corporations may not be part of the mapping that is identified in Table 10.1, as their commitment to SR is only remotely sincere. These companies seek to strengthen their power in the marketplace and have intentionally turned SR into a marketing tool. Their involvement in SR, therefore, is anything but ethical. About a thousand years ago, Al-Ghazali (2006, p. 409) identified those who engaged in *sedakah* and came up with six categories of people who are not sincere in their commitment to SR. His writings are still relevant. Though he focused on individuals, the message underlying each category can be applied to modern corporations. These categories are:

1. Those who spend on buildings and on what people are able to see and admire like mosques, schools, water towers, etc. They engrave their names on these objects so their fame will last after their death. They think that by their contributions they will be forgiven for their misdeeds. This might not be the case for two reasons:
    a. They gained their wealth through abuse, doubtful means, bribes, and whatever is prohibited. If they obtained their money through unlawful means, they should ask for forgiveness and return the money to those who deserve it, like the poor and the needy, instead of spending it on buildings.
    b. They might think that in spending money on buildings and towers they have engaged in worthy activities. If this was the case, they would not refrain from spending one dinar on the deprived; alleviating poverty should be given priority.

In the context of business, this applies, from an ethical perspective, to corporations that contribute to building museums, schools, roads, etc. just to improve their public image and use these contributions to effectively market themselves as responsible citizens.

2. Those who contribute *sedakah* might acquire wealth through lawful means but this might not be the case for two reasons:

    a. The contributor seeks fame and admiration. Instead of building mosques or schools, the money should be distributed to the poor and needy in the area.
    b. The contributor unnecessarily spends money on ornamentation and decorating mosques.

In the business world, this implies that corporations must consider social priorities first. The focus should be on activities that improve the living standards of members of the community, like creating employment opportunities or enabling them to gain needed skills and easing their professional mobility.

3. Those who spend their wealth on the poor and the needy but seek a prominent social position and to win public praise and thanks from the poor. Moreover, they have no intention of keeping their charity secret.

At the corporate level, this means that corporations should avoid using their SR contributions primarily to boost their image. Likewise, if possible, such contributions should not be publicized. Rather, their contributions should be discreetly given.

4. Those wealthy contributors who focus on ritual aspects of worship rather than on spiritual aspects. They are driven by greed, which overcomes their ability to help the poor and the needy.

Corporations should internalize spiritual aspects and be driven by optimally serving the public without expecting anything in return. That is, corporations should have a culture that sanctions engagement in sociopolitical activities because these might serve public interest and eradicate poverty.

5. Those whose greed obstructs their vision and motivates them to pay only alms. The alms are usually handed to those in important positions, in order to obtain future favors.

Corporations that fulfill only what is required by regulations fall short of meeting social expectations and changing economic and social conditions. Meeting legal obligations in today's world does not mean corporations are not responsible for inflicting harm to society or that they not should help members of the community where they operate who are in need.

6. Members of the general public, including the capable and the poor who think that attending religious sermons instead of paying *sedakah* is enough.

Participating in public ceremonies and attending public meetings with government and civic leaders is not an alternative to contributing to SR. Rather, corporations must actively seek to address public concerns and fulfill societal expectations through various SR activities and other means that promote public good.

Stakeholders' Approach and Islamic Ethics

Stakeholder theory, in the last few decades, has gained attention and has been promoted as instrumental in enhancing connectivity between corporations and society. As we have shown in the discussion above and reiterated in the previous chapters, in Islamic ethics societal concerns are intertwined with business affairs. The question that might be asked is "Is there a link between stakeholder theory and the Islamic view of societal interests or common good?" In terms of financial matters, for example, both perspectives underscore the necessity of investment and growth of capital to benefit individuals and society. Likewise, both approaches place priority on value creation and trade and stress that business activities and ethics must not be separated (see Al-Mawardi, 2002, died 1058, p. 335; Freeman, 2000, p. 174). Indeed, Freeman's four principles of stakeholder theory (stakeholder cooperation, complexity of human being, business as an institution continuously seeks to create value to society, and emergence of competition in the marketplace) are integral elements in the discourse on societal interests in the Islamic approach (see Glaachi, 2000; Osman, 1995; Raghib, 1995). Al-Mawardi (2002, p. 214) further indicated that the welfare of an individual is not independent of that of his society. He stated, "And know that the betterment of public interest in this world is contingent on two aspects: the enhancement of the welfare of the society and the improvement of the well-being of each individual. These are interrelated where the betterment of each does not take place without the other."

The Islamic view seeks to ensure open access to opportunities and minimize inequality. As was demonstrated in Chapter 1, the Islamic approach to common good treats the acquiring of benefits and the avoidance of harm to society as an obligatory rather than voluntary goal. There are two important economic aspects that evidence that both the Islamic view and shareholder theory share significant similarities though they differ in the scope of their domain, with the Islamic view being much broader. The first concerns economic objectives. Al-Mawardi (2002, p. 335) argued that the objective of economic activities is to realize happiness and broaden public interests or public good. He further asserted that satisfying needs and obtaining benefits can be achieved by utilizing material objects (tools, machines, etc.) and making a living. The first is possible by owning assets that generate earnings. The making of a living is possible, too, through actions that lead to acquiring assets and through behavior that satisfies needs either by engaging in commerce or engaging in industrial activities (e.g. generating knowledge, generating material, or a mix of these industries).

The second aspect revolves around the concept of profit. In Islamic thinking, profit is not exclusively an economic matter. Profit considerations are not independent of an ethical system. Rather, they are part of prevailing norms that govern conduct and exchange functions. In fact, ethically sanctioned profit (modest) enables businesses to survive and grow without creating difficulties for others. Profit consideration takes a central place in Islamic ethics and, therefore, Islamic prescriptions do not condone profit that stems from exploitation and mischief in the marketplace (Ali, Al-Aali and Al-Owaihan, 2013). In this context, the Islamic view is similar, though broader, than stakeholder theory in advocating that the concern "for profits is the result rather than the driver in the process of value creation" (Freeman, Wicks, and Parmer, 2004, p. 364).

COMPONENTS OF SOCIAL RESPONSIBILITY

The issue of SR is dynamic in nature and often a reflection of social and economic sophistication, along with political openness. For example, in the early formal discourse on SR, in the US, the focus was on environment protection and moral responsibility of firms, especially toward their employees. With the rise of social awareness, sovereign consumers, stakeholder activism, civic organizations, and increasing business and social interaction and connectivity across the world (e.g., globalization of business), the scope of SR has broadened significantly to include fair trade, human rights, eradicating corruption and fraudulent practices, etc.

In Islamic thought, because the focus is on serving and providing benefits to society, the scope of SR since the rise of Islam has been broad and comprehensive in its coverage. This is manifested in the logic of public interest, especially repulsion of harm, the virtue of moderation, and *ehsan*. The first or public interest situates public good at the core of the SR agenda and the repulsion of harm makes it obligatory for corporations to think about possible future consequences of current actions. The logic of *ehsan* complements both the public interest and moderation logics by explicitly reaffirming that goodness implies alleviating distress and participating in activities that enhance well-being. Unfortunately, in most CMM societies, a clear understanding of SR, in the context of Islamic ethics, is not common. In Indonesia, for example, the UN (see Kemp, 2001, p. 34) reported that "At this point in Indonesian history, CSR itself can only remain an image projected onto a screen—an outline with little depth." Likewise, Waagstein (2011) demonstrated that laws requiring the implementation of CSR have created much confusion pertaining to their substance and procedures. Similarly, in Iran, Najati and Ghasemi (2012) found that CSR is in its infancy among organizations. Salehi and Azary (2009) state that the practice of CSR in Iran is far from expected levels. In Saudi Arabia, Ali and Al-Aali (2012) found out that participants' view of CSR is largely shaped by the principles of capitalism, rather than religious prescriptions. In Malaysia, Atan and Abdul Halim (2011) found that level of awareness of the importance of CSR among the stakeholders in Malaysia was low. The authors found that stakeholders' perception of CSR focuses on corporations meeting their legal responsibilities with less emphasis on ethical and religious requirements.

The aforementioned studies reveal that in a CMM society an understanding of CSR that is ethically sound and practically relevant has not yet been realized. Indeed, the results of these studies prove that today's stakeholders in general, and executives in particular, have no clear understanding of CSR and of the degree of involvement of companies in social responsibility. Both the general public and executives are not expected to take the CSR program seriously without being themselves involved in a learning process pertaining to changing trends in society and the marketplace. This is possible only when these actors become familiar with their faith principles and the changing economic and social conditions at home and abroad.

As was demonstrated in the previous chapters, Islamic ethics places considerable emphasis on serving people's interests. These are expressed in one general Islamic premise and two sayings of the Prophet which are:

1. **"Whatever serves people, serves God."** This saying serves as a motivational factor for both individuals and corporations to do their best in serving customers and society. Furthermore, since Islamic ethics address the issue of serving in terms of people, it does not differentiate between customers and employees, suppliers and competitors; all must be treated fairly and social and economic justice should be the guiding principles. That is, in discussing components of CSR, the emphasis should be on issues that are relevant to the welfare and

happiness of members of the society. These aspects enhance human interests and safeguard the welfare of future generations.

2. **"The best people are those who benefit others."** In the business world, this implies that corporations that treat CSR as part of their strategic actions and initiatives are ones that actually provide tangible benefits to society. Their participation in CSR, therefore, improves their public image and enhances their strategic position in the marketplace.

3. **"He who does not thank people, does not thank God."** This sends a powerful message that an appreciation of whatever a company does depends solely on the approval of people. Therefore, it is the people who legitimize the existence of any company in the market. Without this legitimacy, a company cannot be a vital market actor. That is, CSR serves as a mechanism for lending creditability to corporations in society. It is the stakeholders, therefore, who either give or withhold approval for a company to operate and conduct business.

The most important components that should be addressed in CSR, therefore, are ones that are relevant to sustaining social and economic justice, fulfilling evolving human needs, and easing human development and professional growth. At the societal level, corporations should take a lead in eliminating bribery, corruption, and fraudulent practices, and protecting and sustaining the natural environment. At the organizational level, corporations should seek to improve work and labor conditions and guard human rights and dignity. They should help market actors in disadvantaged positions, especially farmers in developing countries through fair trade practices, create employment opportunities, and conduct economic affairs without inflicting injustice on other market actors (e.g., through monopoly, profit maximization, child labor, exploitation, etc.). These issues are grouped in different categories and are briefly discussed below:

1. **Ethical responsibility**—Corporations have a duty to act in ways that benefit society and prevent harm to stakeholders. Corporations should not only respond to current stakeholders' norms and expectations, but should rethink the long-term consequences of their actions without overlooking their ability to survive.

2. **Sustainability responsibility**—Protecting and sustaining the natural environment. The Prophet stated, "Do not waste water even if you are near a running stream." This implies the need for conservation even during a time of plenty. Furthermore, Islamic thinkers prohibit any major changes that might destroy the natural setting, like clear-felling,

polluting the environment, etc. Even building huge towers is considered a threat to the beauty and greening of the land. Utbah ibn Ghazwan, a companion of the Prophet (died 639) stated, "Do not burden a land with huge buildings as the magnificence of the earth is in its surface" (quoted in Al-Deinori, 1999, p. 290).

3. **Economic responsibility**—Creating employment opportunities and developing needed skills to improve standards of living and reduce income inequality, along with engaging in traditional business oriented activities such as production and marketing. While the teaching of the faith underscores the significance of creating employment, it also considers skill improvement as part of CSR. The Prophet instructed, "Give *sedakah* to your brother by providing knowledge to guide him and an idea to enhance his vision."

4. **Civic responsibility**—This encompasses two general obligations: ensuring human dignity and defending human rights. The concern about human dignity is a cornerstone of the Islamic faith. Both the Quran and the Hadith outlawed oppression, suppression of thought and abuses, while underscoring the rights of individuals in the workplace for fair treatment and good working conditions. The Prophet argued that poverty and oppression obliterate human dignity. The second Caliph, Omer, stated, "Since when have you enslaved people, knowing that they were born free?" The concern with defending human rights obligates corporations to raise issues with governments and international organizations when the rights of people and where they operate are violated or seriously threatened.

5. **Sedakah responsibility**—The obligatory aspect is spiritual and its voluntary aspects are ethically recommended. This involves giving charity and pursuing and promoting what is good.

6. **Legal responsibilities**—Fulfilling or observing these aspects that are set by government regulations and rules is considered a minimum requirement for any responsible company. These are necessary but never sufficient for acting responsibly. There are many more obligations than merely meeting legal ones. The three typologies of the ethically driven corporations—generous, bountiful, and altruistic—usually go beyond the legal aspects, with the last two exceeding what is normally required in the typical Western perception of CSR.

As was discussed in this chapter, the economic and social dimensions are interrelated. The objective of economic activities is to realize happiness and broaden public interests or public good. Satisfying human needs socially and economically and acquiring benefits can be achieved through active pursuit of business operations and making a living. This particular aspect, while highlighting the social and economic significance of CSR, treats corporate CSR as a normal duty.

The above six components imply that corporations have duties other than economic ones and that in a world where changing social, economic, and political conditions often merge, differentiating between economic and non-economic issues becomes an impossible and fruitless task. Thus, corporations must have mechanisms for anticipating social changes and emerging legal pressures and should be attentive and receptive to the ecological and human rights concerns of citizens. Corporations and their executives should seriously consider all the possibilities surrounding their actions, both today and in the future. They should use their capabilities to sensitize other actors to the fact that a marketplace free of deception and abuses optimally serves the interests of all who are involved, be they competitors, governments, suppliers, customers, employees, or general citizens.

CONCLUSION

In this chapter, the general aspects of SR were outlined and discussed at the individual, corporate, and government level. While the chapter covered the centrality of SR in Islamic thinking, it also shed light on the evolution of SR in contemporary Western thinking. We elaborated on the concept of *sedakah* as a form of SR. The types and conditions for ethically sound *sedakah* were identified and evidence borrowed from early Muslim scholars was provided.

The concept of CSR was discussed. Three types of corporations that are ethically driven (generous, bountiful, and altruistic) were specified and their implications were outlined. In addition, six components of CSR in Islamic thinking were presented. These components are often ignored by practitioners and neglected by researchers.

In the context of CSR components, it was argued that corporations should safeguard human dignity, while pursuing economic and non-economic activities that benefit all stakeholders without impairing their business vision and future generations' abilities to meet their needs. In recent years, and in many countries, business fraud and deception and corporate scandals have multiplied. This not only manifests the shortcomings of social responsibility, but also the failure of business executives to learn and take note of changing business conditions, the rise of social and legal activism, the danger of underestimating customers' reactions and changing priorities, and the dialectic relationship between allowing business to thrive and serving societal needs.

Bibliography

Abdalla, I. (2006), 'Human resource management in Qatar', in P. Budhwar and K. Mellahi (eds), *Managing Human Resources in the Middle East*, London, UK: Routledge, pp. 121–44.

Abdul-Rauf, M. (1984), *A Muslim's Reflections on Democratic Capitalism*, Washington, DC: American Enterprise Institute for Public Policy Research.

Abela, A. (2001), 'Profit and more: Catholic social teaching and the purpose of the firm', *Journal of Business Ethics*, **31** (2), 107–16.

Abu Dawod, E. (1996), *The Directory of Inquirers*, Jedha, Saudi Arabia: A.A. Abu Dawood.

Abu-Saad, I. (2003), 'The work values of Arab teachers in Israel in a multicultural context', *Journal of Beliefs and Values*, **24** (1), 39–51.

Abu Yusuf, Yaqub ibn Ibrahim (N.D.), *Treaties of Taxation*, Beirut, Lebanon: Dar Al Marafa.

Ahmad, K. (1976), *Islam: Its Meaning and Message*, London, UK: Islamic Council of Europe.

Ahmad, M. (1995), *Business Ethics in Islam*, International Institute of Islamic Thought, Herndon, VA and the Islamic Research Institute, Pakistan.Ahmed, A. (2006), 'Human resource management in Sudan', in P. Budhwar and K. Mellahi (eds), *Managing Human Resources in the Middle East*, London, UK: Routledge, pp. 219–32.

Al-Anbari, A. (1987), *The Position of Chief Justice During the Abbasid State*, Beirut, Lebanon: Al Dar al Arabia Le aLmouswat.

Al-Barai, A. and A. Abdeen (1987), *Management in Islamic culture*, Jeddah, Saudi Arabia: Modern Service Library.

Al-Bukhârî, Abû 'Abd Allâh Muhammad (1996), *Sahih Al Bukhari*, summarized, trans. M. Khan, Riyadh: Maktaba Dar-us-Salam.

Al-Deinori, Abû Muḥammad Ibn Qutaybah (1999), *Uyun al-Akhbar*, Beirut, Lebanon: Dar AlKetabAl Arabi.

Alderman, Liz (2010), 'Fiat pushes work ethic at Italian plant', *New York Times*, available at www.nytimes.com/2010/07/23/business/global/23fiat.html?pagewanted=alland_r=0 (accessed 23 July 2013).

Al-Ghazali, A.H. (2006), *Collection of Letters*, Beirut, Lebanon: Dar Al-Fikr.

Al-Ghazali, M. (2004), *Muslim Character*, (trans. M.A. Usmani), Chicago, IL: Kazi Publications.

Al Hakeem, M. (2008), 'Saudi Arabia faces manpower shortage', *Gulf News*, available at www.gulfnews.com (accessed 12 January 2014).

Al-Hamadi, A.B., P. Budhwar and H. Shipton (2007), 'Management of human resources in Oman', *International Journal of Human Resource Management*, **18** (1), 100–13.

Al Hasani, A. (2013), 'Seizing a warehouse where rotten meat was stored', available at www.okaz.com.sa/new/Issues/20130516/Con20130516601109.htm (accessed 30 July 2013).

Al-Hashimi, A. (2001), *Selected Hadiths of the Prophet*, Beirut, Lebanon: al-Maktaba Alysyria.

Al-Hasiany, M. (2000), *Pricing Rules in Islamic Jurisprudence*, Beirut, Lebanon: Dar al Bashaer Al Islamiah.

Ali, A. (1982), 'An empirical investigation of managerial values systems for working in Iraq', unpublished doctoral dissertation, Morgantown, WV: West Virginia University.

Ali, A. (1986), 'Labor immigration in the Arab Gulf States: Patterns, trends, and problems', *International Migration*, **24** (3), 675–84.

Ali, A. (1988), 'Scaling an Islamic work ethic', *Journal of Social Psychology*, **128** (5), 575–83.

Ali, A. (1989), 'A comparative study of managerial beliefs about work', in B. Prasad (ed.), *Advances in International Comparative Management*, **4**, 95–112.

Ali, A. (1992), 'Islamic work ethic in Arabia', *Journal of Psychology*, **126** (5), 575–83.

Ali, A. (1995), 'Cultural discontinuity and Arab management thought', *International Studies of Management and Organization*, **25** (3), 351–61.

Ali, A. (2005), *Islamic Perspectives on Management and Organization*, Cheltenham, UK: Edward Elgar Publishing.

Ali, A. (2008a), 'Rethinking business culture', *International Journal of Commerce and Management*, **18** (3), 205–206.

Ali, A. (2008b), *Business and Management Environment in Saudi Arabia: Challenges and Opportunities for Multinational Corporations*. New York, NY: Routledge.

Ali, A. (2011), 'Marketing and ethics: What have Islamic ethics contributed and challenges ahead?', paper presented at Global Islamic Marketing Conference, Dubai, 20–22 March.

Ali, A. and A. Al-Aali (2012), 'Corporate social responsibility in Saudi Arabia' *Middle East Policy*, **19** (4), 40–53.

Ali, A. and A. Al-Kazemi (2006), 'Islamic work ethic in Kuwait', *Journal of Cross Cultural Management*, **13** (35).

Ali, A. and M. Al-Shakhis (1989), 'Managerial value systems for working in Saudi Arabia', *Group and Organization Studies*, **10** (2), 135–51.

Ali, A. and M. Al-Shakhis (1989), 'The meaning of work in Saudi Arabia', *International Journal of Manpower*, **10** (1), 26–32.

Ali, A., A. Al-Aali and A. Al-Owaihan (2013), 'Islamic perspectives on profit maximization', *Journal of Business Ethics*, **117** (3), 467–75.

Ali, A., T. Falcone and A. Azim (1995), 'Work ethic in the USA and Canada', *Journal of Management Development*, **14** (6), 26–34.

Ali, Imam (1989), *Nahjul Balagah*, (trans. and ed. by F. Ebeid), Beirut, Lebanon: Dar Alkitab Al-Lubnani.

Ali, Imam (1990), *Nahjul Balagah* (illustrated by Imam Mohamed Abda), Beirut, Lebanon: Mouassasa Al-Maarf.

Al-Jahiz, Abu Othman Omer ibn Bahr (1998), *Book of Misers*, Beirut, Lebanon: Dar Sader.

Al-Jasmani, A. (1996), *The Psychology of Quran*. Beirut, Lebanon: Arab Scientific Publishers.

Aljazeera Net (2013), 'Spending on consumption in the Gulf', available at www.aljazeera.net/home/print/0353e88a-286d-4266-82c6-6094 (accessed 22 December 2013).

Al-Kuwari, A. (1985), *Nahwa Istrategiea Badela Litanmeia Shamela* (Towards an Alternative Strategy for Development), Beirut, Lebanon: Center for Arab Unity Studies.

Al Mahami, S. (1987), *Auditing Business Administration*, Cairo, Egypt: Dar Al faker Al Arabi.

Al-Maki, A.T. (1995), *Guot al-Gwlob* (Nourishment of Hearts), part 2, Beirut, Lebanon: Dar Sader.

Al-Maqrizi, Taqi al-Din (1999), *Rescuing the Nation by Illuminating Darkness*, Cairo, Egypt: Maktaba Al adab.

Al-Mawardi, Abu al-Hassan (1986), *Nasihat al-Mulk* (Advice to Rulers), Baghdad, Iraq: Dar Al Shawoon Al-Thaqafia Al Ama, Ministry of Information and Culture.

Al-Mawardi, Abu al-Hassan (2002), *Kitab Aadab al-Dunya w'al-Din* (The Ethics of Religion and of this World), Damascus, Syria: Dar Ibn Khather.

Al-Nawawi, Abu Zakaria Mohiuddin (2001), *Riyadh as-Saaliheen, 'The Gardens of the Righteous'*. Beirut, Lebanon: Al Asrahia Bookstore.

Al Pashehi, S. (2004), *Al Mustatrif*, Beirut, Lebanon: Al Noor Publishing Institute.

Al-Qurni, A. (1987), *Selling in Islam*, Cairo, Egypt: Dar Al Zahwa for Publishing and Distribution.

Al-Ṣabi, Abu'l-Ḥassan Hilal b. Muhassin (2003), *Al wazers* (Ministers), Cairo, Egypt: Dar al afaq al Arabia.

Al-Sadr, B. (1983), *Islam and School of Economics*, Huntington, NY: Islamic Seminary.

Al-Salhy, Suadad (2013), 'Insight: Iraq security forces outmatched as "open war" returns', *Reuters*, available at www.reuters.com/article/2013/07/30/us-iraq-security-jailbreak-insight-idUSBRE96T0X020130730 (accessed 3 August 2013).

Al-Shatibi, Ibrahim ibn Musa (2011), *The Reconciliation of the Fundamentals of Islamic Law*, vol. 1, trans. Imran Ahsan Khan Nyazee, Reading, UK: Garnet Publishing Limited.

Al Shaybani, Mohamed Ibn Al Hassan (1986), *Earning a Livelihood*, Beirut, Lebanon: Dar al Ketab Al Alymeya.

Al-Sulami, Abu 'Abd al-Rahman (1968), *Categories of Sufis*, Cairo, Egypt: Al-Madani Printing.

Al-Suyuti, J. (1996), *History of Caliphs*, Beirut, Lebanon: Institute for Cultural Books.

American Marketing Association (N.D.), *Dictionary*, available at www.marketingpower.com/_layouts/Dictionary.aspx?dLetter=M# (accessed 10 January 2014).

Amiantit Group (N.D.), 'Our vision', available at www.amiantit.com/en/Amiantit_Group/Mission_and_Vision/default.php 9 (accessed 17 October 2013).

Amnesty International (2013), 'Qatar: End corporate exploitation of migrant construction workers', available at www.amnesty.org/en/news/qatar-end-corporate-exploitation-migrant-construction-workers-2013-11-17 (accessed 29 January 2014).

Anderson, N. (1984), *Dimension of Work*, New York, NY: David McKay Co.

Aon Hewitt (2012), 'Qudurat TM', available at www.aon.com/human-capital-consulting/thought-leadership/talent_mgmt/survey_2012-aon-hewitt-qudurat-research-study.jsp (accessed 15 March 2013).

Arab News (2005), 'Low-salaried civil servant rejects SR2 million bribe', available at www.arabnews.com/node/274062 (accessed 5 August 2013).

Arab News (2006), 'Don't trade in stocks while at work, grand mufti tells workers', available at www.arabnews.com/node/288110 (accessed 6 August 2013).

Arab News (2008), 'Enforcement of new recruitment rules delayed', available at www.arabnews.com (accessed 8 January 2014).

Arkoun, M. (1986), *The Historical Base of Arab-Islamic Thought*, Beirut, Lebanon: Center for National Growth.

Aristotle (1998), '*The Nicomachean Ethics*', New York, NY: Oxford University Press.

Armstrong, K. (1992), *Muhammad: A Biography of the Prophet*, New York, NY: Harper Collins Publishers.

Asaf, M. (1987), *The Islamic Way In Business Administration*. Cairo, Egypt: Ayen Shamis Library.

Asharq Al-Awsat (2009), 'Imitating traditional banking will destroy Islamic banking', available at www.aawsat.net/2009/11/article55252729/print (accessed 6 December 2013).

Asharq Al-Awsat (2010), 'Machiavellianism in Islamic finance', available at www.aawsat.net/2010/04/article55250983 (accessed 10 December 2013).

Ashmawy, M. (1992), *Islamic Caliphate*, Cairo, Egypt: Siena Publisher.

Atan, Ruhaya and Nurul Akmal Abdul Halim (2011), 'Corporate Social Responsibility: The perception of Muslim consumers', paper presented at the 8th International Conference on Islamic Economics and Finance.

Aycan, Z. (2006), 'Human resource management in Turkey', in P. Budhwar and K. Mellahi (eds), *Managing Human Resources in the Middle East*, London, UK: Routledge, pp. 160–79.

Bahrampour, T. (2010), 'Muslim immigrant fills niche raising goats on Virginia farm', *Washington Post*, 13 April, B1.

Barbash, J. (1983), 'Which work ethic? in J. Barbash and P.J. Andrisani, *The Work Ethic: A Critical Analysis*, Madison, WI: Industrial Relations Research Association, pp. 231–60.

Barton, D. (2011), 'Capitalism for the long term', *Harvard Business Review*, **89** (3), 85–91.

Belk, R.W., T.M. Devinney and G. Eckhardt (2005), 'Consumer ethics across cultures', *Consumption, Markets and Culture*, **8** (3), 275–89.

Berkovits, E. (1964), 'When man fails God', in A.E. Millgram (ed.), *Great Jewish Ideas*, Clinton, MA: Colonial Press Inc., pp. 183–97.

Bershidsky, L. (2013), 'Islamic finance can save the world', *Bloomberg*, available at: www.bloomberg.com/news/2013-10-29/islamic-finance-can-save-the-world.html (accessed 6 December 2013).

Blau, P. (1963), 'Critical remarks on Weber's theory of authority', *American Political Science Review*, **57**: 305–15.

Bowmen, D. (2008), 'Retailers, banks under fire over consumer spending', *Arabian Business*, available at www.arabianbusiness.com/retailers-banks-under-fire-over-consumer-spending-47537.html (accessed 17 January 2014).

Brodbeck, F. (2000), 'Cultural variation of leadership prototypes across 22 European countries', *Journal of Occupational and Organizational Psychology*, **73** (1), 1–29.

Budhwar, P. and K. Mellahi (2006), 'Human resource management in the Middle East: Emerging HRM models and future challenges for research and policy', in P. Budhwar and K. Mellahi (eds), *Managing Human Resources in the Middle East*, London, UK: Routledge, pp. 291–301.

Burhan G. (1991), *The State and Religion*, Beirut, Egypt: Arab Institute for Studies and Publishing.

Carney, F.S. (1983), 'Some aspects of Islamic ethics', *The Journal of Religion*, **63** (2), 159–74.

Carroll, A.B. and K. Shabana (2010), 'The business case for corporate social responsibility: A review of concepts, research and practice', *International Journal of Management Reviews*, **21** (1), 85–105.

Chapra, M. (2001), *What is Islamic Economics?*, Jeddah, Saudi Arabia: Islamic Research and Training Institute.

Chew, Y.T. (2005), 'Achieving organisational prosperity through employee motivation and retention: A comparative study of strategic HRM practices in Malaysian institutions', *Research and Practice in Human Resource Management*, **13** (2), 87–104.

Conger, J.A. and R.N. Kanungo (1987), 'Toward a behavioral theory of charismatic leadership in organizational settings', *Academy of Management Review*, **12** (2), 637–47.

Dauten, D. (2007), 'Today's work ethic just no longer works', *The Boston Globe*, available at www.boston.com/jobs/news/articles/2007/03/25/todays_work_ethic_just_no_longer_works/ (accessed 5 July 2013).

DesJardins, J. (2010), *An Introduction to Business Ethics* (4th edn), New York, NY: McGraw-Hill.

Diddams, M. and J.L. Whittington (2003), 'Book review essay: Revisiting the meaning of meaningful work', *Academy of Management Review*, **28** (3), 508–17.

Dierker, E. and B. Grodal (1996), 'Profit maximization mitigates competition', *Economic Theory*, **7** (1), 139–60.

Dodd, E.M. (1932), 'For whom are corporate managers trustees?', *Harvard Law Review*, **45** (7), 1145–63.

Doran, C. (2009), 'The role of personal values in fair trade consumption', *Journal of Business Ethics*, **84** (4), 549–63.

Dow, T. (1969), 'The theory of charisma', *Sociological Quarterly*, **10**: 306–18.

Drucker, P. (1974), *Management: Tasks, Responsibilities, Practices*, New York, NY: Harper and Row. *Economist* (2002), 'Is greed good? Only if it is properly governed', available at www.economist.com/node/1119945/print (accessed 12 July 2013).

Emerson, T. and J. Mckinney (2010), 'Importance of religious beliefs to ethical attitudes in business', *Journal of Religion and Business Ethics*, **1** (2), 1–14.

Emirates Group (N.D.), 'Responsibility', available at www.theemiratesgroup.com/english/our-vision-values/responsibility.aspx (accessed 17 October 2013).

England, G. (1984), 'Work centrality in Japan and USA', paper presented at the Academy of Management Meeting, Boston, MA, 12–15 August.

Erikson, E. (1964), *Childhood and Society*, New York, NY: Norton.

Ernst and Young (2013), 'World Islamic Banking Competitiveness Report 2013–14'.

Fakkar, Galal (2008), 'Many land lucrative jobs dodging rules', *Arab News*, available at www.arabnews.com (accessed 15 January 2014).

Ferguson, N. (2004), 'Economics, religion and the decline of Europe', *Economics Affairs*, pp. 37–40.

Fisher, G. (1988), *Mindsets: The Role of Culture and Perception in International Relations*, Yarmouth, ME: International Press.

Fletcher, J. (1966), *Situation Ethics*, Philadelphia, PA: The Westminster Press.

Fletcher, J.K. (2004), 'The paradox of postheroic leadership: An essay on gender, power, and transformational change', *The Leadership Quarterly*, **15** (5), 647–61.

Foroohar, R. (2013), 'The original wolf of Wall Street', *Time*, **182** (25), 20–26.

Freeman, E.R. (2000), 'Business ethics in the millennium', *Business Ethics Quarterly*, **10** (1), 169–80.

Freeman, E.R., A.C. Wicks and B. Parmar (2004), 'Stakeholder theory and "The Corporate Objective Revisited"', *Organization Science*, **15** (3), 364–69.

Friedland, W. (1964), 'For a sociological concept for charisma', *Social Forces*, **43** (1), 18–26.

Friedman, M. (1970), 'The social responsibility of business is to increase its profit', *New York Times Magazine*, available at www.colorado. edu/studentgroups/libertarians/issues/friedman-soc-resp-business.html (accessed 7 July 2013).

Gallup (2103), 'Engagement: Managers also show greatest improvement in engagement', available at www.gallup.com/poll/162062/managers-boast-best-work-engagement.aspx (accessed 5 December 2013).

Ghafour, P.K.A (2008), '8 health officials accused of graft', *Arab News*, available at http://arabnews.com/node/314220 (accessed 5 August 2013).

Glaachi, M. (2000), *Studies in Islamic Economy*, Kuwait: Dar An-Nafaes.

Glass, A. (2008), 'UAE tops Arab consumer spending', *Arabian Business*, available at www.arabianbusiness.com/uae-tops-arab-consumer-spending-122297.html?service=printerandpage= (accessed 17 January 2013).

Global Financial Integrity (2012), 'Illicit Financial Flows from Developing Countries: 2001–2010', Washington, DC, USA.

Graafland, J., M. Kaptein and C. Schouten (2006), 'Business dilemmas and religious belief: An explorative study among Dutch executives', *Journal of Business Ethics*, **66** (1), 53–70.

Grant, C. (1991), 'Friedman fallacies', *Journal of Business Ethics*, **10** (12), 907–14.

Graves, C.W. (1970), 'Levels of existence: An open system theory of values', *Journal of Humanistic Psychology*, **10** (2), 131–54.

Groom, B. (2011), 'Bosses put profit before ethics, says survey', *Financial Times*, available at www.ft.com/cms/s/0/ceb08890-edd8-11e0-acc7-00144feab49a.html#axzz2hVURb72K (accessed 12 October 2013).

Hamedan, Z. (2011), 'All what is related to fardh kifia and ayen and comparison among them', available at www.alhodaway.com/index.php?page=replyandf=55andt=1163 (accessed 28 July 2011).

Hanson, M.J. (1999), 'Indulging anxiety: Human enhancement from a Protestant perspective', *Christian Bioethics*, **5** (2), 121–38.

Haroon, Muhammad, Hafiz Fakhar Zaman and Waiza Rehman (2012), 'The relationship between Islamic work ethics and job satisfaction in healthcare sector of Pakistan', *International Journal of Contemporary Business Studies*, **3** (5), 6–12.

Hartley, J. (2009), 'Lawyers claim taking commission on property deals not prohibited', *Arabian Business*, available at www.arabianbusiness.com/lawyers-claim-taking-commission-on-property-deals-not-prohibited-78991.html (accessed 6 August 2013).

Hartley, R.F. (1993), *Business Ethics: Violations of the Public Trust*, New York, NY: John Wiley and Sons, Inc.

Hashim, J. (2009), 'Islamic revival in human resource management practices among selected Islamic organisations in Malaysia', *International Journal of Islamic and Middle Eastern Finance and Management*, **2** (3), 251–67.

Hasan, Z. (2002), 'Maximizing postulates and their efficacy for Islamic economics', *American Journal of Islamic Social Sciences*, **19** (1), 95–118.

Hill, A. (2012), 'Work 2.0', *Financial Times*, available at www.ft.com/intl/cms/s/2/4f5b4b30-02b7-11e2-9e53-00144feabdc0.html#axzz2SkBbnyDa (accessed 7 May 2013).

Hill, R. (1996), 'History of work ethic', available at http://rhill.coe.uga.edu/workethic/hist.htm (accessed 15 April 2013).

Hofstede, G. (1980), *Cultures' Consequences: International Differences in Work-Related Values*, Beverly Hills, CA: Sage.

Hofstede, G. (1987), 'Cultural dimensions in management and planning', in D.R. Hampton, C.E. Summer and R.A. Webber (eds), *Organizational*

Behavior and the Practice of Management, 5th edn, Glenview, IL: Scott Foresman and Co., pp. 401–22.

Hofstede, G. (1999), 'Problems remain, but theories will change: The universal and the specific in 21st-century global management', *Organizational Dynamics*, **28** (1), 34–43.

Hooker, J. (2011), *Business Ethics as Rational Choice*, Upper Saddle River, NJ: Pearson Prentice Hall.

House, R., M. Javidan and P. Dorfman (2001), 'Project globe: An introduction', *Applied Psychology: An International Review*, **50** (4), 489–505.

Howell, J.M. and B. Shamir (2005), 'The role of followers in the charismatic leadership process: relationships and their consequences', *Academy of Management Review*, **30** (1), 96–112.

Hughes, R., R. Ginnett and G. Curphy (2006), *Leadership*, Boston, MA: McGraw Hill.

Human Rights Watch (2003), 'Saudi Arabia/GCC states: Ratify migrant rights treaty', available at www.hrw.org (accessed 31 January 2014). Human Rights Watch (2013), 'South Asia: Protect migrant workers to Gulf countries', available at www.hrw.org/news/2013/12/18/south-asia-protect-migrant-workers-gulf-countries (accessed 31 January 2014).

Hunt, J.G. and J.A. Conger (1999), 'From where we sit: An assessment of transformational and charismatic leadership research', *Leadership Quarterly*, **10** (3), 335–43.

Huntington, S. (2004a), 'The Hispanic challenge', *Foreign Policy*, (141), 30–45.

Huntington, S. (2004b), 'American Creed', *The American Conservative*, **3** (7), 8–16.

Ibn Abed Raba Al-Andelesy, Ahmed (1996), *Al-ʿIqd al-Farîd* (The Unique Necklace), vol. 2, Beirut, Lebanon: Dar Ahya Al-Tiourath Al Arabi.

Ibn Abed Raba Al-Andelesy, Ahmed (1996), *Al-ʿIqd al-Farîd* (The Unique Necklace), vol. 3, Beirut, Lebanon: Dar Ahya Al-Tiourath Al Arabi.

Ibn Al-Josie, Abu Alfaraj (1995), *The Organized in the History of Kings and Nations*, vol. 4, Beirut, Lebanon: Dar Al kitob Al Alymaeha.

Ibn Hajar al-Asqalani, Ahmed ibn Ali (1947), *Attainment of the Objective According to Evidences of the Ordinances*, Cairo, Egypt: Al Salfaiah Printing.

Ibn Hazm, Abu Mohamed (1982), *Murateb al ijma*, Beirut, Lebanon: Dar Alafaq alJadedah.

Ibn Khaldun, Abd al-Rahman (1989), *The Magaddimah*, (trans. by Franz Rosenthal and edited by N.J. Dawood), Princeton, NJ: Princeton University Press.

Ibn Khaldun, Abd al-Rahman (2006), *The Magaddimah*, Beirut, Lebanon: Dar Al-Kotob Al-IImiyah.

Ibn Taimiyah, A. (1900), *al-Hisba fi al-Islam (Public Duties in Islam)*, Cairo, Egypt: Al-Mu'ayyad Print.

Ibn Taimiya, A. (2002), *A Lawful Policy in Reforming the Leader and Followers*, Beirut, Lebanon: Dar Al-fakr Publishing.

Idemudia, U. (2011), 'Corporate social responsibility and developing countries. Moving the critical CSR research agenda in Africa forward', *Progress in Development Studies*, **11** (1), 1–18.

Ikhwan-us-Safa (1999), *Letters of Ikhwan-us-Safa*, vol. 3, Beirut, Lebanon: Dar Sader.

Imam, A., A. Abbasi and S. Muneer (2013), 'The impact of Islamic work ethic on employee performance: Testing two models of personality X and personality Y', *Science International* (Lahore), **25** (3), 611–17.

Inkeles, A. and D. Smith (1974), *Becoming Modern*, Cambridge, MA: Harvard University Press.

Ip, P.-K. (2008), 'Corporate social responsibility and crony capitalism in Taiwan', *Journal of Business Ethics*, **79**: 167–77.

Iqbal, Z. (1997), 'Islamic financial systems', *Finance and Development*, **June**, 42–45.

Iraqi Business News (2011), 'Canadian firm wins $1.7bn Iraqi power contract', available at www.iraq-businessnews.com/2011/07/04/canadian-firm-wins-1-7bn-iraqi-power-contract/ (accessed 3 August 2013).

Jasim, A.S. (1987), *The Tormented Flower*, Baghdad, Iraq: Al-Yagdha Al Arabia Bookstore.

Jasim, A.S. (1990), *Sufi of Baghdad*, Baghdad, Iraq: Shrekit AlMuarifa for Publishing and Distribution.

Jenkins, P. and C. Binham (2013), 'Barclays in probe over links to Saudi prince', *Financial Times*, available at www.ft.com/intl/cms/s/0/61b8fa16-b98c-11e2-bc57-00144feabdc0.html#axzz2axJnBbM4 (accessed 3 August 2013).

Kami, A. (2011), 'Iraq electricity minister resigns over power deals', *Reuters*, available at www.reuters.com/article/2011/08/18/iraq-electricity-minister-idUSL5E7JI30220110818 (accessed 6 August 2013).

Kanter, R.M. (2002), '"Rising to rising expectations". Strategy for living in a changing world', *World Link*, **15** (1), 70–74.

Kanoo, M. (2006), 'Open your eyes, thieves are everywhere', *Arabian Business*, available at www.arabianbusiness.com/open-your-eyes-thieves-are-everywhere-125074.html (accessed 10 July 2013).

Kaplan, H. and C. Tausky (1972), 'Work and Cadillac: The function of and commitment to work among the hard-core unemployed', *Social Problems*, **19** (4), 469–83.

Karns, G. (2008), 'A theological reflection on exchange and marketing: An extension of the proposition that the purpose of business is to serve', *Christian Scholar's Review*, **28** (1), 97–114.

Katona, G., B. Strumpel and E. Zahne (1971), *Aspirations and Affluence*, New York, NY: McGraw-Hill.

Kayed, R. and K. Hassan (2011a), 'Saudi Arabia's economic development: Entrepreneurship as a strategy', *International Journal of Islamic and Middle Eastern Finance and Management*, **4** (1), 52–73.

Kayed, R. and K. Hassan (2011b), *Islamic Entrepreneurship*, New York, NY: Routledge.

Kemp, M. (2001), 'Corporate social responsibility in Indonesia: Quixotic dream or confident expectation?', paper number 6, *Technology, Business and Society: United Nations Research Institute for Social Development*.

Khaleeej Times (2008), 'Kuwait parliament to hold emergency session on labour unrest', available at www.khaleejtimes.com (accessed 20 January 2014).

Kohlberg, L. (1981), *Essay on Moral Development. Volume I: The Philosophy of Moral Development*, San Francisco, CA: Harper and Row.

Koplin, H. (1963), 'The profit maximization assumption', *Oxford Economic Papers*, **15** (2), 130–39.

Kurd Ali, M. (1934), *Islamic Management in the Golden Age of the Arabs*, Cairo, Egypt: Egypt Press.

Kushner, H.S. (2001), *Living a Life that Matters: Resolving the Conflict Between Conscience and Success*, New York, NY: Alfred A. Knopf.

Landau, R. (1938), *Search for Tomorrow*, London, UK: Nicholson and Watson.

Leat, M. and G. El-Kot (2007), 'HRM practices in Egypt: The influence of national context?', *International Journal of Human Resource Management*, **18** (1), 147–58.

Lee, K., D. McCann and M. Ching (2003), 'Christ and business culture: A study of Christian executives in Hong Kong', *Journal of Business Ethics*, **43** (1/2), 103–10.

Lewison, M. (1999), 'Conflicts of interest? The ethics of usury', *Journal of Business Ethics*, **22** (4), 327–39.

Li, D. (1964), 'The objectives of the corporations under the entity concept', *The Accounting Review*, **39** (4), 946–50.

Lipset, S. (1990), 'The work ethic-then and now', *Public Interest*, **Winter**, 61–9.

Lowry, R. (1998), 'The dark side of the soul: Human nature and the problem of evil in Jewish and Christian traditions', *Journal of Ecumenical Studies*, **35** (1), 88–101.

Mahmud, H. (2000), *Financial and Economic System in Islam*, Riyadh, Saudi Arabia: Dar Al Naser Al Dawely.

Mellahi, K. (2003), 'National culture and management practices: The case of GCCs', in Monir Tayeb (ed.), *International Management: Theory and Practices*, London, UK: Prentice Hall, pp. 87–105.

Metwally, M.M. (1980), 'A behavioral model of an Islamic firm', Research Series in English no.5, King Abdulaziz University, Jeddah, Saudi Arabia: International Center for Research in Islamic Economics.

Micewski, E.R. and C. Troy (2007), 'Business ethics: Deontologically revisited', *Journal of Business Ethics*, **72** (1), 17–25.

Moore, E. (2013), 'Should you buy into Islamic finance?', *Financial Times*, available at www.ft.com/cms/s/0/2061a806-4159-11e3-b064-00144feabdc0.html (accessed 6 December 2013).

Morris, B. (2008), 'Trader, father, veteran, convict', *Fortune*, **157** (12), 92–102.

Morse, N. and R. Weiss (1955), 'The function and meaning of work and job', *American Sociological Review*, **20**, 191–8.

MOW International Research Team (1981), 'The meaning of work', in G. Dlugos and K. Weiermair (eds), *Management under Differing Value Systems*, Berlin, New York: Walter de Gruyter Co, pp. 565–630.

Muhammad Ali, M. (1977), *A Manual of Hadith*, Ithaca, NY: Olive Branch Press.

Muller, A. and A. Kolk (2009), 'CSR performance in emerging markets: Evidence from Mexico', *Journal of Business Ethics*, **85** (2), 325–37.

Muncy, J.A. and J.K. Eastman (1998), 'Materialism and consumer ethics: An exploratory study', *Journal of Business Ethics*, **17** (2), 137–45.

Muncy, J.A. and S. Vitell (1992), 'Consumer ethics: An investigation of ethical beliefs of the final consumer', *Journal of Business Research*, **24** (June), 297–311.

Murphy, P.E., G.R. Laczniak, N.E. Bowie and T.A. Klein (2005), *Ethical Marketing: Basic Ethics in Action*, Upper Saddle River, NJ: Pearson Prentice Hall.

Najati, M. and S. Ghasemi (2012), 'Corporate social responsibility in Iran from the perspective of employees,' *Social Responsibility Journal*, **8** (4), 578–88.

Namazie, P. and M. Tayeb (2006), in P. Budhwar and K. Mellahi (eds), *Managing Human Resources in the Middle East*, London, UK: Routledge, pp. 20–39.

Naqvi, S.N. (1981), *Ethics and Economics: An Islamic Synthesis*, Leicester, UK: The Islamic Foundation.

Nasr, S. (1984), 'Islamic work ethics', *Hamdard Islamicus*, **7** (4), 25–35.

Numani, S. (2010), *Al Farooq: The Life of Omar the Great*, New Delhi, India: Adam Publisher and Distributors.

Osman, M. (1995), 'Some principles that govern public administration in Islam', in M. Al-Barai and M. Marcy (eds), *Management in Islam*, Jeddah, Saudi Arabia: Islamic Institute for Training and Research, pp. 105–40.

Ottaway, M. (2001), Reluctant missionaries, *Foreign Policy*, (125), 44–54.

Parboteeah, K.P. and J.B. Cullen (2013), *Business Ethics*, New York, NY: Routledge.

Pava, M. (1998), 'The substance of Jewish business ethics', *Journal of Business Ethics*, **17** (6), 603–17.

Peterson, M.F. and J.G. Hunt (1997), 'International perspectives on international leadership', *Leadership Quarterly*, **8** (3), 203–27.

Petroleum Development Oman (N.D.), PDO, available at www.pdo.co.om/pdoweb/tabid/131/Default.aspx (accessed 20 November 2013).

Pew Research Center (2007), 'Muslim Americans: Middle class and mostly mainstream', available at www.pewresearch.org/2007/05/22/muslim-americans-middle-class-and-mostly-mainstream/ (accessed 30 December 2013).

Pew Research Global Attitudes Project (2012), 'Pervasive gloom about the world economy', available at www.pewglobal.org/2012/07/12/chapter-4-the-casualties-faith-in-hard-work-and-capitalism/ (accessed 6 December 2013).

Porter, M. and M. Kramer (2006), 'Strategy and society: The link between competitive advantage and corporate social responsibility', *Harvard Business Review*, **84** (12), 72–98.

Primeaux, P. (1997), 'Business ethics in theory and practice: Diagnostic notes B. "A prescription for profit maximization"', *Journal of Business Ethics*, **16** (3), 315–22.

Primeaux, P. and J. Stieber (1994), 'Profit maximization: The ethical mandate of business', *Journal of Business Ethics*, **13** (4), 287–94.

Raghib, H. (1995), 'Islamic values and beliefs and their impact on marketing policy: Comparative analysis study', in M. Al-Barai and M. Marcy (eds), *Management in Islam*, Jeddah, Saudi Arabia: Islamic Institute for Training and Research, pp. 307–55.

Rahman, K. (2012), 'Recycling medical wastes', available at www.thefinancialexpress-bd.com / index.php?ref = MjBfMTFfMTFfMTJfMV8yXzE0OTYyNg == 9 (accessed 5 August 2013).

Ralston, D. (2008), 'The crossvergence perspective: Reflections and projections', *Journal of International Business Studies*, **39** (91), 27–40.

Rice, G. (1999), 'Islamic ethics and the implications for business', *Journal of Business Ethics*, **18**: 345–58.

Richter, F. (2010), 'Top Islamic finance scholars oppose reform effort', *Reuters*, available at www.reuters.com/article/2010/12/01/islamicfinance-scholars-idUSLDE6B015920101201 (accessed 6 December 2013).

Rizk, R. (2008), 'Back to basics: An Islamic perspective on business and work ethics', *Social Responsibility Journal*, **4** (1/2), 246–54.

Rizvi, M. (2013), 'Islamic banking to double market share in Pakistan', *Khaleej Times*, available at www.khaleejtimes.com/kt-article-display-1.asp ?section=uaebusinessandxfile= data/uaebusiness/2013/november/uae business_november365.xml (accessed 6 December 2013).

Rokhman, W. (2010), 'The effect of Islamic work ethics on work out-comes', *Electronic Journal of Business Ethics and Organization Studies*, **15** (1), 21–7.

Rose, M. (1985), *Reworking the Work Ethic: Economic Value and Socio-Cultural Politics*, London, UK: Schocken.

Rost, J.C. (1991), *Leadership for the Twenty-First Century*, London, UK: Praeger.

Sabanci (N.D.), 'Corporate Social Responsibility', available at www.saba nci.com/en/sabanci-group/corporate-social-responsibilty/corporate-soc ial-responsibility-policy-and-principles/i-144 (accessed 3 October 2010).

Salehi, M. and Z. Azary (2009), "Stakeholders' perceptions of corporate social responsibility: Empirical evidences in Iran', *International Business Research*, **2** (1), 63–72.

Salem, O. (2013), 'FNC call for action on Ramadan price rises in UAE', *The National*, available at www.thenational.ae/news/uae-news/fnc-call-for-action-on-ramadan-price-rises-in-uae#ixzz2b7Hmkz5P (accessed 5 August 2013).

Samad, A. (2008), 'Market analysis from an Islamic perspective and the contribution of Muslim scholars', *Journal of Islamic Economics, Banking and Finance*, **4** (3), 55–68.

Sambidge, A. (2011), 'Saudi Arabia pledges to stamp out corruption', *Arabian Business*, available at www.arabianbusiness.com/saudi-arabia-pledges-stamp-out-corruption-390520.html (accessed 10 July 2013).

Saudale, V., N. Lumanauw and F. Putra (2013), 'Food prices soar during Ramadan', *Jakarta Globe*, available at www.thejakartaglobe.com/news/food-prices-soar-during-ramadan/ (accessed 5 August 2013).

Saudi Gazette (2008), 'Govt plans minimum wage for Saudi workers', available at www.saudigazette.com.sa (accessed 7 January 2014).

Schein, E. (1980), *Organizational Psychology*, Englewood Cliffs, NJ: Prentice-Hall.

Shariati, A. (1979), *On the Sociology of Islam*, Berkeley, CA: Mizan Press.

Shaw, J.B. (1990), 'A cognitive categorization model for the study of intercultural management', *Academy of Management Review*, **15** (4), 203–27.

Shaw, W.H. (2008), *Business Ethics* (6th edn), Belmont, CA: Thomson Wadsworth.

Shelaq, A. (1990), *Heritage of Islamic Economy*, Beirut, Lebanon: Dar al Hadatha.

Sibley, A. (2009), 'Should profit be maximized? Daily estimate', available at www.dailyestimate.com/article.asp?id=22975 (accessed 28 August 2010).

Siddiqui, M. (1987), *Organization of Government Under the Prophet*, Delhi, India: Idarah-i Adabiyet-i Delli.

Sihite, E. and L. Tambun (2013), 'Civil servants warned not to use govt cars for private trips', *Jakarta Globe*, available at www.thejakarta globe.com/news/civil-servants-warned-not-to-use-govt-cars-for-private-trips/#more-%27 (accessed 5 August 2013).

Steenhaut, S. and P. van Kenhove (2006), An empirical investigation of the relationships among a consumer's personal values, ethical ideology and ethical beliefs', *Journal of Business Ethics*, **64** (2), 137–55.

Steers, R. and L. Porter (1983), *Motivation and Work Behavior*, New York, NY: McGraw-Hill.

Stogdill, R. (1974), *Handbook of Leadership: A Survey of the Literature*, New York, NY: The Free Press.

Tamari, M. (1991), '*In the Marketplace: Jewish Business Ethics*', Southfield, MI: Targum Press.

Tilgher, A. (1930), *Homo faber: Work Through the Ages*, trans. by D.C. Fisher, New York, NY: Harcourt Brace.

Torchia, A. (2013), 'Corruption worsened in Arab countries since uprisings: poll', *Reuters*, available at www.reuters.com/article/2013/07/09/us-mideast-corruption-survey-idUSBRE96805U20130709 (accessed 10 July 2013).

Transparency International (2012), *Corruption Perceptions Index 2012*, www.transparency.org/cpi2012/results.

Trenwith, C. (2013), 'Kuwait appoints first anti-corruption chief', *Arabian Business*, available at www.arabianbusiness.com/kuwait-appoints-first-anti-corruption-chief-504082.html (accessed 10 July 2013).

Triandis, H. (1979), 'Values, attitudes, and interpersonal behavior', in H. Howe (ed.), *Nebraska Symposium on Motivation*, Lincoln, NE: University of Nebraska Press, pp. 195–260.

Twenge, J., S. Campbell, B. Hoffman and C. Lance (2011), 'Generational differences in work values: Leisure and extrinsic values increasing, social and intrinsic values decreasing', *Journal of Management*, **36** (5), 1117–42.

Uhl-Bien, M. (2006), 'Relational Leadership Theory: Exploring the social processes of leadership and organizing', *The Leadership Quarterly*, **17** (6), 654–76.

Ul-Haq, S. and R. Westwood (2012), 'The politics of knowledge, epistemological occlusion and Islamic management and organization knowledge', *Organization*, **19** (2), 229–57.

United Nations Industrial Development Organization (2007), *Building Linkages for Competitive and Responsible Entrepreneurship. Geneva*: UNIDO.

Van Burns, H. (1999), 'Acting more generously than the law requires: The issue of employee layoffs in Halakhah', *Journal of Business Ethics*, **19**: 335–343.

Vitell, S. and J. Paolillo (2003), 'Consumer ethics: The role of religiosity', *Journal of Business Ethics*, **46** (2), 151–62.

Waagstein, P.R. (2011), 'The mandatory corporate social responsibility in Indonesia: Problems and implications', *Journal of Business Ethics*, **98**: 455–66.

Wang, L. and K.J. Murnighan (2011), 'On greed', *The Academy of Management Annals*, **5** (1), 279–316.

Weber, M. (1905), *The Protestant ethic and the spirit of capitalism*, New York, NY: Scribner's.

Wilber, K. (1999), *The Collected Works of Ken Wilber*, Boston and London: Shambhala.

Wilensky, H. and C. Lehbeaux (1965), *Industrial Society and Social Welfare*, New York, NY: Free Press.

Wilkie, W.L. and E.S. Moore (2007), 'Marketing's contributions to society', in G.T. Gunlach, L.G. Block and W.L. William (eds), *Explorations of Marketing in Society*, Mason, OH: Thomson, pp. 2–39.

Willner, A. (1984), *The Spellbinders: Charismatic Political Leadership*, New Haven, CT: Yale University Press.

Wolpe, H. (1968), 'A critical analysis of some aspects of charisma', *Sociological Review*, **16**: 305–18.

World Bank (2013), 'Corruption', available at http://web.worldbank.org/WBSITE/EXTERNAL/EXTABOUTUS/0,,contentMDK:23272490~pagePK:51123644~piPK:329829~theSitePK:29708,00.html (accessed 8 July 2013).

Wrightsman, L.S. (1992), *Assumptions About Human Nature: Implications for Researchers and Practitioners*, Newbury Park, CA: SAGE Publications Inc.

Yousef, D.A. (2000), 'The Islamic work ethic as a mediator of the relationship between locus of control, role conflict and role ambiguity: A study in an Islamic country setting', *Journal of Managerial Psychology*, **15** (4), 283–302.

Yousef, D.A. (2001), 'Islamic work ethic: A moderator between organizational commitment and job satisfaction in a cross-cultural context', *Personnel Review*, **30** (2), 152–69.

Yousef, F.R. (2011a), 'Dr. Lal al-dean: The absence of strategic vision prevents seizing advantage of the financial crises by Islamic Banks', available at www.aawsat.com (accessed 6 December 2013).

Yousef, F.R. (2011b), 'Faris Murad to Asharq Al-Awsat those responsible for banking industry ignored Islamic financial planning', available at www.aawsat.com/print.asp?did=621988andissueno=11858 (accessed 6 December 2013).

Yousef, F.R. (2012), 'The widespread of reverse loan in some Islamic banks obscures industry principle', *Asharq Al-Awsat*, (12432), available at www.aawsat.com/print.asp?did=708298andissueno=12432 (accessed 10 December 2013).

Y-Sing, L. and R. Kasolowsky (2009), 'Islamic banks: Trouble beneath calm waters?', *Reuters*, available at www.reuters.com/article/2009/06/01/us-islamic-financial-idUSTRE55005W20090601 (accessed 6 December 2013).

Yu, D. and R. Srinivasan (2013), 'Employee engagement increases in china, but still very low', *Gallup*, available at www.gallup.com/poll/160190/employee-engagement-increases-china-low.aspx (accessed 14 December 2013).

Yu, D., J. Harter and S. Agrawal (2013), 'U.S. managers boast best work engagement: Managers also show greatest improvement in engagement', *Gallup*, available at www.gallup.com/poll/162062/managers-boast-best-work-engagement.aspx (accessed 5 December 2013).

Name index

Amiantit Group 71
Anderson, N. 123
Aon Hewitt 197
Aristotle 42
Arkoun, M. 91
Armstrong, Karen 87, 90,
    93
Asaf, M. 65, 103–6, 111, 153–5, 160,
    180, 185, 188
Ashmawy, M. 91
Atan, Ruhaya 213
Aycan, Zeyneb 192
Ayoun, B. 193
Azary, Zhila 213
Azim, A. 136

Bahrampour, Tara 158
Barbash, Jack 128
Barton, D. 62
Belk, R.W. 141
Berkovits, Eliezer 192
Bershidsky, Leonid 98
Binham, Caroline 38
Blau, P. 82
Bowie, Norman E. 9
Bowmen, Dylan 163
Brodbeck, F. 83
Budhwar, Pawan 178, 194
Burhan, Ghalioun 201

Campbell, S. 122
Carney, Frederick S. 17
Carroll, Archie B. 200
Chapra, M. 70–71
Chew, Y. T. 178
Ching, M. 1, 63
Conger, J. A. 82–3
Cullen, John B. 4
Curphy, Gordon 82

Dauten, Dale 137
DesJardins, Joseph 4, 7
Devinney, T. M. 141
Diddams, M. 128
Dierker, E. 63
Dodd, E. Merrick 200
Doran, Caroline 140
Dorfman, P. 83
Dow, T. 82
Drucker, Peter 63, 72

Eastman, J. K. 140
Eckhardt, G. 141
El-Kot, Ghada 194
Emerson, T. 1, 63
England, George 123–4
Erikson, E. 29–30

Fakkar, Galal 187
Falcone, T. 136
Ferguson, Nial 128
Fisher, G. 142
Fletcher, Joseph 18
Fletcher, J.K. 93
Foroohar, Rana 102
Freeman, Edward R. 64,
    211–12
Friedland, W. 82
Friedman, Milton 62–3

Ghafour, P. K. Abdul 40
Ginnett, Robert 82
Glaachi, M. 12, 54, 60, 71, 74, 103,
    111, 146, 152, 154–5, 160–61, 189,
    205, 211
Glass, Amy 163
Graafland, J. 63
Grant, C. 64
Graves, C. W. 29–30
Grodal, B. 63
Groom, Brian 62

Hampton, D. 124
Hanson, M. J. 193
Haroon, Muhammad 136
Harter, Jim 138
Hartley, Joanna 41
Hartley, Robert F. 2
Hashim, Junaidah 178
Hassan, Kabir 71
Hill, Andrew 130
Hill, Roger 127
Hoffman, Brian 122
Hofstede, G. 19, 83, 123–4,
    194
Hooker, John 4
House, R. 83
Howell, J. M. 82–3
Hughes, Richard 82
Hunt, J. G. 82–3
Huntington, Samuel 127

Subject index